LABOUR REBUILT

D0246319

LABOUR REBUILT

THE NEW MODEL PARTY

Colin Hughes
and
Patrick Wintour

Fourth Estate · London

First published in Great Britain in 1990 by
Fourth Estate Ltd
Classic House
113 Westbourne Grove
London W2 4UP

British Library Cataloguing in Publication Data
Hughes, Colin
    Labour rebuilt : the new model party.
    1. Great Britain. Political parties: Labour Party (Great
    Britain). Reforms
    I. Title   II. Wintour, Patrick
    324.24107

    ISBN 1-872180-70-1

Typeset by York House Typographic, London W7
Printed by Richard Clay Ltd, Bungay

Reasons for *[handwritten]*

CONTENTS

Introduction   1

PART ONE: *Preparing the ground*

1   First Time Around: 1983-87   6
2   Campaign '87   22
3   Blueprint for Change   36
4   Glitznost   48
5   Aims and Values   64
6   Long Hot Summer   76

PART TWO: *Labour Rebuilt*

7   The Listening Party   98
8   Defence: Leave it to Gerald   104
9   The Economy and Tax: Fit to Govern   128
10   Industrial relations: The Policy of Discontent   143
11   People Politics: Citizens and consumers   153
12   Private Agenda, People's Agenda   166

PART THREE: *The New Model Party*

13   The Turnaround   176
14   Perestroika   188

Conclusion   202

INTRODUCTION

MIDWAY THROUGH the afternoon of 7 June 1987 Glenys Kinnock stood smiling amid crowds of celebrating Labour activists in the 'Aggy Hall' business design centre – a symbol of publicly-funded modernity in Islington, north London. She was smiling because the sense of success was tangible at the climactic rally of Labour's general election campaign – the 'Coming Up Roses' rally, as it was called. Labour had entered the election race a month earlier against a muttering chorus of predictions that the party – and Mrs Kinnock's much-criticized husband – were accelerating into terminal decline. Instead, by what felt a miracle to many who were present at that rally, Labour had accumulated unprecedented accolades for the professionalism of its campaign. Neil Kinnock himself had won tributes from unlikely quarters for the energy and verve he had poured into his tour of the country. The party itself had remained more or less united.

Mrs Kinnock turned to the young man at her side – Peter Mandelson, one of those responsible for the party's transformed campaigning style. 'You know,' she said, in the heat of the moment: 'I really think we can win. Neil's never taken on anything that he's lost.' The estimate of her husband's strength of will was incontestable; a single-minded determination to succeed had become his overriding personal and leadership characteristic. But Mrs Kinnock's judgment of the impending polls outcome proved devastatingly awry.

Neil Kinnock had never allowed himself to believe that Labour would win the 1987 general election. The height of his real hopes, given Labour's parlous position in public opinion polls during the preceding winter and spring, was that the Tory majority could be limited to somewhere between, maybe, 40 and 60 seats.

In the early evening of polling day Mandelson was sitting in his room at the party's Walworth Road headquarters enjoying one of the first peaceful, solitary moments he had spent for a month, when Vincent Hanna, the BBC's celebrated and loquacious election presenter, came on the line. Hanna was eager to impart astonishing news. According to the BBC exit poll, Labour was heading to finish five percentage points behind the Conservatives, leaving Margaret Thatcher with a projected Government majority of only 26 seats. There was, on that basis, every reason to suppose a hung parliament. Mandelson could not believe it; he pleaded with Hanna not to tell Kinnock, for fear of cruelly raising the leader's expectations. When the ITN exit poll results were telephoned through later, Mr Kinnock's assembled aides felt justified in their scepticism: ITN's figure of a 68-seat Tory majority fitted their prognosis. Worse was to follow. By the early hours of the morning it became clear that all the effort expended on what Tony Benn later called the most professional Labour campaign since 1959, had achieved less even than the ITN poll suggested. Mr Kinnock faced, not only a towering 102 – seat Conservative majority, against which his 229 MPs would feel frustratingly impotent; he also faced a party which had suffered its third election defeat in succession. It would urgently need leadership direction if it were not to fragment.

Within a year, Kinnock's leadership did in fact falter alarmingly under challenge. At one point he personally sank so low into dejection that many close colleagues suspected him of being on the verge of surrendering his ambitions. The policy review which he launched immediately after defeat seemed at times to be drifting like a becalmed raft; the party appeared sullenly resistant to change, and the public's judgment was so long suspended that party strategists wondered whether voters could ever again be persuaded of Labour's electability.

Yet, paradoxically, the scale of the 1987 election defeat opened the way for a comprehensive review. Labour's failure in 1987 was, in certain crucial ways, quite different from the '79 and '83 defeats. It was the defeat without excuses: there had been no winter of discontent, no Falklands war, no ageing leader, on which to blame the electorate's refusal to embrace Labour. The campaign had been a triumph of image over substance. The most revealing feature of Labour's 1987 general election manifesto had been its margins. Not only were they extremely wide, so as to keep the policy text to a minimum, but they also contained brief summary pointers to the text which – notably on subjects such as defence – bore only a tangential relation to the policy being summarized. It was impossible for any remotely thoughtful party member to avoid concluding that the party had this time fallen down on policy; indeed, that it was the very character of the party itself which voters rejected. Labour was out-of-date and out of line with people's most strongly-felt aspirations.

Out of that disappointment, the ensuing self-analysis, and the compelling need to restore purpose and electability to the Labour Party, grew the most comprehensive policy review that the party had ever undertaken. Out of it too, grew a determination to restructure the party's organization, and unify its restyled campaigning with streamlined policy-making methods. The seeds of that change lay in the run-up to the '87 campaign. Kinnock had quietly changed much of the policy-making machinery, and rather less quietly fought and beaten back the Trotskyist Militant left. His command over the party, even then, was extraordinary. But few people believed the day after polling day in June 1987 that Neil Kinnock would, inside two years, change Labour's defence policy from unilateralism to multilateralism. Or that he would propose reforming the trade union block vote and survive.

A month after the 'Aggy Hall' rally, and the day before the party's national executive began considering for the first time proposals for that policy review, Mandelson wrote a ten-point note to Charles Clarke, Neil Kinnock's chief of staff. Clarke and Mandelson were long-standing friends and political associates. Both – Clarke in particular – knew Kinnock's mind instinctively. The note was Mandelson's first attempt to help think Labour out of its post-defeat torpor, and was headed 'Moving Ahead'. It was not the origin of the review: the political spark came later from Tom Sawyer, chairman of the national executive's home policy committee. But it was about a strategy which was arguably more important than, and certainly indivisible from, the review process. It was about the presentation plans for the coming four or five years – what Mandelson and his associates called the post-election 'communications strategy'.

The roughly-drafted two-page memo began by arguing: 'The attractive dynamic is of a listening, innovating, forward-looking party. Looking at Britain living, working, earning its way in the 1990s. A party with an understanding of Britain 2000, able to analyse change and manage change. This dynamic needs to be seen in what we are doing now, and for the duration of the parliament. We need to carry forward the momentum of the election campaign – our strategy should be to project the image of moving ahead. The obvious elements of this communications strategy are democratic constitutional change, reorganization, policy renewal, and leadership enhancement.' Moving Ahead in fact became the slogan for the autumn 1987 party conference.

Mandelson proposed ideas for implementing that strategy. Assuming that one member, one vote plans went through conference that autumn, the party should identify 'a series of more or less significant constitutional changes' to 'expand/reform/involve the membership – youth, women, trade unionists'. Reorganizing regions, agents, head office, 'would have some appeal', but a high-profile membership drive 'would be more exciting'. Mass membership proposals were indeed adopted, mostly because the powerful trade unions pushed it on the party leader. Mandelson merely suggested at the time that every party member be challenged to recruit at least three more, with promotional rewards for the most successful. He added: 'If it could be linked to a direct mail, listening and learning from the voters questionnaire exercise all the better.' Listening and learning were to be the watchwords for the 'Labour listens' exercises which ran alongside the first phase of the review. More important, however, would be the party's pure policy. Point eight of the hasty note argued that policy modernization would be the key to Labour's 'next election image', particularly in fields affecting wealth creation, taxation, and work. The party 'should make a virtue of change, be as forthright and open as (internally) possible . . .'

Then came the campaigns and communications director's clinching point: 'I think this requires switching from a policy committee based process to a communications-based exercise. The elements could be public survey work, consultation with interest groups, foreign experience, research projects. This activity is the core of campaign 90 – the longest-running general election campaign, which runs for four years . . . Neil's role in implementation is crucial – it's his means of further enhancement. He needs to instigate, participate, guide and finally present to the nation. The last building blocks of the new model party.'

There, at the moment of the review's devising, the central question was posed: how could Labour create a Cromwellian political army – a disciplined 'new model party' devoted to common principle and purpose? An army whose strength would lie in unity and determination to enter a new model world? Could such a drastic transformation in the culture of the Labour Party be real, or sustainable? Labour's opponents argue that the review is merely a superficial implant, barely below the skin, accepted by the party only for so long as it takes to cross the next general election winning line. The Kinnock-led revival, they say, is merely a brilliant mirror trick perpetrated by the image-makers on the commentating classes. If they are right, neither the review nor Kinnock's leadership is likely to endure the crucible heat of the next election campaign. If they are wrong, and Kinnock has indeed built a new model party, then Labour is once more electable. It is that question which this book seeks to answer – by identifying the key players and their motives, and by describing how they, under Neil Kinnock's leadership, renewed the party's electoral fortunes by implementing the policy review.

FIRST TIME AROUND: 1983-87

THE GENERAL election defeat in June 1983 was no less traumatic for being the most widely predicted since the war. That the party ran an inept and disorganized campaign, led by one of the least appropriate figures ever to head either of the two dominant political parties, merely exacerbated an already disastrous prospect. Even 28 per cent of the vote, the party's lowest share since 1918, seemed more than Labour deserved. Vicious internal warfare over the collapse of the Callaghan Government, the formation of the Social Democratic Party breakaway of Labour right-wingers, and the intensive campaign by Tony Benn and his followers to take over the party, had led to the most protracted period of self-mutilation in Labour's post-war history. The Falklands war simply guaranteed Margaret Thatcher an overwhelming majority.

Though the transformation of the Labour Party mostly took place after the 1987 general election defeat, it is important to recognize the extent to which those later advances were founded on attempts and mistakes made by Neil Kinnock's leadership during the preceding four years. His struggle to rebuild the Labour Party began the day he was elected leader in 1983. The style and approach of his leadership grew directly out of the need to staunch the wounds still flowing after three years of uncontrollable civil war in the party, and out of the need to revive a party that was devastated by that general election defeat.

Young, confident, ebullient, and brimming with energy, Kinnock presented the sharpest available personal contrast to Michael Foot. In his speech to the 1983 party conference, hours after being elected successor, Kinnock made it his mission to ensure that Labour never repeated the trauma of the early 1980s. He told delegates that the party had to recapture its innate common sense and realism: 'If anyone wants to know the reason why we must conduct ourselves in this fashion, just remember the old times and old temptations and remember how each and every one of you felt on that dreadful morning of June 10 and think to yourselves "June 9, 1983 – never again will we experience that".' He went on: 'Unity is the price of victory. Not unity for four weeks before the general election, not unity for four weeks before the European Assembly elections, but unity here and now and from henceforth, not a cosmetic disguise, but a living, working unity of people of a movement, of a belief and conviction, who want to win in order to save our country and our world.' Thereafter the words varied only slightly; the sentiment was to be repeated by Kinnock from public platforms and in private meetings more frequently than any other single political assertion.

Kinnock's huge leadership election victory – winning at the first ballot with 71 per cent of the votes cast – gave him an extraordinary authority to set about rebuilding the party. Unity was a primary aim. But modernization and change were the overriding imperatives from the outset. His leadership election speech was greeted with a standing ovation, but that warmth was short-lived. Kinnock's first serious attempt at party reform, only a year later at the 1984 conference, ended in embarrassment. He pressed the party to move towards one member, one vote democracy for the selection of parliamentary candidates – a major change for a party founded on representative and delegate decision-making. At that early stage Kinnock's advisors – Dick Clements, the former editor of *Tribune*, and Charles Clarke, who had been Kinnock's researcher when he was education spokesman – were inexperienced. They misjudged the mood of the unions, the interest group most threatened by the change; their block votes, alongside the opposition of suspicious constituency activists, inflicted a wounding defeat. Kinnock suffered an early blow – albeit by a narrow margin – that crucially changed his perspective. He discovered that he could not secure change simply by appealing to loyalty. He promised himself that he would never again risk his authority in that way unless it was absolutely necessary. Clarke, too, learnt from the experience. Kinnock decided that in future he would first ensure that he could build the required majority before he embarked on proposals for change. Indeed, where possible he would seek to persuade and manoeuvre the party toward unanimity, isolating enemies where necessary. Clarke – who became not only Kinnock's closest advisor, but also one of the most influential men in the party – argued that the leader's first task was to establish unquestioned control. Defeats merely reinforced the perception either of a rudderless or disloyal party, or of a weak leadership. If Kinnock was to boost his status as party leader with the electorate, he needed not simply to win votes, but to win them handsomely. Narrow 15 to 12 victories on the national executive were not good enough. Only emphatic margins would do. Anything less risked perpetuating the impression of division, as well as encouraging the notion that the Bennite left really still held sway.

To achieve that aim, Kinnock quite deliberately set about constructing a new leadership-supporting alliance on the party's national executive. It might have seemed an obvious strategy, but it had eluded his two predecessors, Callaghan and Foot. Their neglect of the executive as a power base enabled Benn and his supporters to retain a hold on the party's policy-making machinery and organization. Kinnock was more fortunate than they, in that many on the left were turning away from confrontation anyway, and the right-wing unions had successfully organized to recapture the national executive in 1982. More and more of Benn's former acolytes started to back out of what they began to see as a cul-de-sac.

The break-up began to formalize itself with the establishment of the Campaign Group as the organization of the hard left. It clearly distinguished itself from the soft left, represented by the Tribune group of MPs (from whence Kinnock himself came), and the Labour Co-ordinating Committee, which formed to represent the soft left in the constituencies. By 1984 those divisions began to manifest themselves on the executive, as its members adopted conflicting attitudes to the miners' strike, and the tactics employed by Arthur Scargill, the miners' union president. Three distinguishable blocs emerged. The right-wing was led by Gwyneth Dunwoody and Roy Hattersley, the left by Tony Benn, Dennis Skinner and (initially at least) Eric Heffer. But a new LCC/Tribune-oriented group – sympathetic to the miners' cause, but privately uneasy about the failure to ballot NUM members – was beginning to mark out distinctive ground in the middle. The primary achievement of the first period of Kinnock's leadership was to weld that newly-emergent soft left grouping into an alliance with the right. That isolated the hard left, and forged a new, centrist unity in the party. Three figures on the national executive played a key role at that time – Tom Sawyer, the newly-elected deputy general secretary of the National Union of Public Employees, David Blunkett, the blind leader of Sheffield city council, and Michael Meacher, the defeated challenger for the deputy leadership against Hattersley in 1983. Kinnock attempted little without first obtaining their prior support, usually by speaking to them himself before crucial executive and committee meetings.

The understanding between that triumvirate and Kinnock was finally sealed in the battle to expel leading members of Militant, who had been pursuing their entryist tactics inside the Labour Party since the late 1960s. Largely unchallenged by a preoccupied Callaghan, and a dormant party bureaucracy, Militant had dug down firm roots in some areas of the party during the 1970s. By the early '80s, Militant dominated the youth wing and many inner city constituencies where the local party had atrophied through right-wing neglect.

Most on the left, though strongly hostile to Militant, were reluctant to launch the kind of heavy-handed purge carried out by the right-wing against Nye Bevan's followers in the 1950s. Foot, himself an old Bevanite, was weak on party discipline. In 1983 the party conference upheld the expulsion of the five members of the Militant editorial board. But Foot's disciplinary measures were so limited that they served merely to advertise Militant's strength. Convinced that Militant was a malign cancer in the party, Kinnock decided to concentrate his mind on slicing out the growth by challenging the organization in its main power base, Liverpool. Not only did Kinnock detest Militant's politics; he calculated that its defeat would display to voters his determination to take a grip on the party machine and erase left-wing extremism. Kinnock seized his chance when the Militant-run Liverpool city council exposed itself to attack by making a series of tactical misjudgements in the fight against rate capping. In a famous passage of his speech at the 1985 party conference in Bournemouth Kinnock lashed Militant, saying that their campaign 'had ended with the grotesque chaos of a Labour council – a Labour council – hiring taxis to travel around a city handing out redundancy notices to its own workers'.

The party leader knew that his speech would be greeted with delight by the Militant-hating press. He was more anxious about the reaction of those on the soft left on whom he still relied for his command over the executive and the party. If they backed him, the realignment into a majority alliance of the centre-left and the right wing would be complete. If they recoiled from scourging Militant, the unity which Kinnock sought would prove elusive.

A key figure on the executive at that time was David Blunkett. At the 1985 Bournemouth conference he topped the section of the executive elections reserved for constituency representatives. After eight consecutive years as the favourite of the constituency parties, Benn was displaced. Blunkett's own rise to eminence was symbolic of the soft left's new ascendancy. As chairman of the national executive's local government committee, and chairman of the Association of Metropolitan Authorities, Blunkett played a central role in the efforts made jointly with the trade union national organizations, to try and pull Liverpool away from incipient chaos.

The Sheffield leader was deeply unhappy with Kinnock's speech, feeling that it had not acknowledged the financial crises being imposed on local councils like his own. He theatrically appealed to Derek Hatton, the Militant deputy council leader who was sitting in the hall, directly from the conference podium. Blunkett's blindness meant that he could not even see whether Hatton was still there; he certainly did not know where in the hall Hatton was sitting, and had to stand on the platform begging, 'Will you do it Derek? Derek?' He did not know that Hatton, realizing he was being upstaged, was running to the front of the hall to agree to Blunkett's offer of a

compromise, whereby Liverpool would allow in independent auditors to study the city council's books. Kinnock was infuriated. He
wanted no half measures over Militant and felt Blunkett's spur of the
moment conciliation irresponsibly undermined the leadership
attack. Blunkett, however, believed that, if it could be shown that
Militant had spurned a realistic means of balancing the books, then
the case against the organization would be strengthened. The
subsequent inquiry by council treasurers and independent auditors,
reporting to Blunkett, and to John Edmonds, general secretary of the
GMB union (which was dominant in Liverpool), found that the
council could have found a way out of its financial difficulties if
Militant had not been intent on a confrontation with the government.

   Those events convinced Blunkett that Kinnock was right after all.
Not only was it essential to expunge Militant; the party's revitaliza-
tion also depended on isolating those on the executive who were
willing to defend or protect Militant. Blunkett, long after the event,
regarded Kinnock's decision to destroy Militant's base as an effective entryist force as the bravest and most perceptive act of his
leadership. On the initiative of Blunkett and Sawyer, the national
executive, at its November 1985 meeting, agreed by 21 votes to 5 to
set up an inquiry into Militant's control of Liverpool city council.
The recommendations of the inquiry were accepted after long
debate by 19 votes to 10 in February 1986. Sawyer was one among
the eight strong inquiry committee; he was converted to the need for
expulsions after listening to the evidence of systematic entryism and
bending of the rules. Genuinely shocked by what he had seen and
heard, Sawyer told his union's conference just how its members had
been treated by Militant in Liverpool. 'In an atmosphere of intimida-
tion fuelled by parading security guards and hundreds of non-
delegates, Nupe representatives were threatened and intimidated
because they would not toe the Militant line. Some of the things I
saw as a member of the Liverpool inquiry have more in common
with the extreme right in European politics than with the left.'
Sawyer's conversion in 1985 from opposition to disciplinary action
was mirrored by a similar experience for another key Kinnock
loyalist in the trade unions – Eddie Haigh, the assistant general

secretary of the Transport and General Workers Union. Haigh also sat on the inquiry, and came to similar conclusions.

Both men went on to form part of a phalanx of Kinnock loyalists from the unions filling vital posts on the national executive sub-committees. The bulk of the work of these trade union second stringers rightly attracted little publicity. But the role they played in stabilizing Kinnock's regime should not be underestimated. Their presence meant that little emerged from sub-committees, for consideration at the full monthly meetings of the national executive, in a form that was unwelcome to Kinnock. Haigh was placed in charge of the organization committee; Sawyer took the chairmanship of home policy; Tony Clarke, the deputy general secretary of the Union of Communication Workers, chaired the international committee; Gordon Colling, the political officer of the National Graphical Association, ran the finance and general purposes committee. Colling later ensured, as the right-wing whip on the executive, that most of the twelve trade union representatives acted in concert. Kinnock's hold on the party bureaucracy was tightened when Jim Mortimer, the general secretary, was replaced by Larry Whitty, the respected head of research at the GMB.

Kinnock used his control to build a new relationship between the executive on one side, and the Shadow Cabinet and other front-benchers on the other, by replacing the ramshackle collection of executive policy committees – largely ignored by frontbenchers – with joint policy teams. They later became the model on which the policy review groups were based.

The party leader further cleared the way for modernization by deciding to take responsibility for campaigns away from the head-quarters organization department, and create a new communications and campaigns directorate by blending campaigns with the publicity and press office operations.

It was to the directorship of that new department which Peter Mandelson – who became the figure most publicly associated in Tory demonology with the review – was eventually appointed. Mandelson was working voluntarily for the party, helping its candidate in the Brecon by-election, when he was joined in the front of his car in the Welsh town's market place by Charles Clarke. The pair first became friends when Clarke was president of the National Union of Students and Mandelson ran the British Youth Council. Mandelson moved on to become a TUC researcher and then a television producer, but was becoming frustrated with his highly-paid job, and wanted to move back into politics. The comprehensive school and Oxford University educated grandson of Herbert Morrison, Mandelson was regarded by his London Weekend Television colleagues as one of the sharpest young brains in the business. He was tipped for a rapid rise in the intensely competitive broadcasting world. But Mandelson was, from an early age, soaked with a passion for politics. It was his first love – the gossip and the glamour, the machinations and the power. His most thrilling boyhood memories were of his neighbour in Hampstead Garden Suburb, Harold Wilson, inviting him and his parents to tea at Number 10. Boy Peter spent the 1964 election, Wilson's great victory, touring polling stations on his bike.

Mandelson's colourful and mischievous conversational manner, tinged with a kind of flirtatious wit, contrasted with his companion. Clarke – public school, but also Oxford-educated – was a large, bearded, bear-like and burly figure. His brusque manner belied a natural civility, and warmth. He was the son of a high-ranking Treasury civil servant, Richard 'Otto' Clarke, who was the architect of the public expenditure scrutiny system in the early 1950s. Otto was once described by Lord Croham, former Treasury permanent secretary, as the most restless of officials: 'Ruthless in the pursuit of effective solutions, ruthless in the demolition of soft advice, soft decisions, soft colleagues, and soft Ministers.' Those words could easily have been applied to his son. Although Charles could sometimes be seen late at night in the party conference headquarters' hotel in jeans and an open-necked shirt, relaxing and drinking beer out of a straight glass, he more often acted with the cool reserve of a praetorian lieutenant. No one enjoyed such closeness to Kinnock as Clarke: the leader's chief of staff in return worked to a strict code of personal loyalty and discretion.

The Brecon market place conversation was an example of just

such reserve. Clarke told Mandelson that a new job was coming up
running the party's reconstructed communications directorate.
Mandelson asked Clarke how he would rate his chances if he
applied. Clarke sternly replied: 'I'm sure your name would be
considered along with the rest.' The conversation led to Mandelson's appointment; and he in turn led a revolution in Labour's
publicity image, and the party's campaigning verve.

BY SEPTEMBER 1986, therefore, there were many reasons for Kinnock to feel moderately optimistic about his chances of delivering a
general election success for Labour at his first attempt. The party
had enjoyed an opinion poll lead over the Conservatives for eight
unbroken months. The Government had been shaken by the West-
land affair and the consequent resignations from Cabinet. The
marginal Fulham seat had been stolen from the Conservatives in
April 1986. Although the poll gap never opened wider than 6
percentage points, Kinnock intended to lever it further apart in the
run-up to the election with a succession of economic policy statements designed to proclaim Labour's abandonment of dirigiste
planning.

However, instead of maintaining a steady upward climb towards
the general election summit, Labour's hopes of preventing a third
term of Conservative government tumbled away. The speed with
which the party's fortunes crumbled demonstrated how fragile and
restrained the Kinnock reformation had been to that point.

Oddly, problems began at the Liberal Assembly in Eastbourne on
23 September, when Liberal delegates voted by 652 to 625 to reject
the defence policy proposals which David Steel and David Owen
had carefully assembled as a joint Alliance package. The Alliance
split concentrated public attention on defence, which was then
directed to Labour's own conference three weeks later. On the
Monday evening of the conference, BBC TV's *Panorama* broadcast
trailed remarks by Caspar Weinberger, the US Defence Secretary,
and Richard Perle, assistant secretary, to the effect that Labour's
defence proposals would mean the break up of Nato. Charles Price,
the US ambassador in London, similarly intervened. On the same

Panorama programme Denis Healey, foreign affairs spokesman, hinted that it was conceivable that the US might persuade Labour to allow its nuclear bases to remain. In one interview during the week Kinnock implied that Labour would accept the protection of the US nuclear umbrella; in another he said it was impossible. However, he did make clear that both Polaris and Trident would be scrapped, and in a passionate speech to the conference he vowed: 'I would rather die for my country than my country die for me.' Labour's conference as a whole was moderately successful – but defence policy was back in the public eye, and that eclipsed Labour's good news. The 1986 conference, which had been designed to highlight the 'unity' theme, in fact emphasized the policy issue on which the party was most obviously divided.

The Conservatives used their own conference the following week to present a stunning public relations obliteration of Labour. Ministers announced a stream of new initiatives – 'the next moves forward', as Saatchi and Saatchi billed them – pointing to an aggressively radical election manifesto. Any impression that Thatcher's Government had lost its thrust was utterly extinguished. The polls turned against Labour. At the start of the Tory conference Labour had been two points ahead: by the end it was trailing badly. Labour's autumn thrust – a campaign titled 'Investing in People' – failed to fire. A month later, in November 1986, it was so clear that a pre-election boom was under way that ministers felt confident enough to predict that unemployment would fall below 3 million the following May.

At the end of November Kinnock flew to America in the hope of re-assuring voters at home that the election of a unilaterally nuclear disarming Labour Government would not precipitate a crisis in Britain's alliance with the United States. In a 7,000-word speech to the Kennedy School of Government in Boston, Massachusetts, he tried to set out in greater detail than hitherto his vision of a Labour Government's relations with the US over defence. It clarified some issues, left others vague, and did nothing to assuage the Reagan administration. The unhappy, though not utterly disastrous trip, was capped with a hostage to fortune. Pestered about why he had not met

Reagan at the White House, Kinnock said that had never been planned; he would return before the general election to talk to the President.

On 10 December, shortly after Kinnock arrived back in London, Labour launched the defence campaign which unilateralists in the party had long been demanding. They suspected that the leadership was deliberately ignoring two successive conference instructions to campaign on defence. They were right: Mandelson in particular was convinced that the less the party said about defence the better. Once the issue blew up during the 1986 conference season, however, a Labour defence campaign could not be avoided. 'Modern Britain in the Modern World: The Power to Defend Our Country' was designed to be a pre-emptive strike against both Tory misrepresentation and internal party dissent.

The campaigns policy document, and the accompanying party political broadcast, laid a new stress on the party's commitment to build proper conventional defences, by trying to argue that the nation had to choose between that and continued reliance on nuclear weapons. Limited resources dictated that Britain could not have both. The policy statement on arms conversion, accepted by the party conference weeks before, had said that only some of the savings from the cancellation of Britain's nuclear defence programme would be committed to conventional defence spending. 'Modern Britain in the Modern World' abandoned all equivocation. Labour would transfer all the savings from the abandonment of the nuclear programme to conventional defence.

Mandelson's salesmanship – spinning his interpretation to the political correspondents – succeeded in winning splash headlines in the following day's newspapers, proclaiming a Kinnock shift towards multilateralism. But the claim was unsustainable. The campaign ultimately served only to underline Labour's lack of either clarity or unity on nuclear defence. Within 10 days of its launch the Tories recorded an 8.5 point lead in a poll conducted by Gallup. It was hopeless to imagine that the party could successfully campaign on a non-nuclear policy, when that policy itself was internally inconsistent, and self-evidently evasive. The leadership's own lack of faith was transparent; it was a standing joke that the campaign was effectively closed the day it was launched.

By January, the Labour leadership was struggling to regain political initiative. Kinnock called a two day meeting of the Shadow Cabinet at Bishop's Stortford on 7 and 8 January 1987 to thrash out the campaign for economic revival and employment creation which Kinnock had long envisaged: 'Jobs, jobs, jobs', his colleagues remember him repeating at every available opportunity.

In the run-up to the 1983 election Foot had promised to reduce unemployment below one million in the lifetime of a Parliament. After the election the target was widely criticized for making the party's whole anti-unemployment policy seem impractical. Yet in his first major decision on economic policy Kinnock repeated the same error but in a new, more modest form: in April 1985 he pledged to reduce unemployment by one million in two years.

No preparatory work was done to establish how that target could be hit. There was even uncertainty within the Shadow Cabinet's ranks about whether the target was to create one million jobs, or to cut the unemployment figures by one million – two very different things. It was not until May 1986 that Roy Hattersley, the Shadow Chancellor, John Smith, the industry spokesman, and John Prescott, the employment spokesman, agreed that Labour should say it would cut registered unemployment by one million within two years. Having finally agreed what the target was to be, no one was charged with the task of working out how it might be achieved. Five months from the election and 21 months after Kinnock first announced the new target, no comprehensive statement existed on how the target was to be met. Kinnock charged Prescott with the task of devising one, but the employment spokesman came up with only a rough model, based on Southwark council's job creation programme in South London. It was shot down at the Shadow Cabinet meeting by John Cunningham, environment spokesman, as jobs on the rates. Denis Healey, who lived in Southwark, scorned Prescott's proposals by pointing out that Southwark council was unable even to keep its own Town Hall jobs filled.

Kinnock extricated himself from Prescott's proposals by appoint-

ing Bryan Gould, then shadow to the Treasury Chief Secretary, to
the task of co-ordinating the jobs package. Gould was given three
pre-conditions: the package had to meet the 1 million off the dole
target; it had to cost less than £6bn, the maximum already set by
Hattersley as Shadow Chancellor; and its first draft had to be ready
within three weeks, in time for a public launch as 'New Jobs for
Britain' at the end of the following month.

Gould delivered. His package proposed four means of creating
the 1.16m jobs which the party said would be needed to reduce
registered unemployment by one million. But even at that time there
were doubts within the leadership about the credibility of the
package. A private paper prepared in Kinnock's office and presented
to a joint meeting of senior union leaders and Shadow Cabinet
members said that a Labour Government might need to create more
than 1.3 million jobs to reduce registered unemployment by one
million, because many jobs might be filled by unregistered female
workers. The internal paper, headed 'Target One Million', pointed
out that the National Institute of Economic and Social Research
suggested that as many as 2 million jobs might be needed.

The jobs and industry pre-election policy package was largely
flam – a one-night stage set made of balsawood. The priority was to
decide a policy objective, without first attempting to work out
whether it was either convincing or achievable. After the election
Mike Craven, Prescott's advisor, wrote to John Eatwell, Kinnock's
chief economic advisor, to condemn the way in which the package
had been prepared. He told Eatwell: 'There must be doubt that it
was a serious programme for a Labour Government, and whether it
could have achieved the one million job target in the first two years. It
was cobbled together at the last minute and was not the result of a
detailed economic analysis. Nor was it tested on an economic
model.' As Craven said, the programme made no mention of private
services – 'an area which most economists agree will be the principal
source of jobs'. Tourism did not feature, even though that single
sector of services was expected to produce 150,000 new jobs in the
next three years. It ignored part-time employment and concentrated
too much on private manufacturing. The party's four leading econo-

mic spokesmen had been arguing that manufacturing could not be expected to produce a net gain in jobs – but the campaign policy contradicted that, by claiming that Labour could create 250,000 full time manufacturing jobs.

Up to that point Labour was stumbling, but still on its feet. The death on Christmas Eve of Guy Barnett, Labour MP for Greenwich, knocked the party flat on the floor. Kinnock strove to prevent Deidre Wood, a former councillor with a long hard left history, being selected to run in the by-election – where she was being challenged by Rosie Barnes, the SDP's apple pie marketing researcher. But a Nupe official told him that the constituency party would back Wood. After a meeting at the Commons with the union, Kinnock told Mandelson: 'It's Wood. Do what you can.' Mandelson and Hewitt, Kinnock's press secretary, forlornly tried to sell their candidate as 'an Earth Mother figure, very popular in Greenwich'. Wood strove hard and was effective on the doorstep. But she was an inappropriate candidate, at probably the most vulnerable moment in Labour's general election run-up. Having started the by-election campaign with 60 per cent of the vote – according to a Harris poll – Labour ended up losing to the SDP by 5,000 votes.

Norman Tebbit, as Conservative party chairman, ran a brutal and compelling propaganda campaign throughout autumn 1986 and early 1987, using Tory-sympathising tabloid newspapers to fix the impression of a Labour Party still dominated by the 'loony left'. A confidential memorandum by Patricia Hewitt – written on 26 February, the day of the Greenwich result and sent privately to the senior members of the parliamentary and London Labour Party – was leaked to the *Sun*. It warned that the 'loony left' image was taking its toll, partly because the message was being repeated so frequently by the Tories, and partly because there was an element of truth in it. 'The gays and lesbians issue is costing us dear among the pensioners, and fear of extremism and higher taxes is particularly prominent in the GLC area,' Hewitt wrote. The leaker's identity and motive were never known, despite heavy inquiries within the office. Insiders gave two opposite accounts, one suggesting that Kinnock's office itself leaked the letter to put a bomb under the London left, and the other that the letter was lifted from someone's desk and leaked to discredit the leader's office in the party's eyes. Either way, Tebbit's attacks on the loony left received the public endorsement of the Labour leadership.

The Greenwich defeat caused a temporary delay in the launch of the 'New Jobs for Britain' package; it was postponed to 10 March. However, on 9 March, John Prescott became embroiled in a row with Jim Callaghan over the former Prime Minister's attack on the party's defence policy in the Commons. Prescott lost control of his notoriously quick temper and accused Callaghan – in what the tabloids called 'the tea-room tiff' – of snookering Labour's election chances.

The other economic frontbenchers and Mandelson wanted to exclude Prescott from the following day's launch. But the employment spokesman, catching wind of that, insisted on being present. In the end he was allowed on the platform, but left by the back door immediately afterwards. Despite Prescott's silence, the turmoil among Labour MPs dominated the press coverage. The one million jobs commitment – intended as the jewel of Labour's election appeal – was overshadowed by a frustrated Kinnock lecture to the party on the will to win. He told them: 'Since becoming leader, I've set myself a code of self-discipline which is the only way for a voluntary movement such as this to obtain victory. The precondition of making ourselves credible, electable and victorious is self-discipline. The objective of winning is greater than ego, and any vanity, and shortage of memory can be no excuse.'

Kinnock's struggle was complicated by his outstanding commitment to a second visit to the US to meet Ronald Reagan. None of Kinnock's advisors regarded the trip with anything but foreboding. They all feared that it would only serve to redouble public attention on the party's unpopular defence policy. There was also the strong probability that the Reagan White House would regard it as a favour to Margaret Thatcher to embarrass Kinnock. A number of options were considered by Kinnock's team, including announcing either a postponement, cancellation, or an attempt to combine the visit with a balancing trip to Russia. Clarke and Mandelson advised Kinnock to cancel altogether and ride out the Tory taunts of not having the courage to meet the leader of the western world, but Hewitt and Eatwell argued it would be more damaging to back out.

Kinnock himself decided that there was no choice but to press ahead. Typically, he abhorred the prospect of being accused of cowardice. That Reagan gave Kinnock less than the allotted half hour on 27 March was only one of many petty humiliations. Clarke had struck a deal with the State Department on arrangements for dealing with press briefings after the meeting, but on the day the department had to admit that it was being overruled by the White House. The President's press staff gave a dismissive briefing afterwards, conveying a powerful impression of Kinnock's irrelevance on the world stage. That was underscored by the enthusiastic welcome which Mrs Thatcher received in Moscow a week later.

The party leader returned to London at the weekend in bitter mood, to find that his party was still sliding uncontrollably backwards: Gallup showed that the Alliance, riding on its post-Greenwich high, had pushed Labour into third place. On the Monday afternoon following Kinnock's return from Washington, Mandelson, Clarke and Hewitt presented the party leader with an April recovery plan. Each day had a pinpointed fingerhold of a press launch, or a toehold of a speech, which the party could use to scramble and clamber back to a position from which it could prepare to contest the general election.

But, the sequence of accidents and blunders in the run-up to the 1987 general election could not hide the underlying truth that the first phase of Kinnock's leadership had failed to drag the party out of its chronic malaise. The 1984 miners' strike rubbed out the first year of his leadership; the battle with Militant erased most of the second. In the end there was simply too little time to pull the party round. After four years of Kinnock's 'reforming' leadership, Labour had come full circle. There seemed once again, as there had in 1983, a real danger that the Alliance were set to become the main opposition party.

2
CAMPAIGN '87

PREPARATION FOR the three and a half weeks of the election campaign began in early 1985, when Patricia Hewitt suggested that Labour should be ready and equipped by March 1987 at the latest. Her proposal led to the formation of the general secretary's committee, later retitled the campaign management team: the inner core of staffers from Walworth Road and the leader's office, chaired by the campaign co-ordinator (at that time Robin Cook, subsequently Bryan Gould) who would be responsible for planning the campaign, and running it day-to-day. The creation of the campaign management team proved to have a longer term significance. Once in place, it became the central group organising the post-election strategy and overseeing implementation of the policy review.

Each campaign day was planned in fine detail by Mandelson, Andrew Fox (his deputy) and Hewitt – to an extent that would have seemed inconceivable five years earlier. In March 1987 Hewitt wrote a memo pointing out that it would be the first British election campaign covered by the electronic news-gathering technology which had been relatively recently adopted by television news. ENG enables camera crews to be fully mobile on their own two feet. Whereas formerly each TV bulletin would have to be worked out carefully in advance, with politicians pre-booked, this time crews would need only a reporter at hand to ask the questions, and a despatch rider to whisk the tape away for processing. As Hewitt warned, the 1987 election would more than ever before be conducted by ENG, 'with news editors demanding – and getting – virtually instant responses to every key speech and statement'. She also emphasized that, with breakfast television running for the first time in a general election, the 1987 campaign would be exposed to all-day television coverage.

Each campaign day would need to provide 'one frontbencher making a major policy statement, possibly with a policy document (short) to accompany it'. There should be 'one terrific photo-opp with the Leader or key campaigner'. Either Kinnock or a key campaigner should be on *Election Call* or *Question Time*, or a similar national programme: Hewitt predicted that people who were otherwise bored by the campaign would lap up occasions when ordinary voters directly questioned politicians, live on air. As far as Kinnock's tour was concerned, 'good photo-opps for the stills photographers, and good locations for the TV should be the top priority' – which as far as possible should be linked to Labour's chosen theme of the day. In an early 1986 memo headed 'Finding the Best Places to Visit' Hewitt said the locations should be positive: '. . . we want places that are modern, that show the best of Britain and, in particular, the best of what Labour councils are doing; places that encapsulate Kinnock's Britain'. She went on: 'We do **not** want any closed factories, derelict housing sites, run-down hospitals, industrial wastelands or other wrecks of Thatcher's Britain'. Hewitt also wanted 'people – bright, attractive people presenting an image of the broader base Labour has to capture – not people who present an image of old-fashioned Labour die-hards'. The party spent £15,000 on appointing two location researchers to seek out the right upbeat venues for Kinnock to be photographed.

Key campaigners would, according to that early 1986 note, be ' "the team" that Labour will be presenting to the country'. There would be 'an A Team of, say, half-a-dozen who will be given the best possible backing for their campaign days, media appearances etc; with a much larger team (including selected candidates) for regional media, specialist outlets and lower-audience programmes'. Each would need to 'be aware very early on of their starring role, and, with very few exceptions, should go through a one-day TV training course'. The themes, Kinnock's locations, the identities of the key campaigners, back-up advertising, were eventually planned by

Hewitt into a grid which mapped the course of the campaign by
counting down one column 'polling day minus 30, polling day minus
29', and so on.

So Hewitt was in no doubt: Labour had to set its own press and
broadcasting agenda, and be able to react on its own terms to
breaking stories. In a February 1987 note to the Leader's Committee she and Mandelson argued that Labour should 'abandon the
fixed routine of daily London press conferences'. It was a potentially
controversial decision, because, if followed through, Kinnock would
inevitably be accused of running away from the London press. The
main Hewitt/Mandelson argument was that daily press conferences
by Kinnock would demand 'a large investment of resources which is
simply not justified by results'. But they were also thought
'unnecessary for TV, which will be far more interested in a good
photo-opportunity coupled with a brief "on-site" interview with the
Leader or other senior campaigner'. Stories launched at the morning press conference rarely survived beyond the lunchtime news;
they would restrict the schedules of the leader and other key
campaigners. 'They merely provide the Fleet Street political correspondents – and the foreign media – with half-an-hour's daily knock-
about with senior Labour Party spokespeople who could be better
occupied.' Kinnock accepted the advice, and Labour opted for his
conducting a regular regional press conference, with only half of his
appearances being in London. The other morning press conferences
would be held by either Bryan Gould, as campaign co-ordinator, or
Roy Hattersley, as deputy leader. The decision to abandon the usual
routine was taken with considerable trepidation, but in the event it
proved brilliantly and unpredictably effective in disarming broadcasting and newspaper news editors. Hewitt and Mandelson had
also been worried that political commentators would find it difficult
to 'get a feel' for Labour's roving campaign, and would therefore
comment critically. As it turned out, despite Tory scorn for Kinnock's evasion of the London press, the commentators mostly found
the break in routine innovative and appealing.

The campaign schedule began at 7am with Mandelson and Bryan
Gould meeting the shadow communications agency (Labour's

volunteer helpers in the marketing and advertising world, see Chapter Four), followed by the campaign management team (including Hewitt and Clarke when they were in London). The campaign committee (comprising key figures from the national executive and the Shadow Cabinet) met twice a week, and more lengthily with Kinnock in the chair at weekends. Its role was less crucial. Bryan Gould acted as anchorman in the television sense of the word – the smiling, calm presenter who provides reassuring continuity. The small-featured handsomeness and relaxed anti-podean charm of Gould – an Oxford administrative law academic, and former presenter of Thames Television's *TV Eye* – appealed perfectly to middle Britain. Personal computer technology was exploited for the first time; Walworth Road sent out briefings to candidates via Telecom Gold three times a day. Bryan Gould and Mandelson met every day in the afternoon, too, to ensure that they were still on top of the main events of the day. It was the Vodaphone election; they were, like the campaign teams in the other parties, and all the journalists covering the campaign, in constant portable telephone contact with one another. All of that was revolutionary for Labour.

Even more revolutionary was Kinnock's acceptance of the advice he received from the shadow agency, that the '87 campaign would be presidential in style. Never before had Labour allowed the presentation of its party platform to be overridden by purely personal projection of the party leader. But Labour's new image-making team knew that the Conservatives would aim to build up Thatcher's image as a world leader of post-war stature comparable only with Churchill; Labour had to respond by building up Kinnock. Before Kinnock became party leader he had made his name as a fiery, exciting Welsh orator: he was flatteringly compared with Nye Bevan, his political hero. But the hard grind and frustration of the run-up to the campaign, on top of his changed leadership personality, appeared to have drained the sap from his speaking style: close supporters were distressed that his platform manner had become torpid and flat. At the first campaign strategy committee meeting David Blunkett urged Kinnock to speak from the gut during the campaign, to re-discover that former fire. Blunkett need not have bothered: once the adrenalin of contest was flowing, Kinnock's natural speaking style returned. And the shift of gear, because it was so conspicuous, attracted immediate comment: Kinnock was starting the campaign in fighting mood, while Thatcher seemed lacklustre. That sense of revived purpose in the leader made its impact at the outset of the campaign with his speech at Labour's first rally at Llandudno on 15 May when he coined the self-written line 'why am I the first Kinnock in a thousand generations to go to university?' – which was plagiarised by Joe Biden, one of Michael Dukakis' rivals for the Democratic Party nomination the following year.

The Kinnock revival was dramatically reinforced by the party election broadcast a few days later – which quickly became known as the *Chariots of Fire* PEB after its director, Hugh Hudson. It lifted Kinnock's personal rating by 19 percentage points overnight. A PEB devoted to Kinnock's leadership style and personality had long been planned; Hewitt, for one, strongly felt that the public saw Kinnock only through the prejudiced distortions of broadcasters and newspaper journalists, few of whom respected or liked him much. Hudson approached Mandelson in August 1986 saying he would like to help, having been converted to Labour's cause on the set of his *Chariots of Fire* film by Colin Welland, the screenwriter. Andrew Fox asked Hudson if he would make the take-away video of Kinnock's speech to the 1986 conference. Hudson duly turned up with a camera crew, all working completely voluntarily, and ran around the conference hall filming. The shots Hudson produced the following day delighted Mandelson and Hewitt; they asked him to begin work on a 'real Neil' party election broadcast.

With Hewitt preparing the brief and Welland acting as writing guide, Hudson gathered the basic material by viewing reels of library film on Kinnock. They singled out the sequence at the 1985 party conference when Kinnock scourged Liverpool Militant. That perfect example of Kinnock's oratory at its most excoriating was underlined in Hudson's completed production with a throbbing soundtrack; it subtly reminded viewers of the way the *Chariots of Fire* running races had been scored with the film's pulsing theme tune.

Film of Neil and Glenys on the cliffs walking hand-in-hand as the seagulls wheeled overhead was taken on the Welsh coast during the afternoon before the Llandudno speech.

By the time Hudson sat down to spend three days rough-cutting his film, Mandelson's attention had long wandered: he was wrapped up in the day-to-day campaign, and so had no idea what to expect when those involved all gathered in his room late on a Monday evening to view. At the end of the showing there was total silence. Hudson nervously jumped up, saying he could see they did not like it, he could re-edit it, there was plenty of time. 'Hugh ... ' Mandelson replied: 'We are knocked out.' But the following evening, as they sat together completing the editing, neither could decide how to title the broadcast. Mandelson suggested they borrow from Edward Heath's famous party election broadcast, and call it 'The man and his vision'. Hudson looked distressed at that, but could not immediately find an alternative. Eventually the director diffidently asked: 'Why don't we just call it "Kinnock"?' Mandelson, too tired to think of anything more clever, agreed. As a talking point the broadcast was unquestionably successful. At the campaign committee at which the broadcast was approved, Gerald Kaufman said it was so good the party should run it a second time during the campaign: David Blunkett turned to Tom Sawyer and asked him, *sotto voce*, to pass a sick-bag. At a Fabian Society conference at the end of the year Peter Mandelson said that the Hugh Hudson *Chariots of Fire* party election broadcast had been 'the most effective piece of political communication in recent political history': someone in the audience shouted out – 'But it didn't work, did it?'

LABOUR'S CAMPAIGN was therefore well-planned, and began confidently. But it was only ever expected to achieve relatively modest ends. In reality the primary aim was to ensure that Labour emerged the clear challenger to the Tories. Party strategists were in no doubt that, if the Alliance pulled away at the outset, there was a serious risk of Labour being squeezed into a corner where it could only delay its ultimate oblivion as a political force. That danger evaporated quickly when the Alliance campaign ran into the mud; but it was

probably Labour's accelerated start which left the Alliance adrift, for
the simple reason that the Liberal/SDP campaign fell instantly to a
reactive third place in news bulletins once Labour's campaign found
its stride.

Labour's successful campaign launch was the critical factor in the
party's survival as the main opposition force. Once the Alliance had
been beaten, Labour's objective turned to limiting the Tory majority.
No one close to Kinnock – except his wife, and even she only briefly
– believed Labour had any real hope of winning. Even within the
leader's camp there were staff who felt that, because a victory in
1987 would have been undeserved, it would probably also be in some
ways undesirable. A fluke win would have been based on weak
foundations; a Labour Government elected in '87, they felt, would
have been vulnerable to the faintest seismic tremor in the political
substratum. Kinnock and his team knew that, for all their pre-
campaign effort, the edifice of the Labour Party had only really been
redecorated, and moderately refurbished. Labour was, as yet, ill-
equipped for power.

One of the flakiest facades of that edifice was the defence policy.
There had been an early attempt to set the defence issue aside by
putting Denis Healey up during the first week of the campaign to
make a speech on non-nuclear defence. Mandelson had hoped that
that would draw and dissipate the Tory fire. It failed. Norman
Tebbit, Conservative party chairman, was too sharp to rush into
attacking Labour on defence. He waited until the target was out in
the open.

In fact, when that moment came, it took a couple of days for
Central Office reacted swiftly and efficiently. On the Sunday morning of 25 May David Frost interviewed Neil Kinnock on the
implications of Labour's non-nuclear policy. It was a gently-con-
ducted, unaggressive interview, with a small live audience. Kinnock
was relaxed, though he was tightly-briefed on what everyone in his
entourage knew would at some stage be a point of Labour vulnerabi-
lity. Frost took Kinnock steadily down the non-nuclear defence path
until he arrived at a moment where Russian soldiers were ready to
invade Britain. Instead of dismissing the scenario as preposterous,

Kinnock ambled into a prolix reply, saying that at the last resort, defence would be guerrilla warfare. What he meant to convey was that there would, because of the inevitability of such resistance, be little for the Russians to gain by invading Britain. But the remark became a sore protrusion, as much because it was clearly ill-considered and confused as for its content. It ensured that Labour's policy became a campaign highlight. Conservative Central Office media watchers snapped up the opportunity, and conducted intensive telephone briefings of political reporters – many of whom would otherwise have paid scant attention to an interview so early on a Sunday morning. The Tories' efforts ensured that the Frost interview was prominently covered in the Monday morning papers. The following day L. Cpl. Colin Ragman succeeded in making the normally unflappable John Smith – then Labour's trade and industry spokesman – squirm in the Election Call studio, by insisting that he needed the protection of a nuclear weapon. Then, on the Wednesday, the Tories co-ordinated their attack, with a Thatcher speech scourging the defence policy, while Tebbit wielded his rhetorical boot, accusing Labour of waving the red flag of socialism and the white flag of surrender. The Conservative campaign, which had suffered from a slow and seemingly aimless start, woke up. And the Kinnock TV-am interview lent additional impact to the Tories' final week posters – the most memorable campaign image – of a soldier surrendering with both arms in the air, and the simple slogan: 'Labour's Defence Policy'.

Labour's planning had always included a moment during the penultimate week when the campaign management team would assemble to decide a strategy for the final leg up to polling day. It was there that the inexperience of the Kinnock team showed. For all their communications talents, and the sharpness of their advance assessment of the changed nature of 1980s' election campaigning, Kinnock's aides had not reckoned with their own weariness. None of them had ever been involved at the heart of a general election campaign before. Kinnock himself had been a mere education spokesman during the '83 election; Clarke had been his research assistant. Hewitt had stood as the Labour candidate for Leicester

East; Mandelson was a television producer. Bryan Gould had held
the post of an academic, and Larry Whitty had been a GMB fixer.
None of them knew from their own experience what Margaret
Thatcher and all her team knew; that they would need to conserve
their energies for the final week.

Labour's 'final week' strategy meeting was held on the Tuesday of
the week before polling, in the Bevin Room at the TGWU's
Transport House headquarters in Smith Square, Westminster, less
than a stone's throw from Conservative Central Office. Clarke and
Hewitt had been on the campaign trail almost continuously, attending central planning meetings only when the leader's programme
allowed – often late at night. It was, therefore, harder for them to see
a complete picture of the campaign's progress. Mandelson had
anticipated that a particular issue – health perhaps – would take off
during the campaign, and that that could be made to run for the final
stage. He had also hoped that, like runners on relay, batons could be
handed over to fresher people for the last week. In fact, when it came
to the point of deciding the 'final week' strategy, there was no single
issue around which the campaign was turning. Hewitt had imagined
that, if it looked like Labour could win, they would adopt a 'preparing for Government' mantle; if Labour was dragging behind, some
desperate measure would be necessary. If Labour was holding up,
she thought, Kinnock would appeal to Alliance voters.

That was, in fact, the decision taken at the Bevin Room meeting.
Labour's message during the final week would be that the anti-Tory
majority should unite behind Labour. The message would be
unveiled by Kinnock himself at the Friday morning press conference, in London. For the day before, the campaign team had two
months previously planned a 'health shock' into the grid. Though no
one knew until close to the day what that would be, Mark Burgess
proved a hit. The boy who had been waiting 13 months for an
essential heart operation enabled Labour to maintain pressure on
Thatcher, particularly since she allowed herself to voice her personal
preference for private health during the Tory campaign press conference later that morning. Labour's team saw her confession as the
most damaging slip-up in the Conservative campaign. Even more

encouraging for Labour – at least until it became clear that it was a brief blip – was the *Daily Telegraph* Gallup poll that Thursday morning, showing that Labour had closed the gap on the Tories to four points. The poll, plus Burgess, brought 'wobbly Thursday' on Central Office. Tory jitters turned into an all-out fight for the conduct of their campaign between Thatcher (backed by Lord Young) and Tebbit.

Labour's team knew little of that. All they knew was that Kinnock's appeal to Alliance voters failed to take off on the Friday morning, largely because his presentation was tired and uninviting. Kinnock had drafted his own press conference address the previous night; it lacked conviction. Television news editors were unexcited. Labour would anyway have had difficulty backing up its chosen 'final week' strategy with an advertising blitz; there was no time to order new materials to match the message. New posters were ordered, depicting Kinnock in apocalyptic pose against an electric storm background, with the slogan 'The Country's Crying Out For Labour' underneath. The posters did achieve an impact – not least on Kinnock himself. The shadow agency had not dared show him the posters in advance, for fear that he would veto them – so the first Kinnock knew of his translation into a Nordic myth was when he saw one from the window of his campaign car.

In the course of that Saturday before polling, Labour lost its initiative. It was not merely a matter of fading away: by the evening Labour's campaign had broken into several pieces, cracked apart by a Tory attack on Labour's precarious tax policy. John MacGregor, the Chief Secretary to the Treasury, had been gaily claiming that Labour's 'hidden' programme (the manifesto, plus all the historic pledges in conference resolutions, ad hoc policy papers and occasional pamphlets that had been left out of the manifesto) would cost the taxpayer an extra £35bn to implement. Nigel Lawson's aides assiduously fed the figures out to reporters. Labour had consistently shrugged off that fully-anticipated attack, saying that spending priorities would be determined according to what a Labour Government could afford. Voters' scepticism about Labour's competence to run an efficient economy was evident, but remained relatively submerged in the active campaign until the final weekend. Roy Hattersley, as Shadow Chancellor, had agreed with John Smith, Bryan Gould, and Kinnock himself, a tax package which would substantially redistribute wealth from the best to the worst off. It had been closely costed by the front bench research advisors – in particular, Doug Jones, then working for Hattersley, and Henry Neuberger, then working for Kinnock. But Hattersley persuaded his colleagues to agree that the details – and the figures which went with them – should remain undisclosed, on the grounds that precision would provide the Tories with mounds of material that could quickly be processed through Treasury computers, and then used to claim that almost every voter stood to lose under Labour. Instead, Hattersley suggested, the front bench and leader should stick to the repeated assertion that no one who earned less than £25,000 a year, or £500 a week, would be worse off as a result of Labour's tax plans.

The seeds of the destruction of Labour's tax policy were sown on the same day as Mark Burgess scored Labour's greatest campaign success. In answer to a question from a *Guardian* reporter about the effect of national insurance contributions on the tax levels which Labour would levy, Kinnock broke the front bench agreement. He admitted that lifting the national insurance ceiling would mean that, 'a few extra pence a week' would be paid by people earning £15,000 to £17,000. Kinnock further conceded that Labour's abolition of the married man's tax allowance would mean that childless couples earning more than the average wage of £10,000 a year might lose. The abolition of the allowance had originally been in the manifesto, but was struck out by Kinnock and Hattersley. Their decision was frankly bizarre, since the party's proposals to increase child benefit had been kept in the manifesto and only made sense if the married man's tax allowance was being abolished.

Kinnock's lapses on Thursday meant that on the following morning, when he was supposed to be appealing to moderately prosperous Alliance voters, the *Daily Mail* headlined its front page 'Labour's Lies Over Taxation'. On the Saturday morning the *Daily Express* – again briefed closely by Lawson's staff – put more convincing detail on the accusation that Labour's tax policy deliberately deceived.

Their arguments were close and cogent – they were not smear
stories, but well-argued pieces, transparently based on competent
Tory research. The central point was that Labour's policy of lifting
the ceiling on national insurance contributions would mean that
many people earning £15,000 a year would lose. £15,000 was a
potent figure: though it was considerably more than average earnings
– then about £10,000 a year – it was a salary to which most people
could reasonably aspire. The newspapers were telling Labour's
target voters that they would be clobbered for tax if they succeeded
in earning what seemed a relatively modest income.

That would have been damaging enough. But it was immediately
compounded by muddle among Labour's senior politicians over
what the party policy actually meant. On the Wednesday – the day
after the 'final week' strategy meeting – the campaign team had sent a
message to Hattersley instructing him to turn up in Cambridge on
the Saturday for a big evening rally at the Guildhall – billed as the
'Come Home to Labour' rally. Cambridge was thought apt for the
final week strategy of appealing to Alliance voters, because it was a
three-way marginal, with Shirley Williams standing for the SDP.

Hattersley was happy to oblige, and broke his campaign tour at
York to meet Kinnock at Cambridge Labour Party HQ. On the way
he received, but only half understood, a message from Bryan Gould
saying that he should emphasize to Kinnock the need to stick to the
originally agreed line: that no one under the £500 a week threshold
would lose under Labour. Gould's anxiety stemmed from a local
radio interview in Welwyn, in which Kinnock had again appeared to
suggest that it was possible that some people earning less than
£25,000 might lose. The question was put to Kinnock because
Nigel Lawson had used that morning's press conference to extend
the Tory attack on Labour's tax plans. Broadcasters took up the story
for the first time, so that the tax policy was the running news story all
day Saturday. Hattersley and Kinnock met alone in a back room,
refusing to allow any of their staff in, but Hattersley went into that
meeting and left it not knowing why Gould had made his anxious
telephone call. At the end of the rally a press officer went up on to the
Guildhall platform and asked Hattersley if he would do an

impromptu piece to camera with presenter Martyn Lewis, who
would be asking questions down a line from London. Hattersley
stepped down, a microphone was taped on to his shirt-front, and
Lewis immediately asked him if it was true that no one earning less
than £25,000 would lose? Hattersley said that was right – at which
Lewis pressed on to say that Bryan Gould was saying one thing at the
London press conference, and Neil Kinnock was saying something
quite different on a local radio programme. Unexpectedly trapped,
and oblivious of the detail of his colleagues' statements, Hattersley
took the only course available; he abused the interviewer. All
Hewitt's anticipation of electronic news gathering counted for
nothing when the politics turned sour.

The sequence confirmed voters' lack of faith in the likelihood of
Labour-led prosperity. At a subsequent Institute of Contemporary
History session on the election, Mandelson said that the campaign
plan so thoroughly enabled Labour to stick to its own social policy
agenda that it was 'thrown only twice – over defence following Neil
Kinnock's interview with David Frost, and then over taxation in the
last week of the campaign'. His verdict on 'Labour's brilliant
campaign' was that 'it proved ineffective in dislodging the Government, but decisive in seeing off the Alliance and re-establishing
Labour as the major contender for power'. However, despite the
modernizing theme, and the adoption of a forward-looking image,
Labour turned voters off by talking endlessly about the divided
society and the unemployed.

Most significantly, Kinnock himself privately blamed the tax
policy for the scale of Labour's defeat. He never accepted that both
he and Hattersley were jointly to blame. Hattersley had to accept
responsibility for insisting on such a high-risk strategy of hiding
behind a veil of barely plausible figures. But it was Kinnock who blew
Hattersley's strategy by giving the wrong answer to the right question. The party leader believed at the time that, had it not been for
the chaos of the final weekend, the Conservative majority might have
been half the actual outcome. In fact the Tories lost only 21 seats,
leaving their majority still in three figures. For Kinnock, that was the
main disappointment: a Tory majority of 40, 50, even 60 seats, would

have been narrow enough at least to frustrate the Conservative manifesto, particularly its most controversial elements, such as the poll tax and education proposals. That would have given Labour backbenchers something to fight for during the first part of the parliament. The disintegration of the tax policy, Kinnock felt, was largely to blame for his party's sense of powerlessness and hopelessness on the morning of Friday 12 June.

The conduct, course and outcome of the 1987 election campaign moulded the policy review. The tone and style of party leadership, backed by the modernized communications techniques which Kinnock had encouraged in the run-up, was fixed by the campaign in people's minds. The 1987 general election wove Kinnock's style into Labour's fabric, even to the extent of becoming more or less acceptable to the party's membership. More importantly, reaction to Labour policy, or the lack of policy, was prime evidence at the election inquest. The main elements of the campaign became reference points for the review.

3
BLUEPRINT FOR CHANGE

THE GOVERNMENT'S 102–seat majority, after such a professional Labour campaign, numbed the party leadership. Labour's opinion poll ratings barely twitched during the campaign: the Tory lead held steady, regardless of Labour's efforts. Tories 42.3 per cent, Labour 30.8, Alliance 22.6: that was dispiriting enough. But the regional distribution gave deeper cause for dismay. Labour's support declined the further south one went. In the crucial marginal seats – in the Midlands, and the north west of England – the party made no headway. And the number of marginal constituencies was declining. Many Conservative MPs in formerly close-fought seats – including some in the north of England – were becoming so entrenched and well-known locally that every Labour defeat made it more difficult to prise them out again.

Apart from Tony Benn lauding the campaign organizers for putting on the best show since 1959, and Michael Meacher rather surprisingly arguing for a top-to-bottom reconsideration of the reason for the slide in Labour's appeal, little of consequence happened at the national executive's election inquest session on 24 June. Kinnock was urged on all sides to adopt a forward-looking stance, review policy, rethink Labour's position, gear the party to the 1990s, modernize. But those were buzz phrases humming around inside a post-election bell-jar, settling nowhere. Although there plainly had to be a post-election review of policy, no one knew how it should be conducted, how wide-ranging it should be, or indeed what real purpose it might have. Rather than sketch out a blueprint of his own, Kinnock let his team cast around among themselves for a common idea, while the party flapped uncertainly on the post-election beach. That was typical of him: Kinnock's ability to make judgments, and to take and execute important decisions, could never be questioned; but he always lacked managerial initiative.

The first written scheme came from Geoff Bish, the Walworth Road policy director, and one of the longest-serving Labour Party bureaucrats. Bish – balding, with straggling side hair and an open shirt – presided from behind a pile of policy directorate filing cabinets and papers at the heart of Walworth Road. Amiable, open, and easy-going, the policy director too often displayed the kind of mild indecisiveness, and traditional view of Labour's internal politics, which most grated with Kinnock. Bish also had the misfortune to have been working at Walworth Road far longer than Kinnock had been party leader – nearly 20 years in fact. The party leader, while labouring under a windbag reputation himself, preferred to surround himself with crisply assertive minds – ones that he had appointed and knew to be fresh, and loyal to him personally.

Bish went away from the 24 June executive to prepare a policy review proposition. His paper was submitted to the 6 July home policy committee of the executive. Headed 'Policy Development for the 1990s', it began by picking up the prevalent view that policy must 'look forward to the needs of the new decade – not backward to the missed opportunities of the seventies and eighties'. But the paper drifted in a way that was guaranteed to annoy Kinnock. The party leader so vigorously dismissed the paper that Bish concluded he did not want a thorough policy review after all. That was not the case: Kinnock was simply prejudiced against Bish, and thought the paper vague, more exhortatory than effective. The leader's office view was that, while the gist of the Bish proposals was right, they could easily turn to treacle.

The real post-mortem tension resolved itself, not in the formal confines of the national executive, but in a flurried contest over objectives between Bryan Gould, Roy Hattersley, and Kinnock himself. The deputy leader envied the publicity acclaim being enjoyed by Gould, and the support which Gould had received during the campaign from the leader. His annoyance intensified when

Gould topped the Shadow Cabinet poll on 8 July. He bridled at not being consulted by Kinnock over the review, and was further irritated by the knowledge that Kinnock blamed his deputy for the failure of the tax policy to stand up to campaign pressure: in Hattersley's view, the blame lay with Kinnock's own failure to hold the agreed line.

Hattersley's discontent found a focus when Gould gave an interview on the BBC radio programme *The World This Weekend* on 5 July – the day before Bish's paper went to the home policy committee. Gould argued that the party needed to approach policy making in an entirely new way. 'We all recognise that too often we have brought in groups of experts who tell us what we ought to be doing or saying. We then agree on that policy, and then we think, almost as an afterthought, of how it is to be sold to the electorate.' Kinnock agreed with that: he had struggled to overcome the labyrinthine and cumbersome structure of vast national executive policy sub-committees, prior to the '87 campaign.

But Gould went on: 'What we ought to be doing is looking at where policies ought to come from, what the demand is, what interests we ought to be serving. In that way we can make sure that the policy includes its popular appeal from the outset.' Those two sentences gave enough meat to commentators inside and outside the party who wanted to show that Kinnock was planning to sell out on socialism, by pandering to voters' most selfish demands, purely for short term electoral gain. The result was that the questioning of Kinnock by reporters after the home policy meeting concentrated on whether he was proposing to water down socialism – to which he was obliged to reply: 'I am not in the trimming business.'

Now it was Kinnock who was irritated. He had been delighted by Bryan Gould's performance as Labour's campaign anchorman. But Gould's newly-identified political closeness to Kinnock meant that every word he uttered was being interpreted as a proxy for the leader's opinion. Kinnock went on to provide some evidence to support that view. He also said after the 6 July home policy meeting: 'Being part of a collective is not as strong as it used to be. Our initial approach has got to be from the party to the individual. They have got to be told that socialism is the answer for them, because socialism looks after the individual.' That was enough to convince Roy Hattersley, at least, that Gould's remarks were in truth a reflection of Kinnock's mind. For all his reputation as a manipulative right-winger, Hattersley felt he could not countenance that degree of electoralism from the leadership. He had stayed in the Labour Party when his closest former allies quit Labour to form the SDP and he had subsequently fought to give the party a distinctive intellectual identity. He was infuriated by the implication that Labour might be converted to the kind of social democracy advocated by David Owen.

Hattersley's political doubts about Kinnock's direction combined with a personal sense of grievance. He became a loose cannon rolling round the deck. On 11 July, in an interview on Channel Four's *A Week in Politics* he fired a warning shot at what he suspected lay behind Bryan Gould's thinking. 'The idea that six weeks after an election defeat, somebody can come along and say: "These are all the things we do; we change this policy, we have a new defence policy, we abandon nationalization, we give up our view of equality. What we do, we send out a lot of marketing men into the country, just as the Democrats in America did 20 years ago, and say, 'what are the policies people want' and then when we find out what they'll vote for, we'll write it into our manifesto" – that is not the sort of politics I want to be involved in.' He added: 'If you were running a religious programme, and there was a bishop sitting here, you wouldn't say to him: "What's all this about the Sermon on the Mount? You've been going on about the Sermon on the Mount for 2,000 years, we need something new to attract the trendy, upwardly mobile middle-classes". What we have to do is stick to our Sermon on the Mount, which is the view of equality, a freer society in which power and wealth is more evenly distributed, and interpret that in language that people understand.' He concluded, in case the message was not altogether clear: 'I've not gone through the last six years – the defeat of '79 as well, the humiliation of '83 – to make the Labour Party into a new sort of Social Democratic Party.'

From Hattersley's point of view, the interview achieved its desired aim, of conveying a message to the party leader. At the parliamentary

Labour Party meeting the following week, Hattersley denied any suggestion of a clash with Gould; he was in a sense being honest – his exchange had been, indirectly, with Kinnock himself.

At that meeting of the parliamentary party, MPs backed the need for a policy review. But Kinnock still did not know what he wanted from it; he only knew there had to be one. The impasse was broken by Tom Sawyer. The Geordie deputy general secretary of Nupe was a former Bennite, who believed passionately that the party had gone astray in the 1970s because the parliamentary leadership lost touch with the rank and file. A compact, bearded and quietly spoken man, Sawyer did not immediately present the image of an active executive. His lack of flamboyance belied him: he thought harder about political strategy, and about what he believed to be politically right, than many more articulate Kinnockites. He had, among them, an often surprising authority that was rarely appreciated by outsiders. Sawyer also possessed a quick sense of disarming mockery and self-effacing diffidence which enabled him to present potentially unpalatable political options without sparking confrontation.

Long before the '87 election campaign, Sawyer began thinking about what the party might need to do after defeat. He started from the view that Labour – and he himself – had travelled down a Bennite blind alley in the early 1980s. In doing so, Sawyer believed the party had come to seem irrelevant as a political movement to most British adults. It had even become irrelevant to many people who, out of nothing more than habit, continued to vote Labour.

In deciding to take the lead – from his position as chairman of the home policy committee of the national executive – Sawyer went further than providing the blueprint for the review. He also offered Kinnock his services in carrying the process through. Often discreetly, certainly with little public proclamation, Sawyer steered the policy review on to its eventual course. He began the process when he returned to the Nupe offices in South London after the 6 July meeting, bitterly depressed by what he had heard and the reception given to Bish's paper. Sawyer spoke first with Adam Sharples, his union's head of research and a former Labour Party headquarters researcher, about how the party should advance and what form the review could take. He widened his discussions to include his closer political friends: David Blunkett and Michael Meacher, with whom he had been allied on the executive prior to the 1987 election; Eddie Haigh, the Transport and General Workers Union executive member whose judgment he trusted; and the sharp new people whose thinking he respected, and who he felt sure would be leading players in subsequent events – Bryan Gould and Peter Mandelson in particular.

Bish's 6 July paper had proposed the preparation of 'a major policy document', to be agreed by the national executive and Shadow Cabinet, for presentation and adoption at a special party conference in 1990. That document should not be too detailed. Bish suggested small study groups, did not believe early decisions needed to be made, and concluded by suggesting that he prepare a more detailed proposal for the November executive, following a short presentation to the party conference in late September.

Sawyer's main anxiety was that the party might lose its way as its most prominent politicians headed off in different directions. There had to be a means of directing the post-election effort; of persuading everyone to set off down the same road, and keep marching roughly in time.

He and Sharples believed that the policies of the party needed radical change. But they also believed that the way in which the party reviewed its policies was almost as important as the final policy product. A more multi-disciplinary approach, they felt, should be adopted to avoid the review going down the familiar tramlines of Labour Party policy. Spokesmen should be prevented from riding their hobby horses. The review should be as open as possible. It should be an educational process for the party membership, who should be drawn in by being asked to talk to the electorate about what they wanted from Labour.

Sharples' draft was sent under Sawyer's name to Kinnock. That paper kick-started the policy review, when it went to the executive in September in place of Bish's earlier proposal. It began with a caveat: 'It would be unnecessary and wrong to rush into public rejections of policies on which we fought the election, simply because we think they were unpopular'. And it would be wrong and impossible to start the review 'with a blank sheet'. Not everyone around Kinnock entirely agreed with that – but Sawyer was sure that the party would reject the review on any other, purely electoralist terms. It mattered little to the scope of the review, since the thrust of the paper was that the need for review grew directly from defeat.

The aim of the review groups should 'not be to embark on wholesale revision of policy, but rather to review some of the key themes and issues'. Those were defined as the relevance of policy to the majority of voters, how to get Labour's message across, how to persuade target voters – 'the people whose votes we need to win over' – and the social changes that Britain could expect over the decade. Sawyer advocated that the party should plug into three main sources. The first was public opinion: 'Our policy must be responsive to the concerns of the voters – particularly those we need to win over.' The paper rushed on to qualify: 'This is not to say we should abandon our programme in favour of a collection of "popular" ' policies. But policy development cannot be divorced from communication of that policy.' The review's inception, then, bore the imprint of the idea that the party's communications strategy could no longer be detached from its policy prospectus. Sawyer's other sources were party members themselves (a programme he pursued in the second phase of the review, with limited success), and overseas experience – by which he meant learning from European, Scandinavian and antipodean socialist parties. The mechanics would be, as Bish had earlier suggested, joint groups comprising representatives from both the executive and the Shadow Cabinet. But unlike Bish, Sawyer added that the whole process should be co-ordinated from Kinnock's office.

Sawyer's proposals for what the review groups should encompass were a long way from the final structure. He suggested that different groups should look at: changes in the electorate, especially the working class vote; public services for the 1990s; industry and enterprise (public ownership, but also wealth creation); fairness at work (part-timers and women, as much as unions); economic and social equality; and a review of the party conference. All those areas were covered in the reconstruction effort conducted by the party over the next two to three years, but not in the form Sawyer originally envisaged. Despite Kinnock's distrust of the Walworth Road policy development director, Bish did in fact strongly influence the final form of the review. He submitted a covering note to the Sawyer/ Sharples paper which advocated three additional review groups: one on economic strategy (which was to become Bryan Gould's group); another on 'centralization, local democracy and the rights of individual citizens' (which was to become Roy Hattersley's group); and one to cover what Bish called 'the international dimension, defence etc'. Under Sawyer's plan no single group would have been specifically responsible for tackling defence policy. Bish added that more detailed longer-term policy groups might be needed to look at areas such as tax and social security: in the final event, a single group covered those two fields.

Sawyer's outline was approved by the 14 September pre-conference executive without a vote – though Dennis Skinner argued against, and Tony Benn warned that the party risked seeming opportunistic. Also approved for submission to conference was a paper arguing the case for review. Though largely written by Bish (who scavenged Kinnock's speeches for his text), its title was provided by the communications directorate: 'Moving Ahead'. The introduction to the paper was compiled by Sawyer and Mandelson. So the scheme that went to the 1987 conference contained all the main ingredients of the review as it was eventually constituted. It was still in fragmentary form, however, a long way from its completed shape. Sawyer told journalists after the September executive: 'Some may mistakenly or unfairly portray these proposals as a new revisionism, and an attempt to swing the party away from traditional principles and socialist values. For those, the only true test of radicalism is a deep conservatism in thought and ideas.' The party knew that Sawyer meant what he said, because his background on the left was unquestionable.

The 1987 conference in Brighton was defined by the sullenness with which the party acquiesced in the leadership project. There was no enthusiasm among constituency activists, who made it plain that they believed the whole enterprise was a cloak for selling out. Equally they had no desire to be blamed for smashing up the prototype on its launching pad. Sawyer knew better than most that the party would be intensely suspicious; he also sincerely believed that the review would fail unless it carried the party along with it. That was why his role was so invaluable to Kinnock. Without that commitment to the review process on Sawyer's part, Kinnock might have faced a more fearsome internal backlash than actually materialised.

On 28 September Sawyer's proposals went through with barely any bloodletting, but Kinnock knew his party's commitment was precarious. He tested the review waters very gingerly when he took the rostrum the next day. The market, he said, was 'adequate for deciding the price and availability of many goods and many services' – an anodyne formula in comparison to the shift he would make the following year. The left detected Kinnock's tone; but his words were too restrained to merit frontal assault.

The day after that, however, gave ample grounds to confirm the left's suspicions. Again it was Bryan Gould who provided a peg on which to hang the accusation that the review's outcome was both preconceived, and a sell-out to Thatcherism. On 30 September, debating industrial policy and the key issue of public ownership in the conference chamber, Gould aired the notion of a 'popular socialism', which would match Thatcher's claim to have established 'popular capitalism'. Gould proposed the creation of a share-owning democracy under Labour, in which power over enterprise would lie in the hands of the mass of ordinary people owning shares as workers and consumers. Sawyer was livid; having succeeded in oiling the passage of the review proposals past the conference, the leadership now found that Gould's speech had enabled the left to present the review as a preparation for socialist betrayal. The only way of hurriedly rowing back was to reinterpret Gould's speech. A fringe meeting was arranged at short notice for the following evening (under the bizarre auspices of a small City of London lobbying group). The packed meeting in a tiny pub backroom heard Gould explain that he had been misinterpreted. He had meant to suggest only that employee share ownership schemes, workers' co-operatives, and other well tried and tested ideas which the left had been advocating as socialist alternatives to nationalization since the mid-1970s, could be converted into a form of popular socialism. Nevertheless the belief was universal among Shadow Cabinet and national executive colleagues that Gould did, in fact, originally intend to say what he was read as saying: that Labour should leapfrog Thatcherism in the field of industrial ownership.

That left defence. In his speech on the Tuesday, Kinnock had sampled reaction to his developing, post-Reykjavik views on options for a redrafted non-nuclear policy, by saying: 'We will work to ensure that we have policies that are capable of dealing with the changed conditions of the 1990s, in a way that will enhance the prospect of removing reliance on nuclear weapons of any description.' When it came to the defence debate on 1 October, however, constituency delegates enjoyed their only real celebration of the week as they emphatically confirmed unilateralism. Right-wing trade union leaders, along with Denis Healey (who had retired in June from the Shadow Cabinet), warned that the party would never win an election unless the policy was changed; the conference majority countered that Labour's unilateralism would have been a campaign asset if the leadership had enthusiastically promoted it. Everyone – including Joan Ruddock, the former Campaign for Nuclear Disarmament general secretary who had been elected MP for Lewisham Deptford – said the policy should be updated. But no one from the unilateralist majority believed that it should be fundamentally changed. The lines were clearly drawn, and Kinnock had no intention of opening up any battle. He told a television interviewer that evening: 'The use of such weapons would ensure our obliteration, and consequently they are not plausible weapons for the defence of our country in the event of war.' Kinnock's colleagues concluded that the leader would never shift far from his long-held and ardently-argued unilateralist position. Though Hattersley, Kaufman, Gould and others felt that the prospects for policy change were healthy in other fields, they did not then believe that Kinnock would change his mind on defence.

The final shape of the review was submitted to the executive by Larry Whitty, the party's general secretary, in October. He suggested that the 1988 conference should receive a 'statement on values, objectives and an outline of Labour's policy programme'. The review groups would 'assess the policy issues and opportunities in the 1990s; make an assessment of the relevance and credibility of existing party policy matched against the need and concerns of groups of voters; and recommend broad themes of political strategy as well as policy areas in which more detailed examination is required'. Although Whitty did not say so, each of those three points again linked formulation of policy directly to the possibility of selling it. Appraisal of the 'opportunities for the 1990s' would rest to a great extent on shadow communications agency forecasting, just as assessment of existing party policy in relation to the needs and concerns of groups of voters could only be achieved through testing voters' opinions, particularly by using qualitative market research. It was, therefore, clear that the broad themes of political strategy were more likely to be devised by professional strategists – such as Mandelson and his agency – than policy researchers.

The October meeting approved that completed version of the review structure: seven policy groups, each with two convenors, one drawn from the national executive, the other from the Shadow Cabinet. All the thinking thus far had been to limit the range of the review to key policies, and to a broad brush approach, though the review groups actually appeared to cover virtually the whole range of policy.

Sawyer's recommendation that there should be an extended effort to engage in dialogue with target voters, and to involve rank-and-file party members, led to the invention of 'Labour listens'. Its objective was 'to tap the fullest possible range of public opinion about Labour's policies as part of the review'. On 4 November, Kinnock told Labour MPs – who had specifically asked for a discussion of the review – that the 'Labour listens' events would be 'a critical part of the whole exercise'. Labour needed 'to convey the message that we are listening, that we are facing up to the real problems that people are experiencing, and that we are ready to receive opinions from the general public and from specialist professional and voluntary organizations'.

The review was now ready to move from drawing board to building site, but what was the architect's aim? At the party conference Kinnock argued: 'The question of whether the policies were right or wrong in 1987 is of course a matter of some interest. But the question of whether the policies will be right or wrong for 1991 will be the matter of the most profound importance. That is the dominant consideration in this review.' A month later he faced the allegation of 'electoralism' – the accusation that the review was simply a cloak for selling out in return for unprincipled electoral gain – by pleading guilty. The party, he said, had to have 'a constant unremitting, unswerving dedication to defeating the Tories'. There, in essence, was the objective as Kinnock saw it. He had no more complex or subtle strategy in mind. Bryan Gould – speaking not for the leader, but for himself – put it rather differently, but equally bluntly, at a Fabian Society conference titled 'Beating the Blues' on 5 December: 'If you insist on positions you had 20 or 30 years ago, if you insist nothing has changed, then you are dead.'

4

GLITZNOST

THE IMMEDIATE task was to shove, cajole and arm-twist the party into looking forward, rather than let it squat about poring over past miseries. That meant someone had to tell the party what opportunities and pitfalls the 1990s might hold for a socialist movement. That role was filled by the shadow communications agency – Labour's secretive but influential image-makers. It was there, among aides and volunteers in the marketing and advertising world, that the idea of building a party fit for the millennium germinated. But there was no question – as some later suspected – of the party being hijacked by a veiled conspiracy of Soho advertising executives and Covent Garden market researchers. The agency could not have carried the concept which lay behind the review unless it precisely fitted Neil Kinnock's personal leadership vision. Any strategic design or image-creation promoted by those around Kinnock would be worthless unless it matched the party leader's style and aims. Without Kinnock's active engagement, no project would long survive public scrutiny. Equally, however, Kinnock's leadership aims – particularly his guiding principle that he should try to carry every change as near unanimously as possible – could not have been achieved without the skills of the shadow agency. Its value lay as much in persuading the party of the need for change, as in persuading the public of Labour's electability.

Detecting the demand, the shadow agency pulled together a team that could tell the party's extended leadership what Britain in the 1990s might look like. On 20 November 1987 it gave a three and a half hour presentation to a joint meeting of the Shadow Cabinet and national executive at Transport House. The presentation, called 'Labour and Britain in the 1990s', exploded on some of those present like a grenade; in the minds of others it smouldered away on a slow-burning fuse. That session alone would make the influence of the shadow agency on the development of the review inestimably strong. But the agency's role in the reconstruction of the Labour Party extended further. Its direct input to Labour's entire strategic outlook, as well as its purely presentational style, was continuous from early 1986. It reached its apogee in the final stages of the policy review, as the thematic cohesion of the completed review was developed to a great extent out of the agency's research and analysis.

The shadow agency originated in October 1985, when a small group of people gathered for dinner at the north London home of Robin Paxton, a London Weekend Television producer. Paxton's role was solely of matchmaker: he had invited two friends, at their mutual request, who had never met each other before. One was Peter Mandelson, with whom Paxton had been working for the past three years on LWT's cerebral political programme, *Weekend World*. The other was Philip Gould, a young advertising executive. Though Mandelson had shown high-flying promise as a young producer, he felt out of place in the television industry. He had originally wanted to work as a political advisor, and began first at the TUC, and then working for Albert Booth, Labour's transport spokesman. But, when the party began ripping itself into shreds in 1980/81, Mandelson followed Denis Healey's advice and quit politics temporarily to acquire an outside skill. By 1985 he was ripe to return to politics. After talking to Clarke, he succeeded in being offered the newly-created post of campaigns and communications director at Labour's Walworth Road headquarters. Mandelson took the job, and a £10,000 salary cut, on his 32nd birthday, in October 1985.

Philip Gould – the other participant in the dinner-table match-making – had left school at 16. He worked for his local Labour Party in Woking, Surrey, took A-levels at nights, and went to study politics at Sussex University. After an MA in London, he decided to learn everything there was to know about advertising. He succeeded to the extent of forming his own agency, and then selling it so that he could

go to the London Business School and study again on a one-year
Sloane Fellowship. Gould, 34 at the time he first met Mandelson,
had shoulder-length and mildly unkempt dark hair. Throughout the
dinner he was nervous and shy. His conversation flitted, rushing at a
point, and then backing off. His enthusiasm and galloping energy,
however, were plainly evident – and he was in deep earnest about
what he wanted to tell Mandelson. He argued that Labour's image,
and consequently its electoral fortunes, could be metamorphosed if
only the party would exploit the kind of modern communications and
marketing methods which the Conservative Party had used to such
effect since 1979. The theme was no armchair fantasy; it was
Gould's private mission – the one job he really wanted.

Mandelson, for all his three years experience on a low-audience
television programme, knew almost nothing about modern mass
communications except what his sharp lay observation had taught
him. In particular, he knew nothing about the techniques and
practices of the advertising industry – something Gould had devoted
a decade to teaching himself. After the dinner Gould wrote a long
letter to Mandelson which led to the new Walworth Road director
spending £750 of the party's money – before he had even taken up
his post in November 1985 – commissioning Gould to carry out a
communications audit on the Labour Party.

Gould began work on 11 November and delivered his report
(partly rewritten in the interim by Mandelson himself) on 22
December. Its 64 pages of analysis of the party's presentation,
political positioning, and campaigning techniques, became the battle plan for a revolution in Labour's image. Gould, under Mandelson's instructions, pulled no punches. The first page of his report
said: 'Positive perceptions of the Labour Party tend to be outweighed
by negative concerns, particularly of unacceptable "beyond the pale"
policies and figures; the party sometimes acts in a way that confirms
these concerns by scoring "own goals"; there is some feeling that the
Labour Party does not, as it once did, represent the majority, instead
it is often associated with minorities; the party has something of an
old-fashioned cloth cap image . . . ' Labour had been producing too
many different leaflets to run too many different campaigns, directed

more at party activists than the voting public. Party officials and
campaigners regarded tabloid newspapers with disdain, even though
they were, Gould emphasized, the main medium for Labour's target
voters. Press officers, instead of actively promoting the party, were
reacting to hour-to-hour, day-to-day problems. There was no co-
ordination of the message Labour was trying to convey to voters, no
political oversight of party political broadcasts. Labour's use of
advertising was poorly orchestrated or non-existent.

Gould recommended the formation of a shadow communications
agency 'to focus and structure outside communications expertise
and assistance'. It would have 'its own monthly steering committee, a
part-time convenor, and eventually its own offices'. Its role would be
'to draft strategy, conduct and interpret research, produce advertising and campaign themes, and provide other communications support as necessary'. The agency would use modern market research
methods: it would, for example, commission monthly qualitative
research 'to monitor the electorate's mood, and supplement polling/
quantitative research'. Hitherto, Labour had used only quantitative
opinion polling conducted by Mori. Quantitative polling finds out
what large, representative samples of people think in response to set
questions; it does not reveal much about why they respond in that
way, nor does it discover the degree to which their opinions are in
flux, or qualified by other unperceived factors. Qualitative research
complements traditional polling by eliciting that additional information. It comprises relaxed sessions with usually six or eight people
selected from a balance of jobs and backgrounds, asking them over a
period of a couple of hours their feelings and views about a range of
topics. Rather than the pollsters' questions determining the outcome, the small sample of interviewees shapes its own questions.
The material is presented, not in the form of majority or minority
opinions, but in the form of key responses which describe most fully
how people are reacting. Qualitative research is often, for obvious
reasons, used to test the likely reaction to prototype products; it
became a valuable tool for testing some of Labour's emergent review
policies as the groups worked towards their final reports in early
1989.

Gould's report continued by arguing that Labour's 'communications message' had to be honed and simplified. There should be one overall campaign theme at any given time, along with priority subsidiary themes, the language and presentation of which should be simplified and refined by the agency. The message then needed to be orchestrated, with regular reiteration of key themes: 'Major speeches, events and PPBs [party political broadcasts] should be followed up by supplementary speeches, a co-ordinated PR push, and the use (where possible) of advertising and direct mail.' Party political broadcasts would stay with John Gau, the party's paid PPB producer, but be client-led (i.e. shaped by the party) for the first time. Hitherto Gau had been left to produce broadcasts on his own, according to very broad specifications; in future the shadow agency would outline creative approaches, in line with the main message Labour was seeking to convey.

The key communications principle was that there should be 'a shift in campaigning emphasis from "grass roots"/opinion forming, to influencing electoral opinion through the mass media'. Under Nick Grant, Mandelson's predecessor, campaigns were conceived as leafletting and door-knocking exercises. Gould argued that in future all campaigns 'should have the influence of electoral opinion as their first priority'. All creative work would go through the shadow agency. Advertising had 'a vital role to play' because it enabled 'direct communication to the target audience in hostile media'. It could help set an agenda, 'raise the flag for party workers, focussing issues and raising morale' and 'attack and destabilize the Government'.

Then Gould laid down the roots of the red rose by proposing that the party adopt a new corporate image. 'A design company should be commissioned (under the auspices of the SCA) to examine all aspects of the "corporate appearance" of the party, including the party logo,' he wrote. Early the following year Mandelson proceeded by writing a note to Larry Whitty, asking the general secretary's blessing for a new 'corporate identity' for the party: 'It is vital to re-inforce the impression of an innovative party shedding old associations and image.' The use of a red rose as party emblem had long been favoured by Kinnock, who regarded the red flag as dated, and

associated with old-style socialism. As early as the 1984 Euro-
elections, Kinnock had quietly displaced the flag and substituted the
Socialist International symbol of a red rose in the grip of a macho
fist. He told Peter Mandelson he wanted the rose to become the new
corporate image, but Gould insisted that the designer – Michael
Wolf, of Wolf Olins – should be allowed to pursue his own creative
thoughts. Wolf spontaneously offered a rose himself. He commissioned the drawing of 200 different roses before he landed on the
design which is now distinctive on all Labour's campaigning material. The flower – which has long been the emblem of several
European socialist parties – even embosses the standard Labour
letterhead. Some less self-conscious Labour MPs regularly arrive at
work with a red rose in their buttonholes; vases of them adorn every
Labour platform. For many the rose is a mildly embarrassing joke.
But Mandelson's earnest faith in the symbol's importance has never
been shaken. He told the Institute of Contemporary History in late
1987 that the red rose was, on its own, a significant factor in the
success of the 1987 general election campaign: 'It created a harmony
and cohesion all of its own,' he claimed. The emergence of the red
rose from Kinnock's own suggestion was characteristic. When
Mandelson went in search of a new theme tune, it was the party
leader who proposed the Brahms passage used by Labour during the
1987 election campaign.

   Mandelson knew the party would be unable to afford a fully-
retained advertising agency, and that it would anyway prove difficult
to find an agency of sufficient calibre and resources willing to be
identified as 'Labour's agency', in the way that Saatchi and Saatchi
had become tagged as the Conservative Party agency. Gould had
talked about the Republicans' 'Tuesday Group' in the United States.
Instead of hiring an agency, the Republicans picked the brains of the
best people they could find throughout the advertising and media
world, who were supporters, and willing to give their services
voluntarily. Gould argued that Labour needed, not only top-class
image-makers, but also ones who were committed to the party's aims
and purpose. That way the message would emerge more confidently
persuasive in tone. It would also be considerably cheaper; and, with

the party spending only 17 per cent of its total budget at the time on communications, Gould knew that in the Labour Party, cash for campaigning came at a premium.

The national executive approved the creation of the shadow agency at its February 1986 meeting, with Philip Gould appointed co-ordinator. Thereafter Labour took the bulk of Gould's energies, and became his main source of income; in effect, he worked full-time for the party, doing other work on the run. Throughout, he regarded Peter Mandelson as his client. He was commissioned by Mandelson, and reported to Mandelson. They spoke to each other every day, and so fused their operations that they often found it hard to distinguish who proposed what. But their division of responsibility was clear: Gould diagnosed and evaluated, Mandelson carried out the surgery. The analysis produced by Gould was delivered with *force majeur* by Mandelson. Sometimes Mandelson openly stated that proposals were coming from 'outside experts', in the belief that the politicians were more likely to swallow their advice than his own. On other occasions he felt obliged to conceal the source of his material, for fear that politicians would shy away from marketing and media manipulators.

Philip Gould's communications ideas were central to Labour's revival, throughout the 1987 election campaign and the policy review period. But it was Mandelson who implemented them, often taking enormous political risks with his own position in order to do so. It follows, therefore, that few of those present at the February 1986 executive knew what they were agreeing to; they only understood that its cost would be minimal compared to its anticipated benefits.

The agency met for the first time that month, under the chairmanship of Chris Powell. Powell was then managing director, subsequently chief executive, of Boase Massimi Pollitt. (He was also, incidentally, the brother of Charles Powell, who, as her ever-present private secretary to Margaret Thatcher, was one of the most influential middle-ranking civil servants in Whitehall. One brother has since early 1986 been Labour's main advertising advisor; the other has been the Conservative Prime Minister's key foreign affairs advisor.) Recognising the cost restraint on Labour, Gould's report

suggested the appointment of a core group of BMP staff who had
worked for Ken Livingstone's Labour group at County Hall, on the
'Fares Fair' and GLC anti-abolition campaigns. Both advertising
campaigns (on which the GLC spent millions) won plaudits for
BMP throughout the advertising world, and grudging admiration
from Livingstone's opponents in the political world. The anti-
abolition campaign, Gould argued, had shown 'that sophisticated
communications techniques, and in particular advertising, can be
used by a radical organization without compromising either the
message, or the policies underlying [it]'. BMP would have been
Gould's preferred choice for Labour's full-time agency, but he had
been told by the Labour sympathisers at BMP that there would be
resistance on the board. Instead, the team who had worked with the
GLC – notably Peter Herd, the account director, Alan Tilly and Paul
Leeves, joint creative directors, and several of the other creative staff
– agreed to work voluntarily to the shadow agency. Other participants at the outset were Colin Fisher, managing director of the
Strategic Research Unit, Leslie Butterfield, planning director at the
Abbott Mead David Vickers agency, Patricia Hewitt, Bob Worcester
and Brian Gosschalk from Mori, and Richard Faulkner of Westminster Communications. Alongside Gould worked Deborah Mattinson, who had quit the Ayer Barker agency to set up Gould
Mattinson Associates in Greek Street, Soho. She, too, ended up
working mostly for Labour. They continued throughout the period
to be the only two who were regularly paid for their services. All
other work was offered free. Gould calculated after the 1987 general
election campaign that volunteer effort and indirect subsidy by
volunteers had saved the party roughly £500,000 in the election
campaign effort – a quarter of what Labour actually spent on its
campaign advertising.

Within two months the shadow agency delivered a new Labour
image. Kinnock had been pressing Mandelson for a campaign which
would reclaim from the Conservatives the political principles of
freedom and fairness. Kinnock felt that Thatcher had thieved and
contaminated those principles: he saw both as fundamental to
democratic socialism. The agency went to work on the 'Freedom

and Fairness' campaign. When the agency finally presented its unifying slogan: 'Labour: Putting People First', to the campaign strategy committee, it won the enthusiastic backing of Dr Jack Cunningham, the committee chairman. But it was the first time the party used the lone word 'Labour' on its campaign literature, without the word 'Party' alongside. At one of the committee meetings called to view the new campaign posters and logos, the health spokeswoman Harriet Harman mildly objected, not only to the loss of the word 'Party', but also to the brutal boldness of the word 'Labour' in capitals, with dark lines above and below. The two young Ayer Barker designers who had drawn it turned to her and retorted: 'It's bloody ballsy, and people like it.' Harman in fact became one of the agency's staunchest supporters on the parliamentary front bench, but Mandelson faced a more serious problem when Kinnock called him in. Kinnock liked the posters, and the picture of a teenage girl reaching upwards after a dove. But he wanted it to be called 'Labour's Campaign for Freedom and Fairness'. That was the whole point, Kinnock said – to reassert those principles on Labour's behalf. Mandelson swallowed hard and told the party leader he could not have what he wanted. The materials were already at the printers. It was too late: 'Putting People First' was what it had to be. Kinnock, not a man famed for his even temper, had no alternative. But Mandelson did ensure, in compensation, that all the campaign literature incorporated somewhere in tiny lettering the words 'Published by Labour's Freedom and Fairness campaign'.

From the outset there was suspicion within the party. Eric Heffer, the left-wing Labour MP for Liverpool Walton, read the advertisers' decision to use grey on the posters in place of Labour's traditional red as the material evidence of incipient dilution of full-blooded socialism. The *Observer* commented, somewhat hesitantly: 'Labour's launching of its new 'Freedom and Fairness' campaign last week was too transparently a cosmetic exercise to be wholly convincing – but it did nevertheless mark something of a sea-change. Labour at last appears ready to be regarded as a consumers' party rather than a producers' one.' The *Guardian* leader writers remarked more fulsomely that the campaign was 'a really positive step forward in the political rehabilitation of a party which three years ago seemed to have lost the will to govern this country by consent ever again'. Even *Tribune* said of the concentration on health, education and social welfare in the 'Freedom and Fairness' campaign, that it was a 'welcome return' to 'bread and butter issues . . . presented in a modern, attractive and relevant way'. *Tribune* added (ironically, given the vitriolic abuse it would later spit at Mandelson's alleged role as the leadership fixer): 'Those voices which have sneered at the use of professional advertising techniques could not be more wrong.' The *Guardian*, similarly, said the campaign's presentation and style were 'light years ahead of anything the Labour Party has managed to get together before'. The comment that most delighted Mandelson and Gould was, however, the *Financial Times* leader of 23 April, which opened: 'The British Labour Party is again beginning to look like a credible party of Government – at least in the sense that it wants office, and may achieve it.'

That was the whole purpose of the campaign: to convince people of Labour's electability. Gould's report had emphasized that Labour's real target audience needed to be the tabloid readers who form the majority of voters. The comments of the FT might not reach them, but the advertising material would, along with the revolutionized press relations. 'Freedom and Fairness' failed to recover Neil Kinnock's two cherished notions as Labour's sole domain; but it certainly achieved the aim which Gould had set. On 2 May 1986 David Blunkett wrote to Mandelson, with a copy to Kinnock, protesting at what he feared would be seen as 'value-free' campaigning on 'isolated and unconnected policies'. Kinnock, in reply to Blunkett, displayed his complete grasp of the genie which had ballooned from the shadow agency's bottle. 'The campaign', Kinnock wrote, 'deliberately selects symbolic policies – such as under-5s provision, cervical cancer screening, a ban on lead in petrol and home improvement grants – to illustrate our commitment to general values.' He continued: 'The reason for this approach is very simple: the extensive research we did before the campaign launch [research carried out by the agency] showed that, in the abstract, people found it difficult to see how our values related to their daily

lives. Linked to particular policies, those values came alive.' Two
years later the party leader was arguing that the search for 'symbolic
policies' should be the central purpose of the review.

The shadow agency worked more like a siphon than a vessel. It
was not an organization, so much as an affiliation of mostly anony-
mous Labour sympathisers to a core group, which in turn was
steered by Gould and Mattinson. Those two worked wholly to
Mandelson, who in turn derived his sole authority from Kinnock.
Many Labour politicians, when they spoke of 'the agency', meant
Gould and Mattinson, usually because they have never met anyone
else. But the agency was much wider. It included, for example, a
sub-group of national newspaper and magazine journalists who were
sympathetic to Labour. The first qualitative research for Labour was
carried out during the 1986 Bournemouth party conference by
Roddy Glen, of Strategic Research Group. Glen tested the reaction
of party members to conference events, as well as the general public.
By the end of the general election campaign agency volunteers had
completed around 200 qualitative research sessions for the party.
One of the best-reputed photographers in the advertising world,
known by his trade-name 'Stak', voluntarily produced a portfolio of
12 pictures for 'Investing in People', the campaign which followed
'Freedom and Fairness' later in 1986. From the creation of the
agency, through to the 1987 general election campaign, its volunteer
helpers provided almost all of the work necessary to conduct modern
campaigns. In many cases they were people who had long before
offered their services: when Mandelson arrived at Walworth Road
he had found a file of letters from volunteers who had never received
a reply.

Labour MPs were themselves confused about what the agency did
and not do. Probably the image-making service best known to
Labour frontbenchers was the personal presentation advice offered
to MPs by Barbara Follett, on dress, make-up, and hair-style. Her
service was, intriguingly, more used by men than women – but the
men do not talk about it. When Harriet Harman first went to see
Follett she was asked to look at a bundle of pictures of herself and
describe how she appeared. Harman had never before looked at

herself in that way. Studying one picture, in which she was wearing her favourite flowery Laura Ashley dress, she found herself describing herself as 'a Welsh peasant woman'. Follett asked Harman what she wanted to look like, and Harman told her: 'Like a confident, assertive, self-possessed woman capable of running things'. Follett told her to go out and buy a dark suit with padded shoulders, which Harman did the next day.

In fact Follett is freelance, and has nothing directly to do with the agency. But the agency does provide a day-to-day political presentation service, as well as a longer-term strategic and election-campaigning one. In 1988, for example, the Government was on the point of publishing its review of health service policy. A copy of the White Paper was leaked to Robin Cook, the Shadow Cabinet health spokesman, who knew that he had been handed a potentially huge political bonus. He and Harman met members of the shadow agency in a room off Westminster Hall at the Commons and told them, in heavily circuitous language, what they wanted to say about the Government's intentions. The agency people listened, wrote it down in silence, and went away. Twelve hours later they returned. Use phrases like 'a healthy bank balance before a healthy patient', they said. Try repeating the phrase 'cash before care'. And so on. Cook and Harman, at their press conference that morning, carried out the agency advice to the letter. That evening the phrases were repeated over and again on television and radio news bulletins. Within two weeks they had been, through the osmotic effect of the mass media, adopted by Labour campaigners; constituency activists, without any headquarters guidance, were using the same phrases on the door-step as they canvassed. The language was eventually borrowed by the British Medical Association, which probably never realized where it came from. The White Paper leak, combined with the agency's advice, enabled Labour's health team to fight £2m worth of Government advertising on equal terms. Two influential Labour politicians never again wanted to return to the days of randomly-produced leaflets, and unsupported, isolated attempts to attack the Government.

ALTHOUGH the agency was little-known outside the party's leading group, its role was fully formed by June 1987. While almost everyone else collapsed with exhaustion at the end of the election campaign, Philip Gould's boyish energy appeared boundless. At his initiative, researchers working for the agency set out to find out what Tory voters thought of Labour; he had the material back in his hands within two weeks. He began closer analysis of the polling Labour had undertaken during the campaign. And he proposed to Mandelson that the agency should prepare, for the politicians' consumption, a huge study of political opinion, projected onto a backcloth of the changed society which Britain could expect to be living in by the time of the next election.

The result, 'Labour and Britain in the 1990s', was produced by a team chaired by Patricia Hewitt, comprising Mandelson, Gould, Deborah Mattinson, and Roger Jowell, of the British Social Attitudes survey. Andrew McIntosh, the Labour peer from IFF Research Limited, contributed data from a survey he had conducted during and immediately after the election campaign for another client. Andrew Shaw and John Curtice at Liverpool University undertook an analysis of all the available polling data over the preceding quarter century. Rex Osborn, the Walworth Road political intelligence officer, also analysed quantitative polling. Predictions of the next decade's changes in lifestyle, economics, and individual aspirations, were compiled by Paul Ormerod, director of the Henley Centre for Forecasting.

The conclusions were so politically explosive (deliberately so) that the team contrived to wrap their bomb in a little meringue before delivering it to the joint executive and Shadow Cabinet meeting in November 1987. Only Kinnock himself, among the politicians, had seen the full presentation before it was made. Hewitt and Mandelson stood back on the day, even though they had largely structured it, because it had to come from the independent specialists. It also had to be delivered independently of the party leader. The agency volunteers themselves were terrified: as Jowell stood up to commence his introductory section, Dennis Skinner muttered audibly – 'another load of bloody rubbish' – and Tony Benn sought to stall the entire affair by criticizing the quality in advance. Benn, creditably, apologized at the end, saying that the methodology had been rigorous throughout. The gathering as a whole applauded.

But the agency's presentation gave little cause for cheer. The main optimistic ingredient, from Jowell, was that 'Thatcherite values', such as an unswerving faith in the superiority of the private sector and the unfettered free market, had failed to take any real grip among the populace. But the downside was that those things to which people most aspired – home ownership in particular – were utterly identified with Margaret Thatcher. The presentation showed that the gender gap was closing. For 20 years the Conservatives had held a clear majority among women voters; now Labour had taken the lead among young women. That was a pinch of saccharine however: overall the gender gap gain was a result of Labour's poor performance among men. Similarly, there was some small solace in the Liverpool University material, which showed that changes in Britain's class structure alone (the decline of the working class and rise of the middle class) would on its own have reduced Labour's share of the vote by 6 points since 1964. In fact the decline was 13.3 per cent, suggesting that Labour's waning support could not solely be attributed to social shift, and that a substantial proportion should be relatively easy to win back. More depressingly, though, Labour voters were three times more likely to be casting their ballot out of class loyalty than Tory voters. The team whisked in to the mixture a suggestion that European socialist parties had managed to flourish in recent years, despite facing similar social trends. But they omitted to mention the extent to which those European parties had revolutionized their policies to reach a wider audience.

All of those elements were included to make the medicine more palatable. Labour was seen as outdated, identified with an old agenda. Its policies no longer matched people's personal and family aspirations. Labour as a party was seen as having an alien internal culture: male-dominated, and intent on telling people how they should run their lives, rather than enabling them as individuals to make their own choices.

The British Social Attitudes survey confirmed what every Labour

politician involved in the '87 campaign instinctively knew: that it was
the sense of rising prosperity, cleverly created by the Tories in the
period running up to 1987, that destroyed Labour's chances at that
election. But Labour's problem ran deeper than one campaign.
Nationalization had never been supported by more than one-third of
the electorate since 1964; 56 per cent of voters believed an economic
crisis would be likely under Labour (Mori during the '87 campaign).
At no stage in the previous five years had more than one-quarter of
the electorate felt that Labour's view on defence came closest to
their own. Labour had been losing its share of the vote among all
classes.

The IFF material was crucial. It showed that a huge proportion of
Labour supporters at the 1987 election had voted out of habit, or
blind brand loyalty. Among non-Labour voters, the most potent
reasons for rejecting Labour were extremism and division, and lack
of strong leadership: 78 per cent of them thought Labour extremist.
Then came domination by the trade unions, with defence, tax, and
economic incompetence following behind. But when people were
asked, rather differently, what they saw as Labour's bad campaign
points, defence rose up the league table: first came the 'loony left',
then union domination, then the feeling that Labour 'wouldn't
defend Britain', and that Labour would undo economic progress.
The agency kept out of the presentation almost all of the material
they had gathered on perceptions of Neil Kinnock and his leadership
(and toned down the 'lack of strong leadership' point) retaining only
the IFF finding that 19 per cent had felt Neil Kinnock would not
make a good Prime Minister.

Ormerod set out to answer the central question about the sort of
society Labour might face in the 1990s. He concluded that all of the
social conditions and attitudes which people associated with Labour
were fading. The long standing shift to home ownership, the transfer
of employment from industry to services, the shift of population from
town to country, boded ill for a party associated with municipal
ownership, heavy industry, and old towns and cities. Inheritance of
personal wealth and property would rise from £10bn a year in 1987
to £20bn in the early 1990s. Qualitative research revealed strong

aspirations for private education and medicine among middle-
income groups (skilled manual workers and routine white-collar
workers), 'including Labour voters'.

Since agency input was integral to the management of the policy
review, both in presenting public opinion and testing out policies as
they emerged from the review, it was essential that its work should be
trusted as authoritative and independent. For the purposes of the
team working to Kinnock, the agency's product gave vital oxygen to
the review process. If its work were too obviously politically manipu-
lated, or manipulative, its potency would drain away. When 'Labour
and Britain in the 1990s' was issued to constituencies as a party
publication in May the following year, Larry Whitty wrote in the
introduction: 'It is important to stress that this information is no
more than background evidence: it is not designed to prescribe any
particular routes for the Policy Review to follow'. That denial of
interventionist intent was attached or addressed to virtually every
presentation the agency made during the review. Hardly anyone
involved in the review ever believed the rubric: they could see that, in
the 'new model party', political demands would be inseparable from
the communications imperative. But the disclaimer was honest in a
sense. Shadow agency advice was presented rather as a psychiatrist
talks to the couch. There was no instruction that Labour must follow
a given course; the party was left to draw its own conclusions.

5

AIMS AND VALUES

THE TERMS of a political resolution of Labour's problems seemed hazily remote. There was an open hostility between those on the party's right who sought a wholesale new revisionism, and those who believed that such an overt conversion would leave the party no longer worthy of its name. Eric Heffer argued that the Kinnock-led Labour Party was already well on the way to becoming an 'SDP Mark II', while Giles Radice, Fabian Society intellectual and former education spokesman, argued that Labour needed a renunciation of Marxism similar to that made by the West German SPD at Bad Godesburg. The leadership felt frustrated by the party's apparent reluctance to recognize the overdue need for change. Activists, including many on the soft left, remained hostile to the accommodation which Kinnock had reached with the centre-right wing of the party in order to entrench his supremacy. Was a challenge being made to Labour's values? Or to the personality and style of the party leadership? The drafting of an 'Aims and Values' document, in attempting to settle the first question, represented an important preliminary skirmish in Kinnock's battle to win over the party.

Kinnock was always sceptical about the merit of devising a democratic socialist 'big idea'. But he agreed in 1985 that an assertion of Labour's basic principles might help to conjure a sense of the kind of society the party sought to create. The project was promoted by David Blunkett, who persistently argued that Labour needed an inspirational idea with which to replough the political landscape. Seizure of an ideological stronghold had, to Blunkett's mind, been the main reason for the political success of Thatcherism. Blunkett's personal preference was that Labour should rally around the notion of a participatory democracy – the approach which he himself had adopted with considerable reward as leader of Sheffield city council. That meant, simply put, that socialism sought to involve every individual in those decisions which affect his or her life. Such participation extended from the most basic level of ensuring that public services acted in the consumer interest, guarded if necessary by consumer groupings, in an unbroken chain to the national levels of political interest, such as the volume of national resources which should be devoted to defence. The same participatory political model applied as much to giving individual tenants the right to choose the colour of their front door, as it did to deciding for or against the continued possession of nuclear weapons.

A committee of the executive was set up in 1985, and various papers drafted, by Geoffrey Hodgson, the professor of politics at Newcastle Polytechnic, Geoff Bish, and by Bernard Crick, professor of politics at Sheffield University. Crick had tutored Blunkett at Sheffield, and the pair worked together on several drafts. Kinnock rejected them all as too abstract and wordy. None of the offerings chimed with his sense of Labour's main purpose. So when the post-election discussions began to revolve around the idea of an 'aims and values' statement being presented as the centrepiece of the review's first phase, the party leader turned to his deputy and asked him to take on the task.

Roy Hattersley and Neil Kinnock were, on a personal level, chemically incompatible: poured into the same test-tube and vigorously shaken, they would almost certainly detonate. Consequently, they had only twice been in each other's home socially. Kinnock acted as a stage-holder in company, regaling his companions with long anecdotes and streams of Welsh jokes, expecting others to act as foils to his energetic performance. He was full of a brash bonhomie that smelt a little too strongly of the rugby changing room for Hattersley's taste. Hattersley sometimes called Kinnock a 'gregarious loner', cleverly encapsulating what many people felt about the party leader: that all his ebullience concealed a core to which few intimates ever succeeded in penetrating. Hattersley's wit was that of the Punch column: he inhabited a world which Kinnock saw as faintly elitist, and politically indolent. Each thought himself better endowed than the other. It was impossible to imagine Kinnock writing a 255,000-word novel set in Victorian Britain, as Hattersley did at his first fiction-writing attempt; it was, on the other hand, likely that Kinnock wondered why Hattersley felt he could spare the time. Hattersley regarded himself as more intellectually wide-ranging, culturally perceptive and articulate; Kinnock in some ways felt threatened by that, because he was hooked on a sense of his own intellectual inferiority. Kinnock, however, mastered political survival skills in the roughest school, the Labour Party of the 1970s and early 1980s. He showed himself a brave political fighter and clever tactician, and therefore looked down on Hattersley's raw political judgment. Those mutually-contested differences were at least arguable. But the key difference between them was irrefutable: Kinnock beat Hattersley in the leadership election of 1983. Hattersley decided then that he would accept the party's verdict, and would not weaken Kinnock's flank by continually behaving as the leader who should have won. Some in Kinnock's office, like many Labour MPs, disliked Hattersley for his pompous self-importance and conniving arrogance. Nothing delighted them more than seeing the deputy leader deflated. They therefore rarely sang Hattersley's main virtue, from Kinnock's point of view – which was that Hattersley had actually stuck by his decision to be loyal, and never to sabotage the party leader. Barring an occasional boat-rocking foray – such as the post-'87 election episode, when Hattersley felt his tax policy was being blamed for the scale of the defeat – the deputy leader declined opportunities to deliberately undermine Kinnock. He naturally could not help but display his pleasure when, on the occasions that he deputized for Kinnock in the Commons, he performed more effectively than the party leader. Privately he reflected on Kinnock's failure to anticipate the second despatch box question, but publicly he said nothing. Hattersley's decision not to undermine the party leader was taken out of self-interested motives: he did not want to waste ten years of his life stewing in the bitter juice of a belief that he

could do the job better than Kinnock. He anyway came to think that
Kinnock was the better man for the particular task of reconstruction
confronting the party in 1983. Hattersley always thought that he
would make a better Prime Minister than Kinnock. But he also knew
throughout that he would never win the political battles necessary to
win the war. In other words, Roy Hattersley took the view that, as
Labour leader, he would probably never get to Number 10 Downing
Street – whereas Neil Kinnock, for all his faults, very likely might.

Kept mostly apart, the two came to produce a creative political
blend, if not a happy personal one. They hardly ever fought; and
when they did, it was usually in private, and face to face. Hattersley
had the good sense to back off from any public confrontation with
Kinnock. He presented no threat to Kinnock's leadership. Kinnock,
equally, felt that he and Hattersley were roped together, and that any
rift between them would damage the party.

Most importantly, Kinnock's and Hattersley's political principles
were closer than most of their colleagues fully appreciated. Kinnock's friends were on the realist left, Hattersley's on the pragmatic
right. But when Kinnock's belief in a politics of proficient caring was
boiled down, it sat only a pigeon-step away from Hattersley's more
loftily articulated philosophies. Ideological compatibility was proved
by the relative ease with which the pair agreed between them the
content of the draft 'Aims and Values' paper.

Fully in character, Hattersley began the task of thinking through
Labour's 'aims and values' by picking up Bernard Crick's most
recent paper, and marking it like an undergraduate essay; he was
unimpressed, and told Crick as much by post. Shortly before the
1987 election Hattersley published his long-gestated personal statement, *Choose Freedom: the Future for Democratic Socialism* (Michael
Joseph), intended as his own answer to the questions about the
purpose and future of socialism which Tony Crosland, the vanished
star of Hattersley's generation, had posed. *Choose Freedom* argued in
its introduction: 'There always has been (and there still remains) a
strange reluctance within the Labour Party to set out a clear
statement of socialist belief against which to measure programmes
and policies. But the time when Labour could take refuge in

ideological agnosticism has passed . . . Without an ethical framework on which to build its programmes, Labour will risk losing its way in the future, as it has lost it in the past.' At Kinnock's behest Hattersley sat down on occasional Sunday afternoons and started to write such a statement of aims and values which could act as a litmus paper with which to test the policy review. After several efforts he went back to Kinnock, and told the party leader it was no use: whatever he produced would be a condensation of *Choose Freedom*. That, Kinnock replied, was exactly what he wanted.

Hattersley's aim was to assert once and for all that socialism was about freedom – or more particularly, the concept derived from the philosopher John Rawls, of extending the sum of freedom in society. Socialism was, therefore, about agency: extending the sum of freedom by enabling individuals to realize their potential more fully. As was evident from Kinnock's insistence on the 1986 'Freedom and Fairness' campaign, the party leader's guiding belief was much the same. He had always talked of socialism as being about the 'enabling state'. Hattersley felt that the assertion of freedom as socialism's purpose would also help release the party from its prevailing identification with bureaucratic controls. Hattersley despised the way in which Labour's most recent left-wing generation believed that degrees of socialist commitment could be tested by the level of faith in either public ownership, or nuclear unilateralism. The very first words of *Choose Freedom* were: 'The true object of socialism is the creation of a genuinely free society in which the protection and extension of individual liberty is the primary duty of the state.' The introduction continues: 'Socialism exists to provide – for the largest possible number of people – the ability to exercise effective liberty.' Equality was the means, liberty the end: 'The achievement of a more equal distribution of wealth and power, and the resultant increase in the sum of freedom for the community as a whole, is the principal goal of socialism.' There was, for example, 'no such thing as a socialist defence or foreign policy – save only for the support of liberty in both the Soviet Union and South Africa'.

The opening words of the final version of 'A Statement of

Democratic Socialist Aims and Values' are precisely redolent of *Choose Freedom*: 'To be truly free a man or woman must possess the ability to make the choices that freedom provides. There is an obvious and undeniable relationship between the resources that an individual can command and the choices which it is possible for that individual to make. That is why freedom and equality – far from being conflicting objectives, as our opponents pretend – are inextricably connected. The Labour Party is, and will remain, committed to the redistribution of wealth and power. Rational consideration and the lessons of history convince us that a more equal distribution of wealth increases the sum of freedom.'

Between Hattersley's first version, and the presentation of 'Aims and Values' to a specially-convened joint Shadow Cabinet/national executive meeting on 5 February 1988, Kinnock and his deputy exchanged endless alternative drafts. The party leader changed little of substance: most of his additions were subsequently erased, as were Hattersley's more prolix bouts of self-indulgence. But Kinnock had thoroughly and personally thought through the document's content, and endorsed it.

Both leader and deputy leader fully anticipated a hard-left assault on the paper. Indeed, Hattersley hoped for such an attack: he believed it would help expose the differences between the principles adumbrated in 'Aims and Values', and the principles which a hard left leadership challenge would be seeking to defend. The paper was, then, ambiguous in its aims. It was at one level a genuine attempt to enshrine an enduring statement of democratic socialist faith that could clearly be distinguished from David Owen's version of social democracy on one side, and Soviet-style command economy socialism on the other. But it was also intended, in part, as a contemporary tactical manoeuvre.

It therefore came as a shock when the document was most pertinently criticised in the meeting by some of the Shadow Cabinet's stalwart right-wingers: not only Jack Cunningham, (who protested against the absence of any statement about science or the environment), but also John Smith – Hattersley's closest political ally. John Smith, Bryan Gould, and Robin Cook all said the document was too enthusiastic about the advantages of the market as a mechanism for distributing most goods. The Shadow Cabinet members asked that the document be tempered with a countervailing scepticism about the market's efficacy in providing long-term investment, equitable distribution, and social balance.

The story that the content of the leadership's 'Aims and Values' paper had been disputed by some of Kinnock's and Hattersley's most loyal supporters took seconds to reach the political journalists waiting on the steps of Transport House: Dennis Skinner made sure of that. Smith was mortified: he dined with Hattersley that Friday night, and apologized profusely, saying that he had not understood how impossible it was for any national executive discussion to be kept private. Hattersley blamed himself: he realized too late that he should have shown the draft paper to his friends, before submitting it to the joint meeting, thereby ensuring in advance that he would have their support. Most coverage, however, latched on to the peg offered by the hard-left: that the argument was over whether or not to scrap the Clause Four commitment to common ownership in the party's constitution. That way the story could be compared to Hugh Gaitskell's doomed and disastrous attempt to erase Clause Four. At the subsequent press conference Kinnock sought to re-educate political journalists in the history and meaning of Clause Four of the 1918 constitution, written by Sidney Webb, and fought over by Kinnock's great hero, Nye Bevan. Kinnock, like Bevan, believed that Gaitskell had pointlessly frittered the party's energy by trying to drop the Clause Four commitment; he was not about to chase down the same cul-de-sac. (The section referred to in disputes over Clause Four is actually only clause four part five of the constitution: 'To secure for the workers by hand or by brain the full fruits of their industry and the most equitable distribution thereof that may be possible upon the basis of the common ownership of the means of production, distribution and exchange, and the best obtainable system of popular administration and control of each industry or service.')

CLAUSE FOUR never was the argument. The central dispute over 'Aims and Values' was on the role of the market, and individual liberty – not the limited and totemic question of public ownership. The party leadership briefly trembled at the prospect of a split opening up within the Kinnock-supporting group when it became known that Robin Cook had agreed to write a piece in the following week's *New Statesman* criticizing the 'Aims and Values' paper. Nothing would have been more likely to anger the party leader – and simultaneously make him pull back from the project he had undertaken. In fact, Cook's gunpowder turned damp over the intervening days, and failed to fire. He applauded the fact that 'the long tradition in socialism of distrust of the state as a real potential agent of repression' had been given 'full voice' in the document's first draft. He hankered only for 'an equally bold challenge to the neoliberalism of Thatcherite market economies'. What the episode actually proved was that, when it came to words in black and white, each leading Labour politician had an intensely strong personal understanding of the socialist creed, accompanied by an equally strong conviction that theirs was the proper understanding of that creed.

So, in the following five weeks running up to the national executive meeting to approve 'Aims and Values', Kinnock and Hattersley accepted extensive amendments to their document. A concession was made to Blunkett's favourite theme, with the addition of a line saying that real freedom could only be extended by 'participation in democratic institutions at work, in the community and in public life'. A section on community (the linked theme promoted by Blunkett and Crick) was added: 'The solidarity which comes from living and working as a community brings with it the obligation of care and service to each other. To live in a community is to enjoy mutual advantages and accept mutual obligations . . . The common sense and common purpose of our community must be emphasized or society becomes fragmented, bleak and brutalized.'

Some of Hattersley's more fulsome phrases were scaled down. The original Government and Freedom section began with the sentence: 'Socialism is the gospel of individual rights.' The executive rephrased it: 'Our concern as socialists is with individual liberty.' The original contained nothing on nuclear weapons; only a line saying that defence of the nation was part of the proper function of the state. That omission was consistent with Hattersley's belief that democratic socialists are properly opposed to war, and in favour of international co-operation, but that unilateralist and multilateralist nuclear disarmament policies could be argued with equal propriety by anyone calling themselves a democratic socialist. The omission was also consistent with Kinnock's wish to avoid opening up a fight over unilateralism at such an early stage in the review. The final draft, however, incorporated a new exhortation against 'the threat of nuclear annihilation'.

Hattersley believed that a democratic socialist's position on the merits and disadvantages of market economies was fundamental. The original section on 'Socialism and the Economy' began with the words: 'We are not, and never have been, committed to any one form of public ownership . . . ' The final version was drastically altered, with five completely new paragraphs added. They covered (to answer Cunningham and Cook) the impact of advanced industrialization on the environment and the collective action necessary to tackle it. Lines were added on the necessity of planning for full employment (a goal unmentioned in the original). And John Smith's most ardently-argued objection was answered with the addition of phrases about the need for a regional policy. If the document was to be used as a litmus for the review, the Shadow Cabinet review group convenors made sure that the test paper was thoroughly stained in advance.

The main change was made to the role of the market. 'It is not possible to lay down any strict and simple rule which governs the way in which the output of the mixed economy should be distributed. There are some areas of economic activity which are wholly inappropriate for the application of market forces. In the case of the allocation of most other goods and services the operation of the market, where properly regulated, is a generally satisfactory means of determining provision and consumption, and where competition is appropriate, socialists must ensure that it is fair and that consumers, workers and investors are protected from commercial and financial exploitation.' The language was uninspiring, but the shift of meaning from the original was exhaustively (indeed exhaustingly) plain: the principle of protection from exploitation, and the assertion that some areas of life were 'wholly inappropriate' for market distribution, were being clearly spelt out. The West German SPD put it more succinctly in their basic programme (the market where possible, rules where necessary). And in case anyone should doubt Kinnock's determination to stifle any appearance of an argument within the leadership, the executive agreed to his suggestion that the whole of Clause Four be printed as part of the new statement.

Hattersley had wanted an ideological battle to be fought and won: he said as much at a Labour Students meeting at Camden Town Hall on 6 February, the day after the original draft was attacked: 'For years we have allowed ourselves to be represented as the enemies of liberty, as the proponents of the centralized soviet economy in which goods and services are allocated by bureaucratic decision, as supporters of monolithic, unresponsive, inefficient state monopolies. We have allowed that libel to go unchallenged because we have singularly failed to set out what we really believe. For far too long, the Labour Party has dismissed ideological argument . . . As a result Labour's image and reputation is decided and determined by the loudest voices in the party – no matter how unrepresentative they may be, and by the leader writers of national newspapers, notwithstanding their chronic prejudice against democratic socialism.' He picked out the argument over Clause Four, saying: 'Our beliefs on public ownership have been intentionally misrepresented since the day on which we published our constitution over 60 years ago. Clause Four has been interpreted by most of our critics and a few of our members as the promise to take the whole economy into state ownership. It means no such thing, and it never has meant any such thing.' He ended by saying that 'Aims and Values' was 'the beginning – no more – of our counter attack in the ideological war which Margaret Thatcher began ten years ago'.

'Aims and Values' could more brutally be described as both the beginning and the end. Kinnock himself barely ever used the document for its designed purpose. At the 9 March parliamentary Labour Party he too argued that the lack of such a statement had enabled Labour's enemies to misrepresent what the party truly stands for. He then summed up what he saw as the document's most contentious message: 'In essence it says that no socialist sensibly proposes that markets are abolished, any more than any socialist holds that markets should be absolute.' That typically vacuous Kinnock sentence reveals one of the reasons for the failure of 'Aims and Values'. Politics is most exciting when it appears innovatory. Anyone who leaps up and down shouting, 'we think markets are sometimes good, sometimes bad, on the one hand efficient, on the other not', is hardly likely to excite much attention. Kinnock anyway believed that politics was not so much visionary utterance, as a matter of what you could win, today and tomorrow. Politics for him was a battleground, on which you deploy according to the demands of the day. His first question in answer to a proposition was always: 'Does it work?' He had a describable end in sight: election victory. He had, for himself, a clear notion of what his political priorities in Government might be.

'Aims and Values' was finally, for Kinnock, a staging post on the way to delivering the policy review. If Kinnock had genuinely wanted to write a new party creed, he could have slugged it out over the ensuing months. When the leadership campaign finally switched from shadow boxing, to open warfare with the left-wing Campaign Group, Hattersley wanted to fight on an 'Aims and Values' leadership platform. Kinnock would not have minded fighting with the hard left over 'Aims and Values', because he would have been confident of winning. But half of his most prominent colleagues had haggled over the detail of the document. They thought they all believed in much the same things; they simply could not agree how to express them precisely. If they did not agree fundamentally, how was it that they found themselves agreeing in practice, day to day, on almost everything? When it came to the point, nobody could quite see the point. Kinnock – whose commitment to 'Aims and Values' had always been half-hearted – lost interest. When the Clause Four argument failed to take off, political journalists and commentators also ignored the document. They were right in a sense: once the document had been doctored, any room for sharp controversy had been eliminated from the text. There was no row, no story, and therefore no lasting impact. The debate on 'Aims and Values' at the 1988 party conference was ill-attended and desultorily conducted. In the introduction to the completed policy review, published in May 1989, the document was referred to as the 'restatement' of Labour's aims and values. The main aim of the review was to persuade the world outside that Labour was changing; 'Aims and Values' was the slipway.

The real challenge Kinnock faced during 1988 focussed, not on the abstractions of the leadership document, but on a bitterly resented contest between the established leadership duo, the Bennite left, and the disillusioned soft left. The battle soured Kinnock personally, and the party generally. Even worse, the mood of futility spilled over into a dismal summer when Kinnock so badly lost his grip that even staunch supporters began to wonder whether he should relinquish the leadership.

6
LONG HOT SUMMER

THE CHALLENGE to the leadership started with John Prescott. The former ferry steward could growl and self-consciously play up to his image as the rough trade of the Shadow Cabinet. He was the first to mock his own unstructured, repetitive speaking style, littered with malapropisms and elisions, by suddenly grinding to a halt and admitting disarmingly he had forgotten what he was about to say next. 'My mind's gone blank', he would say, with a quick rueful smile. Prescott could not claim to have a finely-tuned and articulate intellect – even though he went to Ruskin College and then Hull University as a mature student. But his many warm friends in the trade unions and among the party's activists regarded him as more intelligent than he seemed. They respected his usually hard-headed political judgment, his enthusiasm for devoting time to policy detail, and his willingness to take political risks. He fought hard in the 1960s to bring democracy to the National Union of Seamen. Whatever his brief, Prescott could throw himself in with originality and effect.

Having been kept off the national stage by Kinnock's aides before and during the election, Prescott began afterwards to brood on the feeling that his ability to motivate party activists was being wasted. He genuinely believed the role of the deputy leader, invented to mollify Herbert Morrison, could be transformed into a campaigning post. He believed that he could work outside parliament to build party morale, and extend Labour's mass working class membership in the country. His motives, however, were by no means entirely altruistic. He harboured disdain for the Oxbridge-educated elite around Kinnock, and for the cosmopolitans who led the party's right wing. He particularly resented Hattersley, not only as the overbearing epitome of everything that he most disliked in the Labour movement, but also because he felt Hattersley should have taken the blame for the cardboard flimsiness of Labour's election campaign policy for jobs.

Prescott chose a private chat at the end of the TUC Congress in 1987 with his friend Robert Taylor, Labour Editor of the *Observer*, to float his threat to challenge Hattersley for the deputy leadership. Taylor reported in the paper that weekend that Prescott was considering standing. During the next four months Prescott ran a phantom campaign, quietly stoking the speculation about his intentions. His resolve hardened when he came second in the Shadow Cabinet elections, only to be posted to the relatively low-ranking job of energy spokesman. Aggrieved at having again ended up on the sidelines, Prescott firmed up his decision to challenge. At a briefing with Sunday newspaper reporters, ostensibly called to discuss electricity privatization, Prescott set aside the formal agenda and announced – unattributably – why he would be standing. He had, however, forgotten to take account of the presence of Andy McSmith, the senior Walworth Road press officer, who was there quite legitimately to take a note of the energy briefing. McSmith did indeed take a note of the actual proceedings, and passed it to Mandelson, as he normally would. When Kinnock saw the note he was livid in words of four letters.

A regular stream of MPs, including friends and allies such as Robin Cook and David Blunkett, strongly advised Prescott against standing. They warned that a Hattersley victory over Prescott would push Kinnock further into the arms of the right wing. But there was a stubbornness in Prescott's make-up, and a scratched vanity: he was determined to press on. In the end it took his friend Rodney Bickerstaffe, general secretary of the National Union of Public Employees, and Sam McCluskie – leader of his own union, the National Union of Seamen – to break the deadlock. Bickerstaffe and McCluskie negotiated a private deal with Kinnock which they hoped would enable Prescott to back off without losing face. According to the agreement a debate on the future role of the deputy leadership would be held at the next party conference: Kinnock himself helped draft the terms of the motion to be tabled by McCluskie and Prescott.

Making a brave face of his decision to call off his challenge, Prescott on 20 January 1988 held a press conference at Westminster where he placed heavy emphasis on a deal with Kinnock. Prescott suggested that Kinnock had guaranteed a debate on the role of the deputy leader. As soon as the press conference was over, a tape of Prescott's remarks was played back to the party leader in his office, with Hattersley present. Kinnock erupted at the implication that, in return for Prescott backing off, Hattersley would be asset-stripped. He despatched Hilary Coffman, his press officer, Peter Mandelson, and David Hill, Hattersley's advisor, to tour the press gallery denying that an accommodation had been reached. The terms of Kinnock's press-released statement were caustic enough: 'It's good that John Prescott will not provoke a diverting contest – the pity is that we have had any distraction. My view on the idea of excluding a deputy leader of the Labour Party from a major parliamentary portfolio is well known – I'm completely hostile to it, like, I think, just about everybody else in the trade union and labour movement. I've already turned the idea down flat.' The supplementary briefings by the three leadership aides went even further in their account of Kinnock's fury: the trio, in seeking to reaffirm Hattersley's position on Kinnock's behalf, poured vitriol over Prescott. No deal had been done – at least not of the kind Prescott claimed. They suggested that Prescott stood down because it had finally been drummed into him that he would suffer a humiliating defeat. He would not win more than 20 per cent of the electoral college. The content of their briefings travelled swiftly back to Mike Craven, Prescott's advisor, who embarrassed Mandelson, Coffman and Hill by publishing an account in the LCC's newsletter. The leadership team subsequently regretted their denigration of Prescott, but after four months of being teased by his phantom campaign their patience had worn thin.

HAVING repelled Prescott on the flank, the leadership found itself under direct attack from the hard left. Since its formal launch in 1982 as a breakaway from the increasingly centre-left Tribune Group, the Campaign Group of MPs had tried to muster the forces of the hard-left, inside and outside parliament. The Group's membership, as a result, extended in an ad hoc fashion beyond MPs, to include the leaders of some of the hard-left pressure groups in the party. People like Vladimir Derer, secretary of the Campaign for Labour Party Democracy, Wendy Moore, secretary of the Women's Action Committee, John McDonnell, secretary of the Association of London Authorities, and Les Huckfield, an MEP, were all entitled to attend as honorary members.

Benn, finding himself increasingly repelled by the party's direction, began to issue a string of speeches as single sheet press releases, with the most piquant attacks on the tenor of Kinnock's leadership underlined personally in red ink. 'We dare not sacrifice', he said in one issued on 12 January, 'everything in which we believe, and degenerate into a party scrambling for votes at any price. This is what explains the actual identity crisis within the party which has led many members to feel that even the Labour Listens exercise may lead to an abandonment of some of our basic values leaving a great vacuum at the heart of British politics.'

At the party's local government conference in Edinburgh the following month, Kinnock demanded self-restraint. Winding up the conference, he told delegates that most of the party was exasperated 'at the way in which too much of the good news, too much of the good things that they are doing and the good things they want to do, are being obscured by the bad news of what other people are trying to do'. The press, he said, 'had an avid desire to report everything that reflects division or discredit on the party'. As if to prove the point, Benn won the headlines the next day with a speech in Nottinghamshire listing 'The Ten Deficiencies of Neil Kinnock'. They included 'a consistent failure to support the socialist struggle outside parliament, the abandonment or watering down of basic policies, an over-reliance on polls and pollsters, increasingly authoritarian and intol-

erant behaviour within the party, coupled with the impression of
weakness and indecisiveness conveyed to the country'.

Benn's criticisms were supported in quarters well beyond the
narrow confines of the Campaign Group. Kinnock had to overcome
that pervasive mistrust of the review. The credibility of Benn
himself, however, and of the hard left as an organized force, was
becoming threadbare. In a society which had undergone such
prolonged social change, they seemed intellectually stagnant and
politically regressive.

The Campaign Group even struggled to reach a decision on
whether to mount a leadership contest. Some, such as Clare Short,
felt that a leadership battle was the wrong vehicle for promoting the
left's views. The panatella-smoking feminist, and MP for Birm-
ingham Ladywood, had a rich, Irish-inherited sense of both humour
and passion: she made herself a household name campaigning
against page three nudes in tabloid newspapers. Her distaste for the
old hard-left style was typical of many other left-wingers who were
also unsure that the left's political framework was any longer
applicable. The problem was the group contained an incompatible
mixture of socialists – some with their roots in the 1930s, others
growing directly out of the late 1960s. Ken Livingstone, the former
GLC leader turned Brent East MP, was distrusted as an opportunist
by many in the group. He would not stand anyway, because he
preferred to wait for the contest after next, when he envisaged a fight
between himself on the left, Blunkett in the centre, and a candidate
from the right. Dennis Skinner, the former miner and MP for
Bolsover, refused elected office of that kind. Audrey Wise, suggested
as a woman candidate for the deputy leadership, said her sights were
set on becoming president of her union, Usdaw.

In the absence of an alternative, the decision effectively rested
with Benn. When asked he seemed genuinely reluctant: his family
felt that, at 63, he had given enough energy to leading the left. But he
came under reverse pressure to stand from Jim Mortimer, the
former party general secretary, Jon Lansman, his campaign organizer in 1981, and Skinner. Two Group meetings, a week apart, were
set aside to make the final decision. The atmosphere had already

been poisoned by tensions within, particularly between Clare Short and some of the more aggressive of the men. But the atmosphere worsened when Benn, as chairman, ruled at the second meeting on 23 March that those who had spoken at the previous meeting should not have a second chance. Those who opposed a contest argued either that it would isolate the Campaign Group still further, or that it would be wiser to wait until the following year when the outcome of the policy review provided a more sharply defined target. Lansman argued that a contest would itself help the left strengthen its organization in the constituency parties. That would in turn, he pressed, help improve the left's position on the national executive. Moreover, a contest would wake the party to a debate on its preferred political direction. Benn's own prevarications ended when Kinnock refused to lend unequivocal support to industrial action by health service workers: he was so angered that he swung finally in favour of standing.

At the end of the second meeting, in a small and crowded room off Westminster Hall, Benn left the room to allow the decision to be taken in his absence. The majority was about two-to-one in favour of the first challenge to an incumbent leader since Wilson challenged Gaitskell. A sizeable minority voted against. Several Campaign members also failed to attend. The opponents were Allan Roberts, Dawn Primarolo, Chris Mullin, Audrey Wise, Gavin Strang, Tony Banks, Max Madden, Bob Wareing, Jo Richardson, Clare Short, Joan Ruddock and Margaret Beckett. The last four resigned saying politics was not all about leaders. Only Eric Heffer was willing to stand for the deputy leadership. Kinnock's response was predictably dismissive: 'It will only end in massive defeat for those who have put their self-indulgence above the interests of the party and of democratic socialism.' No one in the Group expected Benn to win, but they expected him to do well enough – at worst a fifth, and at best a third of the electoral college – to reopen the hard left's case and restrain Kinnock.

Benn's agreement to lead a challenge to the leader enabled the aggrieved Prescott to restart his own aborted deputy leadership campaign. Prescott's friends on the Labour Co-ordinating Committee cleared his path by issuing a statement decrying the choice between Eric Heffer and Roy Hattersley. By a margin of 14 to 2 the LCC executive agreed a third alternative was necessary, and invited either Prescott, Cook or Bryan Gould to stand. Gould had briefly considered the possibility the previous summer, but put it out of his mind. After only a weekend of delay following the Campaign Group vote, Prescott announced his candidature. He could, he said, win two thirds of the constituencies, half the unions and therefore needed only 59 MPs to become deputy. Despite fractious relations with Kinnock for more than a year, Prescott sought to sell his bid as the 'Kinnock-Prescott' ticket.

For a short time nerves jangled around Kinnock and Hattersley, as both the leadership staff, and Kinnockite MPs, began to calculate whether Hattersley would survive. John Smith – considered the most managerially presentable politician on Labour's front bench – was asked by several members of the parliamentary party if he would be willing to stand in Hattersley's place. Smith dismissed the suggestions, saying he would never run for the deputy leadership of the party: it was not a post that interested him. Dennis Skinner mischievously toured the Commons lobbies saying that the Campaign Group's real purpose in standing against Kinnock was to try and nudge Smith into standing for the leadership – but there was no likelihood of that happening. Though Smith would have run for the leadership, he would not run against a successful incumbent, whose strategy and politics he strongly admired.

Kinnock, anyway, immediately opted to stand by the distinctly dog-eared 'dream ticket', as the Kinnock-Hattersley combination had been known in 1983. No other permutation was on offer, he said. Kinnock took that decision, however, before he was quite sure of the way MPs would jump. MPs carried only 30 per cent of the voting shares in the electoral college, with 40 per cent going to the unions, and the remaining 30 to the constituency parties, though the response of MPs, particularly those on the soft left, would be crucial. Their reluctance to be identified with Kinnock-Hattersley at that low point in the leadership's fortunes was emphasized when Kinnock called a photocall of the Shadow Cabinet, at which his colleagues were meant to be snapped signing Kinnock-Hattersley nomination papers. Some members of the Shadow Cabinet declined to attend, and the photocall went ahead with Kinnock and Hattersley signing each others' nominations on their own.

Earlier, Robin Cook had signalled to Prescott that he might be willing to back his friend, and told Craven: 'John will need a campaign manager – tell him to give me a ring.' Craven laughed, but Cook said he was serious. But by then Cook was being pressed by Kinnock to run the leadership campaign. He had been the party's campaign co-ordinator during the first three years of Kinnock's leadership. Cook told Kinnock he would be happy to manage the party leader's own campaign, but he fought against Kinnock's insistence that that would mean having to support Hattersley too. Although it had already been decided that John Smith would be Hattersley's campaign manager, Kinnock made it clear that in practice the campaign would be jointly run. Eventually Cook succumbed, telling himself how frequently he had urged Prescott against standing. Prescott, however, understandably took Cook's decision as a personal betrayal: the pair did not speak again socially until a dinner at the TUC Congress in Blackpool more than a year later. As events turned out Cook felt justified. Though he felt no fondness for Hattersley's politics, he ended up admiring the deputy leader's political professionalism. Whenever Cook made demands on Hattersley, for a speech or statement targetted at a specific audience within the party, Hattersley (or his assistant, David Hill) delivered enthusiastically and on time. Kinnock, by contrast, showed little interest in the organization and conduct of a co-ordinated campaign: having decided that the contest was a distraction, he treated it as such, and put in only a small amount of special effort. He believed that the most important aim of the leadership campaign should be to persuade as many constituencies as possible to hold one member, one vote ballots.

THE PARTY leader's performance during the summer was so lifeless and bungling that his capacity to carry through the reconstruction fell into question. The chain of mishap and error, leading to

Kinnock's nearly terminal isolation, began with an invitation to lunch with the political staff of the *Independent*. Kinnock's advisors had been telling him for some time to be less wary of the press, and recover some of the boisterous conviviality which had been the hallmark of his personality before he won the leadership in 1983. Kinnock decided to go. As with all such half-social, half-business lunches between politicians and political journalists, unwritten rules apply. In simple terms, information gathered may be used as the basis for a newspaper story, so long as the politician is never identified as the source. It is a two-way trade. A minister or MP may want a story to appear without anyone knowing where it came from; the journalist has an opportunity to try and peek behind the government or party veil. It also enables politicians to try and explain the background to events or decisions, and sell their own interpretation thereof, without running the risk of being caught out 'on the record'. Some politicians are highly skilled at negotiating three courses without revealing anything more than a taste for French wine and inconsequential gossip. Clearly, opportunities for ambiguity and misunderstanding abound. The politician reveals some fact or opinion it would have been better to withhold; alternatively, the journalist misinterprets a remark, with recriminatory consequences. In the case of the unattributable *Independent* lunch with Kinnock – held in the private room of L'Amico, an Italian restaurant close to the Commons – a failure on both sides to spell out the terms of the discussion set off the chain of disasters.

All four of the *Independent's* political reporters were there, but the discussion was dominated by Anthony Bevins, the political editor, who grilled Kinnock on defence. Bevins – a press gallery maverick who had a special interest in Labour's defence policy running over many years – became convinced as the lunch went on that Kinnock had shifted his position on nuclear weapons. As he understood Kinnock's conversation, the Labour leader was now saying that membership of Nato inevitably implied acceptance of an American nuclear umbrella. Kinnock's inclination to use Trident in negotiation with the Soviet Union implied surrender of the unilateral timetable in Labour's existing defence policy. As soon as Bevins returned to his desk he began to write his scoop for the following day's paper. The headline appeared: 'Kinnock set to modify nuclear weapons policy.' The story said: 'Neil Kinnock is prepared to recognize explicitly the protection of the American nuclear umbrella within the framework of Nato defence strategy.' The point being made in the story was nice, but important.

Kinnock was outraged, and his staff despairing. The story blew a hole in their decision not to open up any debate on defence inside the party during the first phase of the policy review. Indeed, when Mandelson heard that the story was set to run in that night's paper, he had even gone to see Bevins in the *Independent's* room at the Commons and tried line-by-line to persuade the political editor to tone it down. It was less the content of the article, however, that wrought subsequent damage, than the general knowledge among other journalists that the piece had come from a lunch with Kinnock himself. Had the fact of the lunch been kept private the story might have been deniable, but other reporters found out about the lunch, and understandably saw no reason why they should keep it to themselves. Soon the whole of the political world knew where the story had come from.

The *Independent* story might have been hard to follow up had it not been for Kinnock's commitment to address the Council of the Socialist International in Madrid three days later. He intended a straightforward speech pressing the West to help Gorbachev defeat his internal critics by taking a positive approach to his disarmament initiatives. No hidden meanings were intended, but by then the lobby reporters were ready to hold any Kinnock speech to the light and see significance in the placement of commas. One passage, reputedly endorsing a nuclear defence strategy, caught their eyes: 'The Soviet Union and its Warsaw Pact allies may say with complete sincerity that they have no intention of attacking Western Europe or Nato, but meanwhile they do have a military capability so large that it cannot be recognized to be purely defensive in all conditions and all eventualities. For that reason, Britain and its allies must maintain defence forces capable of resisting and deterring any potential military threat.' The word 'deterring', in the light of Bevins' story, leapt from the page – even though it could be read as referring to either conventional or nuclear defence.

The point may have been needle thin, but it was sharp enough for Ken Livingstone to try and impale Kinnock. Quick to seize the opportunity, Livingstone issued a statement: 'An attempt of almost incredible folly is going to be made – to reverse the party's policy on unilateral nuclear disarmament. This would irrevocably divide the party and push it into a state of civil war.' That could have been dismissed as merely malevolent hard-left disruptiveness if the soft-left had not also been alarmed. Blunkett intervened, asserting publicly that the idea of Labour living under a US nuclear umbrella was unacceptable.

The clouds of confusion were rolling in over an already morose and ill-disciplined parliamentary party. Most MPs saw Kinnock as the best leader they had, but they were discovering the impossibility of fighting a 102-seat Government majority – a feeling which was exacerbated by the profoundly distasteful policies on the poll tax, social security and education which the Conservatives were pushing through. Ministers – sometimes patronisingly, sometimes gloatingly – began to bewail the lack of an effective Opposition. Earlier in the year, when disputes over health service cuts and nurses' pay were putting pressure on the Government, Labour had pulled briefly ahead. Now, into the early summer, Mori showed the Tories enjoying a huge 10 point lead. That kind of lead, so soon after a general election, while the Government was delivering an intensely controversial programme of social legislation, was deeply depressing for Kinnock.

In that atmosphere of gloomy speculation the party leader agreed to be interviewed by BBC television's *This Week, Next Week*. No one intended that the discussion should open a new line on defence. The advance briefing, prepared by John Eatwell and Patricia Hewitt, contained nothing fresh on the subject. In the course of the interview on 5 June, however, Kinnock uttered two explosive sentences: 'There is no need now for a something for nothing unilateralism. The idea that there is a something for nothing thrust that can be made is redundant.' The sentences were – unusually for Kinnock –

short, crisp and eminently quotable. The meaning, however, was typically elusive. What on earth was Kinnock trying to say? The phrases 'something for nothing', and 'something for something' came from a recent article by Ben Pimlott in the *New Statesman*. But that did not help clarify their import.

Kinnock was probably not wholly sure what he meant. Though he obviously envisaged updating the pre-'87 defence policy to account for the Gorbachev initiatives, he was not at all clear in his own mind what the details of that might be. He was trying to escape the bind of unilateral versus multilateral terminology, but he used those terms in his interview, because he now assumed that Labour would no longer need to abandon Trident without feeling confident of reciprocal Soviet cuts: the nature of the new leadership in Moscow meant Gorbachev would respond. He had made exactly that point at the end of the 1987 conference. In pure policy terms, Kinnock would only have broken into new ground if Vivian White, the interviewer, had gone on to ask whether British abandonment of Trident was entirely conditional on a reciprocal response from Moscow. If Kinnock replied 'yes', he would have been adopting an unambiguously multilateral stance – but the question was never asked.

As Kinnock left the television studio Patricia Hewitt asked him how he felt the interview had gone. Kinnock was pleased, and predicted the press would run defence and nationalization. He summarized his performance by saying: 'We've not so much slaughtered a few sacred cows today, as quietly put them to sleep.' Hewitt liked that: she interpreted it to mean that she was free to signal a change when she later briefed political correspondents by telephone. She confined her calls to three reporters on the broadsheet newspapers, because it was their interpretation of the interview which would largely set the agenda. Some of Hewitt's colleagues had always found her interpretation of Kinnock's views alarming: 'Kinnock plus 20 per cent', they described her. But Hewitt was operating at a particular disadvantage that afternoon. She had been away on maternity leave between Christmas and April, missing the row which had broken out over the story in the *Independent*. As a result she was less aware of the renewed sensitivity of the defence issue than she

might otherwise have been. Kinnock's remarks, moreover, did not
seem to her a great advance on what he had said at the end of the
1987 conference, the last occasion she had briefed the press on
defence. She rang round, passing on from her own mouth the view
that sacred cows had been put to rest, and doing little to dampen the
interpretation that Kinnock had intended to signal that a shift on
defence was on the way. She pointed to defence as the prime
example and also to some remarks Kinnock had made on public
ownership.

The Following Monday morning Mandelson read the newspapers
in Bournemouth, where he was attending a GMB conference.
Shocked by the consistency with which the idea of a defence shift
had been taken across the coverage, he rang Kinnock's office in
trepidation. He was told that Kinnock was happy with the coverage,
if a little edgy. On returning to London early that evening he went to
the Walworth Road office where he met Hewitt by chance. She was
pleased, saying that Kinnock had made a big step forward and got
away with it. However, by the Tuesday, it was evident that the story
was getting out of control. Kinnock, himself, was becoming anxious
as the story began to reverberate through the parliamentary party.

Mandelson was more than jumpy. Kinnock was in the middle of a
leadership election. On the following Thursday the TGWU executive, possessors of 8 per cent of the entire electoral college and the
most committed of the unilateralist unions, was due to meet to
decide the leadership contest nominations. In quick succession, and
more than once, Robin Cook, David Blunkett and Joan Ruddock –
all confirmed and influential unilateralists – came to Kinnock's door
demanding an explanation and retraction. Cook, additionally,
warned Kinnock that the leadership election campaign might run
into trouble, because Hattersley would suffer from a kick-back
protest against Kinnock himself.

The ensuing fortnight was like running into a quagmire: the
harder Kinnock tried to stay on top, the faster he sank down.
Mandelson, Clarke and Hewitt advised the party leader not to
retract. Though the timing was wrong for signalling a defence shift, a
retraction would, they argued, blow a hole in Kinnock's authority.

He must not be seen to back down, because that would confirm voter's impression of leadership weakness, and make it more difficult to change the policy later. Publicly, Kinnock stood fast: a speech at the annual Durham Miners' gala in Beamish was hastily deployed to mount an attack on Benn's dreamers, while a Fabian Society speech a week later criticized 'frozen attitudes' in the party. In private, though, he told the unilateralist deputations that the phrase 'something for something' had been intended, not to make Labour's nuclear disarmament conditional, but to convey a prediction of disarmament response from the Soviet Union. By verging on duplicity, Kinnock was betraying the weakness of his position.

Nine days after the interview on *This Week, Next Week* it seemed as if Kinnock's feet had settled on solid ground again. Then a 1am telephone call from Denzil Davies, Labour's defence spokesman, to Chris Moncrieff, the Press Association's chief political correspondent, cast him back into the mire. Announcing his immediate resignation, the party's defence spokesman told Moncrieff: 'I am fed up with being humiliated. Kinnock never consults me about anything.' Moncrieff, half awake and stumbling over his cat, rang Mandelson for a reaction at 1.30 a m. Mandelson, stunned by the news, and the manner of its delivery, asked Moncrieff to hold off filing the story until the morning. Moncrieff said he could not do that, but he would wait until Mandelson had talked to Davies before filing the story. Mandelson had seen Davies socializing on the Commons terrace earlier that evening, and feared that the defence spokesman might be destroying his political career in an unclear state of mind. He rang Davies at home, to find him not only resolute, but utterly sharp. There was nothing to be done, and he rang Moncrieff back to confirm the story.

Why did Davies resign? Relations between him and Kinnock had always been tense: one was too clever for his own political good, and the other was not clever enough. The fact that they shared aspects of background – both Welsh, both self-made, both entered parliament at the same time – only intensified a sense of rivalry. Davies, a barrister, was regarded by many of his colleagues as the keenest brain in the parliamentary party. He was the grammar school boy

who won a commission, went to university, took a first-class degree.
Dennis Healy used to introduce Davies as the cleverest man in the
parliamentary Labour Party; Davies himself could not help but
contrasting his own sharpness with Kinnock's verbosity. Kinnock
sympathised with Davies' personal problems – a painful marital
separation – but regarded Davies as undisciplined. Davies rarely told
people where he was or what he was doing, and for some time
previously had left Martin O'Neill, his deputy, to handle relations
with the leader's office. If Davies and Kinnock barely ever spoke, the
fault lay on both sides. But Davies' resignation remarks to Moncrieff
added spice to the left's accusation that Kinnock was running an
authoritarian and remote leadership.

Kinnock finally touched bottom on 20 June when he decided to
keep a long standing engagement for lunch, at the *Independent's*
offices, with the paper's senior executives, leader writers, and
columnists. Though angry with the paper because of his earlier
treatment at the hands of the political editor, he felt it better to
attend. This time, however, he insisted that the whole lunch be
treated as 'on-the-record', and taped. Kinnock nearly pulled out
because he was suffering from toothache and wanted to go to the
dentist. He was in poor temper. The tape recorded a tired man
involved in a disjointed discussion with mostly antagonistic journalists. Under repeated pressure to say whether Trident or Polaris
would be dismantled, regardless of whether or not the Soviets acted
reciprocally, Kinnock said: 'In terms of our defence interests it is
better for us not to be nuclear dependent. If you think that our
defence interests, and our ability to support our obligations in the
Alliance, are better met by using our resources for different objectives, then that is the way in which you will go.' Pressed frequently
on whether that meant his non-nuclear defence policy was free
standing, and would be implemented regardless of the Russian
response, he said that such a description was 'fair enough'. Peter
Jenkins, the paper's columnist, wrote up the interview inside the
paper, while Bevins wrote a front page story announcing that
Kinnock had retracted the suggestion of a shift made two weeks'
previously.

Jenkins, famously, had no love for Kinnock. His account of the interview faithfully reproduced the rambling character of Kinnock's speech, its *non sequiturs* and incoherence. He built his case against Kinnock around the two words, 'fair enough'. Kinnock, hoping to clarify his stance, had emerged looking foolish. Not only had he backtracked on nuclear weapons policy; he appeared as if he was utterly unable to explain his thought processes. Peter Shore immediately likened the party leader to the Grand Old Duke of York, marching his troops down again almost as soon as they had reached to top. The *Daily Mirror* did not fuss with nursery rhyme metaphors: 'What the hell are you doing Neil?' it demanded.

At last patience snapped. Loyalists in the unions began to mutter about whether they should try to replace Kinnock with John Smith. Stories appeared suggesting that Kinnock was temperamentally unreliable, or locked in his office suffering from depression. The dejection spread as far as John Edmonds, general secretary of the GMB, and probably the only man who could successfully organize a leadership coup. He made no move. He had no wish to re-enact the role of unloved king maker, in the manner of David Basnett, his predecessor. There could be nothing worse for the party, Edmonds believed, than the sight of grey-suited men turning up at Kinnock's door to tell him that his time was up. It would reinforce all the stereotypes about the unions' dominance – and Kinnock would not wear it anyway. Edmonds, however, did let it be known within the higher circles of party power that he regarded Kinnock as being on probation. If there was no sign of improvement by spring 1989 his union would be urging Smith, a GMB sponsored member, to stand for the leadership. Smith would never have challenged Kinnock – but he would run if Kinnock was forced to step down.

KINNOCK was saved further anguish by the summer holidays, and the consequent dispersal of his gossip-addicted and gloom-ridden parliamentary colleagues. By the eve of conference, in September, it was clear that Robin Cook's confidence was justified, and that the deputy leadership contest was effectively won. Jeanette Gould, secretary to Stan Orme, chairman of the parliamentary party, was charged with keeping track of the constituencies which had followed the advice of the executive and held some form of individual ballot, either postally, or at branch meetings. Of 586 constituencies which took part in the final vote, 53 per cent held ballots of one form or another. Most of them were in the south, south west, Wales and East Anglia. Ballots were less usual in Labour's traditional strongholds: the north west, Yorkshire and Scotland. The overwhelming evidence was that, the wider the franchise, the more likely were parties to vote for both Kinnock and Hattersley. Hattersley was sitting on the platform of a pre-conference press briefing, held by the AEU, when the first projections of the constituency vote were telephoned through by Jeanette Gould. He found them so unbelievably favourable that he decided not to tell the reporters, for fear of embarrassing himself. In fact, they were to prove to be an underestimate of his vote.

On the Sunday afternoon prior to the conference Benn and Heffer held their final rally, like two ageing stars completing the last date of an ill-advised come-back tour. None of the speakers chose to break the air of unreality by talking openly about the demoralization on the left. Instead the rhetoric was defiant and as empty as most of the seats in the hall. Privately many of those present knew that Benn's campaign had only served to expose and exacerbate the weakness of the hard-left. The Benn-Heffer campaign had, far from consolidating the cause, set it back sharply. This was confirmed hours later when it was announced that Kinnock had won 88.64 per cent of the electoral college and Benn only 11.73 per cent. Benn's result was twice as bad as the most pessimistic forecast made by his campaign organisers back in the spring. Only 38 of the 221 Labour MPs voted for Benn. Among the unions, even the left-led MSF voted for Kinnock. The worst reversal for Benn came in the constituencies, where the results showed the extent to which the politics of the party membership had transformed during the 1980s. Out of the 586 constituencies which voted, Benn won only 112, just 18.8 per cent. No longer would the hard left be able to claim itself to be the activist conscience. It was humiliating. Moreover, Benn's successes were localised within the party: more than half of the constituencies voting for him were within the former Greater London Council area, on Merseyside, and in Scotland.

It might have been possible for the left to explain away the scale of Benn's defeat by ascribing it to reluctant loyalty. That argument could not apply to the deputy leadership contest – where Prescott's candidature gave party dissidents a chance to vote against Kinnock, without actually dethroning him. Hattersley – an unloved figure – would be the coconut that fell. During Kinnock's miserable summer the leadership camp did indeed fear that the deputy leader would fall victim to just such a protest vote against Kinnock. Prescott imagined that Kinnock's messy performance over defence policy might be enough to ensure a run-off between himself and Hattersley. In that event, Prescott assumed all of Heffer's votes would transfer to him, but it did not even come close to a second ballot. Heffer's result anyway proved pitiful – except for the fact that it was self-inflicted. He scored 9.5 per cent overall, and was nicknamed '.007' – a cruelly accurate reference to his vote in the union section.

When Prescott launched his challenge to Hattersley shortly before Easter, the leadership camp trembled for a few days. Their first calculations suggested that Hattersley might win only 54 per cent of the vote – a little close for comfort. But Prescott's campaign was snagged on its own ambiguous purpose. If he was really only trying to change the deputy leader's job description, then the challenge to Hattersley seemed out of proportion to his aim. If, on the other hand, Prescott was really trying to mount a wider political challenge to the direction of the party leadership, rather than register a merely personal objection to Hattersley's political style, why did he not say so?

The effect of Prescott's challenge, as it turned out, was to enhance Hattersley's position in the party. Hattersley actually emerged a stronger figure from the campaign. He won 66.8 per cent of the total electoral college vote, leaving Prescott far behind on 23.7 per cent. The size of Hattersley's vote was not the only factor which confirmed his status. While Kinnock had flailed about through the summer, Hattersley had succeeded in scoring points against Margaret Thatcher at Question Time in the Commons. He had made some effective campaigning speeches, aimed both at the party and the public.

Prescott, as expected, had been unable to win more than half the Tribune Group of MPs. Only two members of the Shadow Cabinet supported him: Michael Meacher and Jo Richardson. He had also suffered a serious blow when the riven TGWU executive – responsible for 8 per cent of the total electoral college – voted for Hattersley during a farcical meeting of the executive in which half its membership walked out in one of the union's interminable disputes over union election irregularities. Even if the TGWU had backed Prescott, he would still have lost heavily.

Again, the most telling result came in the constituency section. Hattersley, the party's leading right winger, had won a majority of the constituencies, traditionally regarded as the left's stronghold. He took 60.9 per cent of the constituencies voting, Prescott 25.9 per cent and Heffer 13.1 per cent. Prescott won a majority of the constituencies in only two of the party's 11 regions: Scotland and Yorkshire.

More significantly, the figures compiled by Jeanette Gould showed how important the widening of the franchise had been. Only 20 of Benn's 112 victories were recorded in constituencies which held ballots. The remainder of Benn's constituency votes came from parties in which the decision was confined to members of the general committee. Hattersley won 250 (76.5 per cent) of the 327 constituencies which balloted their members. Prescott won only 18.65 per cent and Heffer only 4.9 per cent.

Further evidence of the divergence between the politics of the activists and the mass of the membership came from a comparison between the leadership results, and voting for the national executive. However the figures were calculated, they convincingly demonstrated that where members had the opportunity to vote, they backed the leadership, and leadership-supporting candidates. Where the franchise was restricted to delegate activists on general committees, they backed the hard-left candidates. Many constituencies whose general committees backed the hard-left slate for the executive, were transformed into Kinnock-supporting constituencies when they held a ballot of the entire constituency membership.

Internal Labour figures showed that 296 of the 598 constituencies which voted in their executive section backed a majority of the hard-left Campaign Group slate. Those votes were all cast by general committees, without any membership ballot, but 124 of these 296 constituencies voted for Kinnock in the leadership elections. More than a third – 36.9 per cent – of the Campaign-supporting general committees found that their wider membership rejected Benn for the leadership in a ballot of the whole membership.

THOSE figures – the cross-party strength of support – gave both Hattersley and Kinnock an additional authority. It was not simply the quantity of votes, but their quality which mattered to Kinnock. It seemed proof positive that the culture of the party was maturing. The next task was for Kinnock to employ his new mandate by making a challenging speech to conference two days later setting out the directions in which he wanted the second phase of the policy review to go. After an eight-month leadership battle, it was an opportunity to set a new course and cast the party forwards to a 1990s agenda. The speech was compiled from 'building block' passages: John Eatwell wrote passages on the economy, John Newbigin wrote sections on the environment, Hewitt drafted a piece on women, and John Lloyd – the *Financial Times* journalist – offered an initial draft on Europe which was largely incorporated. In preparation by his advisors since September, but not actually completed until the morning of the address itself, it was one of his best speeches as party leader, combining pragmatism with passion. It had to be one of his best, because it was imperative that Kinnock restore his authority and regain the party's confidence. As ever, the final speech was entirely his own language and structure; oddly, he did not feel comfortable with it until it was actually delivered.

Labour's goal, he told the conference, was not to build a fully planned economy, but to make the mixed economy work. 'That is what we will have to deal with, and we will have to make it work better than the Tories do.' Even if Labour had been in power for many years, the market would still exist. In choosing between public or private sector solutions, the country should always apply the same test as that adopted abroad: 'Which works best?' Modernisation of education, investment and training were the only means of restoring the manufacturing base. The speech also accurately pinpointed the splits to come within the Conservative Party on Europe, as well as the quandary that protection of the environment would pose for purely free market economics. Above all it challenged Tory values by movingly spelling out the consequences of Tory atomism. He told the conference: ' "There is no such thing as society", she says. No sister, no brotherhood. No neighbourhood. No honouring other people's little children. "No such thing as society". No number other than one. No person other than me. No time other than now. No such thing as society, just "me" and "now". This is Margaret Thatcher's society.'

However, even before Kinnock rose to speak, his advisors knew he was being upstaged. Half an hour before Kinnock began, Eddie Barrett, Ron Todd's media officer, moved around the press room distributing copies of a speech which the TGWU's general secretary was to make later that night at the annual *Tribune* rally. Relations between Todd and Kinnock had soured when Kinnock had gone to the TUC congress the month before and delivered a strong rebuke to those unions – including the TGWU – which were planning to mount a boycott of the government's new training scheme for the unemployed. Todd had not been forewarned of the speech and was understandably irked by Kinnock's high-handedness. But Todd's speech to the Tribune rally was not intended as a tit for tat response: he simply wanted to argue that the labour movement could modernize without abandoning socialist principles. Naivety, as much as malice, led to his message going horribly awry.

Normally, the Tribune rally – the highlight of the conference fringe – is held on a Wednesday evening. A booking mix-up brought the meeting forward by a day. No one in the TGWU had the foresight to think through the natural consequence – namely that Todd's speech had to be especially carefully phrased if it was not to give the media a chance to report a contrast between Todd and

Kinnock. Instead, the speech was written by Ian Willmore, a young, quick-witted research officer, whose colourful phrasing inevitably attracted news editors' attention. He penned the most-quoted passages, in which Todd mocked sharp-suited Filofax socialists with their cordless telephones. He also wrote a passage in which Todd turned on its head the accusation that trade unions were dinosaurs, by saying that dinosaurs had survived for 200 million years. It took an age for a message from a brontosaurus' brain to reach its tail; it took a lot less time for the message to reach Ron Todd that his speech had trampled over Kinnock's crucial day.

Todd never meant to arouse outrage: on the following day he told friends that he felt leper-like in the way trade union delegates shunned him in retribution. Willmore could not be blamed for the reaction to Todd's speech; if anything he simply did his job too well. It was the unprofessional lack of discipline displayed by the TGWU that incensed Kinnock. It made him all the more determined to go his own way in the remaining year of the policy review. Paradoxically, Todd's mistake worked in Kinnock's favour, by reminding the party of the damage which one ill-considered speech could cause.

Kinnock's staff argued at the end of the week that the leadership election victory gave a mandate for change, and that the conference had therefore cleared the path for the second phase of the review. Most delegates appeared to leave Blackpool feeling merely that the review was a *fait accompli*. There remained little rank and file enthusiasm for it. Activists, and many MPs, assumed that it existed merely as a curtain behind which pre-ordained changes in policy could be conjured. However, the post-election period of struggling for the party's soul – expressed as a contest for power among its leading individuals – was settled. Kinnock emerged incontestably sovereign. The next task was to use that power to build the policy foundation which could uphold his reconstruction strategy.

7

THE LISTENING PARTY

IF PARTY MEMBERS felt uninvolved in the process of the review, they might also be uncommitted to the outcome. There would, in those circumstances, always be some doubt as to whether the change would endure. Similarly, if the party were force-fed with a review that had been concocted in conspiracy, it could easily choke it back again. Against both those dangers, the leadership had to balance the need to manage the review effectively, and ensure that it met its main aims. After all, such a comprehensive reappraisal had never been attempted before.

Kinnock and Sawyer were full of genuine good intentions, but they had to make up their methods as they went along. Before the second phase they told MPs and party activists that they had no reason to feel excluded from the review. Sawyer told the 1988 conference that the executive was determined to make it 'open, responsive and democratic'. There would be consultative regional conferences, review group hearings held to take evidence like select committees, and meetings between Labour MPs and policy group convenors on special subjects. Exhorting backbenchers to take part, Kinnock said there had been 'a certain loss of memory about the basis on which the review was undertaken'. He referred back to the way policy had been decided prior to his leadership, when what he called 'a sort of sprawling conurbation' of dozens of working parties and sub-committees had written policy. They had scores of members, some ex-officio, some with expertise; others were there as beneficiaries of patronage or personal acquaintance with a leading figure in the party. The executive's education and science policy sub-committee – which was typically unrepresentative, uninventive, and cumbersome – had 70 members on its own. At any two consecutive meetings completely different sets of people could, and did, turn up. Labour frontbenchers found the experience not only exasperating, but irrelevant to their day-to-day policy needs.

As Kinnock reminded MPs, those policy committees were far less representative and accountable than the policy review groups. Out of 330 people populating the committees in 1982, more than 250 lived in Greater London. They were overwhelmingly white, male, and middle-class. They had no firm schedules, and no guarantee of publication, and no obligation to consult the party at large: 'Occasionally composite resolutions were added to or subtracted from the process but, except in some very specific and rare cases, that was about the extent of the general membership involvement. The result was the sort of political mail order catalogue that we got in the 1982 programme,' Kinnock recalled. Some progress had been made with the joint policy groups before the 1987 election, he added. The review went further. It solicited a wide input of views. It linked the national executive and Shadow Cabinet formally together. Its time-table was being strictly observed.

Kinnock thoroughly deserved the credit for demolishing Labour's derelict policy-making shambles, in order to replace it first with the pre-'87 joint Shadow Cabinet and national executive committees, and then with the even tighter review machinery. Sawyer, who quietly continued as Kinnock's review overseer on the national executive, also feared that a remoteness would develop between the party leadership and the rank and file. It was that dislocation which had distressed him during the 1970s; he had supported Benn's attack on the party leadership in the early 1980s for that reason. In Sawyer's view it was essential, not only to carry the party, but to engage activists and members in such a way that they and the party changed as a complete and indivisible organism.

Their appeal for wider input to the review elicited little response, either from MPs, or the party membership generally and in reality, little input at that level was solicited by the review groups. The two-way exchange broke down at both ends. Because Labour had no tradition of making policy outside the structure of conference resolutions, no one had any experience of how to do it differently. Comments from within the party which bubbled up through 'Labour listens' were so diffuse that they had only a marginal effect on the thinking of the review groups themselves. The special conferences to which Kinnock referred never came about, partly because they would have been too expensive for too little return, and partly because party members showed no interest.

As a means of enabling target voters to tell Labour what they thought, 'Labour listens' was about as effective as an unplugged hearing aid. The big open-entry 'listening' events were amusing, but nothing more. Most of the people attending them were mildly eccentric individuals who saw the events as a forum to flog their pet obsessions. The format was, anyway, impractical. They were held during the day when most working people could not attend. The Walworth Road organizers soon realized that the moment you put politicians on a platform in front of an audience they find it impossible not to deliver speeches. It was no fault of the politicians who took part. They exist to talk, and are emotionally incapable of listening without responding. At the second big regional event in Plymouth, for example, Roy Hattersley was on the platform 'listening' to a local man tell him that Labour would never get elected until it dropped its opposition to private schooling. Instead of merely noting the man's views, he came back with a ten-minute speech on why he found the private and privileged education sector politically repugnant.

One element of the 'Labour listens' exercise did achieve something: the separately-organized women's consultation brought in a large volume of information which was fed indirectly into a number of the review groups. Most of the review groups also held special sessions with invited experts, many of them from outside the party, or the usual interest groups. Although those 'listening' sessions rarely elicited new ideas, they occasionally helped crystallize the review group agendas. Most groups solicited papers from academics and specialists; all received unsolicited material from individuals and pressure groups. The 'Labour listens' tapes were transcribed and analysed, and written submissions from individual members of the party and the public were catalogued by a specially-established policy directorate unit at Walworth Road. But none of it made much difference to the review groups' thinking.

The practical failure of 'Labour listens' probably mattered little. At worst the events were only faintly embarrassing; at best they let people know that Labour was, at least in principle, willing to listen. Because a willingness to listen implies a willingness to change, the publicity surrounding the endeavour helped soften voters' impressions of the Labour Party.

Sawyer strove to overcome the barriers to open discourse within the party by attempting to convert 'Labour listens' into an internal political education exercise in the second phase. Jim Sutherland, Nupe's education officer, prepared a pack which was distributed at the party conference. It contained papers on the fields covered by the seven review groups, posed contentious questions for debate, and gave briefings on social change. Constituency parties were asked to use the materials as the basis for seminars and discussion days. Some used the packs, and sent back their responses, which were again dutifully processed by the Walworth Road research staff. This time the group convenors did scan the headquarters' analysis. Most of them, however, read it simply as confirmation that they were heading in broadly the right direction; there was no systematic attempt to evaluate the party's views, or compare one constituency with another.

The failure of those consultative experiments convinced most of those at the top of the party – Sawyer in particular – that more pervasive and radical reforms to the party's policy-making machinery would need to be made after the review was complete. Sawyer admitted shortly before the 1989 party conference which approved the review: 'The party just isn't in a position to handle proper membership participation in policy making. That's something we've got to face up to.'

THE MOST important decisions influencing the outcome and management of the review were taken by Kinnock at its outset, when he personally selected the members and convenors of the groups for their interest, expertise, and political position. He designed each group to ensure the kind of political mix which he believed would bring about the results he wanted, while ensuring that dissident views were fairly reflected. He also assigned a member of staff from his office (or rather, Charles Clarke did) to ensure that the groups stayed on track. Those people often merely stayed in touch with the group convenor. Clarke himself, for example, was on the foreign affairs and defence group; he barely attended, but stayed in close contact with Kaufman, the Shadow Cabinet convenor. Clarke also sat on the industrial relations sub-group of 'People at Work'. John Newbiggin was placed on the 'Consumer and the Community' group and on 'Physical Environment'; John Eatwell, Kinnock's economics advisor, and a Cambridge don, sat on 'Productive and Competitive Economy' and 'People at Work'; Kaye Andrews sat on 'Democracy and the Individual' and the training sub-group of 'People at Work'. In the second phase only, Hewitt dealt with 'Economic Equality' and the individual rights section of 'People at Work'. The aim was to stay close to the groups, report back to Kinnock how they were developing, and reflect Kinnock's views to the groups as necessary.

In practice every group was either led by one convenor, or broke up into sub-groups which in their turn were dominated by a single individual. Shadow Cabinet and Walworth Road research staff did the bulk of the work. That 'secretariat' met together every three or four weeks, under the chairmanship of either Geoff Bish or Tom Sawyer. It received regular shadow agency presentations from Deborah Mattinson. Kinnock's only front role in co-ordinating the review arose in his chairmanship of the regular meetings of convenors which were held every five or six weeks during the second phase, from October 1988 to April 1989. Apart from Kinnock himself, no single individual was responsible for managing the review. The campaign management team – Clarke, Bish, Hewitt, Mandelson, and Whitty, under Sawyer's chairmanship – used the meetings of the secretariat and the convenors to carry out that task as best they could. Kinnock kept his eye on the groups, but kept his own hands off, leaving the convenors to organize themselves.

Nevertheless, there remained an uncertainty about the review's purpose even among the secretariat of Shadow Cabinet and Walworth Road bureaucrats who serviced the seven policy groups. That ambiguity developed because the review's remit was never clearly outlined. In October 1987 it was envisaged that the 'Aims and Values' paper would form the centrepiece of the first stage, with the first phase review group reports being preliminary and general in character. In the event 'Aims and Values' fizzled, and the review groups willy-nilly produced more detailed first phase reports than intended. It was unclear whether the groups were supposed to review policy selectively or from scratch, or produce key themes or a comprehensive programme for Government. Each researcher, each convenor and each review group came to different conclusions about the purpose of the review so far as they were concerned. Some set out on an open-ended search for new policy ideas geared to the 1990s; others worked on the assumption that the primary aim was to ditch unpopular policies.

Sawyer himself had no doubt about the review's purpose. He told a Fabian Society conference on 17 June 1988: 'We want to win the next general election. This is the aim of the review. And to anyone who says this is crude or unprincipled, I say that to put Labour into Government, into a position where we can put our principles into practice, is the most sophisticated and principled aim that the party could have.' In his view there were five 'vital components' to the policy review. The first was to anticipate the trends that would shape Britain at the time of the next election. The second was to ascertain the people's hopes and fears. Third, Labour had to clarify its values and objectives – which the party had started to do in 'Aims and Values'. Fourth, the party had to take into account the policies that were already there: 'There was no question of starting with a clean sheet', said Sawyer. Finally, people often had only a 'distorted caricature' of Labour's policies. The party may not like the fact, but it had to start from there.

8
DEFENCE
Leave it to Gerald

LABOUR FOUGHT the 1987 election on a defence policy in which Neil Kinnock no longer wholly believed. The historic meeting between Reagan and Gorbachev at Reykjavik in October 1986 had fundamentally changed his views. Though a long-standing and impassioned unilateralist, Kinnock was enthralled and invigorated by the new era of disarmament Gorbachev offered. The summit opened up possibilities which would have seemed unimaginable only a year or two before. But it was too late to countenance any major changes in the party's unilateral nuclear policy before the 1987 election. Unilateralism had acquired a uniquely untouchable status within the party since it became policy in 1981. The three pillars of the policy – no Polaris, no Trident, no US bases – were deeply embedded, not just in the constituencies, but in the trade unions too. Apart from the strong but publicly unspoken hostility towards unilateralism among some Shadow Cabinet members, no serious multilateralist movement existed within the party. In such circumstances and so close to an election Kinnock could not afford the massive convulsion which would occur if he attempted explicitly to change policy. Instead he attempted to edge Labour towards a new position.

The process began in December 1986 when the party hierarchy presented its defence campaign document. Its central purpose was to show that Britain, as a middle-ranking power, could not afford both strong conventional and nuclear defences. The nation had to make a choice. Labour's preference was for Britain to abandon Trident, and use the £5bn to £7bn savings to buy the most advanced conventional weaponry. Kinnock and Healey as Shadow Foreign Secretary both knew that that policy would not be enough. The policy of unilateral nuclear disarmament, alongside continued membership of the nuclear alliance of Nato, perpetuated the same inconsistencies which had plagued the party during the 1983 campaign. As the 1987 election neared and the political pressure grew, the leadership pair crept further and further away from outright unilateralism. Both began to emphasise the consequences of Labour's unequivocal commitment to Nato. It meant, for instance, Labour would only act after consulting its Nato allies. Writing in *Foreign Affairs* at the time of launching 'Britain in the Modern World', Denis Healey offered probably the most revisionist interpretation of the rationale and timetable of the party's policy. It left open the possibility, he wrote, that a Labour Government could be persuaded away from the removal of US nuclear weapons in the lifetime of a Labour Government. Healey and Kinnock also adjusted the party's stance on the US bases, by making it clear that Labour would continue to allow the Americans to operate all their existing intelligence and communications facilities, and that a Labour Government would welcome nuclear-armed US naval vessels to British ports. Even the enforced removal of the intermediate cruise missiles would be deferred if the intermediate nuclear force (INF) talks between the superpowers at Geneva were making progress.

That position, accompanied by frequent reinterpretations and adjustments by various party spokesmen, probably gave the party the worst of all worlds – neither the strong moral case against nuclear weapons, advanced by the Campaign for Nuclear Disarmament, nor a satisfying technical military case about finite resources requiring a choice between Trident and conventional forces. Mike Gapes, the party's headquarters defence researcher, summed up the frustration of the party in a post-election CND pamphlet: 'The sad fact is that on defence issues most people are not willing to listen to rational arguments. Research indicates that most people would rather not think or talk about these issues at all. When forced to do so, they fall back on crude stereotypes and emotional responses. Einstein said that nuclear weapons had changed everything except the way people think. It appears that in Britain, at least, little has changed in the last 40 years in this respect. As long as British people see nuclear weapons as a kind of national status symbol then it will be extremely difficult to introduce a coherent and rational defence policy to this country.'

Martin O'Neill, then deputy defence spokesman under Denzil Davies, sympathized with Gapes' pessimism: he took the view that, short of the Labour Party threatening in the run-up to an election to bomb Russia regularly, no-one would take its commitment to defence seriously. During his summer holiday in Spain after the election, O'Neill ruminated on what could be done. Gorbachev had convinced the world, after Reykjavik, that he was a new breed of Soviet politician. The imminent completion of the long-running INF talks represented the first successfully-negotiated elimination of nuclear weapons in history. The case for Labour making a unilateral gesture as a means of kick-starting the disarmament process was that much weaker. At least two of the four Trident submarines would be in the water by the time of the next election, and the bulk of the cost would have been expended or committed. It would no longer be possible to take up Healey's option of converting Trident into conventional hunter-killer submarines.

Denzil Davies, O'Neill's boss, hinted at the implications of the superpower Strategic Arms Reduction Talks (Start), aimed at halving the stockpile of long range weapons. He told the 1987 conference that there was no possibility that the Labour Party would go into the next election with anything other than a non-nuclear defence policy. But how the party achieved that in four years' time might very well rest on an agreement between the Russians and the Americans on a 50 per cent cut in strategic weapons. That, Davies said, 'could affect Trident' – a clear signal that Trident might need to be retained for the purpose of negotiations. Gerald Kaufman, appointed foreign affairs spokesman when Healey retired from the front bench after the 1987 election, told friends that he believed a version of Labour's election policy on cruise missiles – keeping them for inclusion in disarmament talks – could now be extended to Trident. Other front benchers were coming to similar conclusions. Hattersley, in line with his long standing private view, wanted to abandon the absurdity of a British independent deterrent, but keep US nuclear bases – therefore accepting the presence of an American nuclear shield.

The key was Kinnock. Could a man who at 16 denounced Aneurin Bevan for advocating multilateralism undertake the same conversion as his fallen hero? Could he turn his back on 27 years of agitation against the possession of nuclear weapons? Would he have the courage to challenge the party, and risk the possibility of a bitter row? And if he did, would Glenys carry out the demand her husband had once made of her – that she should walk out of the house with the kids if he ever renounced unilateralism?

A month after the election there were few immediate public signs that Kinnock was contemplating change. He said the goal would still be non-nuclear, and he rejected the idea of a national referendum on keeping the deterrent – an escape route sought by some of the unions. There were only hints that the changing international scene meant it might be possible to find a forum in which Trident could be negotiated away. In private, however, Kinnock was much more convinced that the policy had to be altered. Both the electoral imperative, and the possibilities for disarmament in the nineties, required change.

Extraordinarily, Glenys Kinnock suggested, soon after the 1987 general election, that her husband should renounce the policy in one big, dramatic speech. She never took the purist view which tabloid newspapers and Tory politicians invented for her. Nor was the Kinnock marriage built, as some critics sought to imply, solely on a mutual faith in the unilateral gospel and other left-wing causes. The couple disagreed on many political issues, and Mrs Kinnock was not always the most 'left', nor the most idealistically inclined. But it was never Kinnock's style to confront the party by trying to change policy with a one-off leader's demand for loyalty. It would not anyway have worked, for the simple reason that he would have been charged with pre-empting the policy review. Whenever change came, Kinnock wanted to ensure that it would be permanent; he would not waste energy on a battle that he felt unconfident of winning.

Kinnock instead used interviews around the 1987 conference to give a further glimmer of hope to those in the Shadow Cabinet who were praying for a sign of change. He told the BBC, for instance: 'I have made it clear many times that the Soviet Union was willing to dismantle a precisely similar weapon system to that of Polaris as a consequence of our doing so.' He added, cautiously: 'It is conceivable that the same kind of arrangement could be undertaken, against the background of strategic arms reduction, in the case of Trident. So that is what we have got to explore.' Asked at the end of the conference whether that amounted to a multilateral approach, he answered: 'Yes. I don't think anybody should get hung up about words. I have been delighted and I think everybody who has been involved over the past 25 to 30 years would be delighted, to be part of a multilateral move. It is now much more of a prospect.' The remarks represented the seeds of a 'something-for-something' deal (a phrase that came to haunt him six months later), but it was by no means clear to Kaufman and O'Neill whether Kinnock now saw the removal of Trident as entirely conditional on either a bilateral arrangement with the Russians or a wider superpower deal.

It was in that context that the foreign and defence policy review team began its work. It had a clean sheet, alongside the knowledge that Kinnock had a comparatively open mind. The membership of the defence review group was probably the most carefully chosen of the seven. On one side were arrayed clear supporters of change: Kaufman; Denzil Davies (later replaced by O'Neill); the national executive right-wing stalwart Gwyneth Dunwoody; George Robertson, the party's European spokesman; Tony Clarke, the chairman of the executive's international committee and number two at the Union of Communication Workers. Ranged on the other side were Joan Lestor, a good personal friend of Kinnock but life-long unilateralist; Stuart Holland, a founder member of European Nuclear Disarmament and trade specialist; and Ron Todd, the inconvertibly unilateralist general secretary of the TGWU.

The group agreed unanimously, almost as its first decision, that it would not discuss defence in the first year of the review on the grounds that too much was moving too fast. The Start talks were under way, Nato was under pressure to take a decision on whether to modernize its short range forces stationed in West Germany, disarmament initiatives were pouring out from Gorbachev almost monthly, and the strong possibility existed that a Democrat would be elected to the White House in November. Postponing consideration of defence policy did not mean the group called a complete moratorium. O'Neill and Kaufman, for instance, began a tour of western capitals to gather first-hand knowledge of international defence thinking.

Kaufman knew no more about the technical details of defence equipment, or the finer points of strategic thinking, than an intelligent and interested newspaper reader. The only difference about Kaufman was that he was a particularly intelligent newspaper reader. The son of a Jewish East European refugee tailor, Kaufman began as a Leeds grammar school boy, working studiously in the day time, and absorbing endless cinema in the evenings. He made good by getting into Oxford University, and then became a *Daily Mirror* journalist, and press secretary to Harold Wilson. Though a small, solitary, and mildly eccentric-looking bespectacled and balding character, Kaufman was one of the most amusing companions in the Shadow Cabinet. Every spare moment he spent collecting rare operatic and classical recordings, going to the pictures (as he preferred to put it), or buying books. He wrote several of the latter too – including *How to be a Minister*, generally regarded as the most caustically witty account of Westminster and Whitehall. He frequently grossly exaggerated in his personalized denunciations of Margaret Thatcher and her supporters – calling them fascists, for example. He regularly headed the Shadow Cabinet poll – a tribute to his dedicated line-by-line attention to legislative detail. As home affairs spokesman, Kaufman was regarded as Labour's most formidable asset in Bill committees.

When the shadow communications agency provided Kaufman and his review group with an analysis of public opinion on defence, he was shocked to discover the degree to which the British people over-estimated the nation's status in the world. Most people thought Britain was still a front-ranking power, only a step behind the US. He was encouraged by the other two main messages from the agency's research: Britons were becoming increasingly pro-Europe, and they were almost exclusively persuaded that Gorbachev meant what he said.

In spite of his aloof exterior, Kaufman felt privately daunted at the task ahead. He told friends that it presented the biggest responsibility of his political career, because it was the only one on which, in his eyes, the whole future of the Labour Party depended. He set his own aim: to construct a policy that was clear, internally consistent (and therefore credible), and electorally saleable. Whatever the outcome, he was absolutely determined that the policy should hang together. He could not face another election watching the defence policy being patched and mended, before finally unravelling. Kaufman, however, confined himself to pure policy, not the machinations needed to deliver it. He did not think it was part of his job to prepare the party for any change of policy, or to become involved in arm-twisting the unions and the executive. Though he stood many times for the national executive, he had never come close to success. All that wrestling would be left to Kinnock's office.

The first attempt to carve out space for a new defence policy was made at the 1988 conference. Kinnock's staff knew that unilateralists would seek to lay down a marker by winning the conference's support for a motion reaffirming the party's existing policy. Gapes was discreetly asked by Charles Clarke to draw up a motion proposing reductions in Britian's nuclear defences by multilateral, unilateral and bilateral means. The resolution was then handed to Tony Clarke, who, it was intended, should submit the resolution to conference. The UCW executive duly adopted the Clarke-inspired resolution but voted 11-10 to make the text more emphatically unilateral. The plan had already come unstuck. The GMB was hastily asked to submit an amendment to the UCW resolution re-inserting the word 'multilateral'. At conference that was duly combined with the UCW resolution to create the text which Kinnock's office originally sought. It seemed an innocent enough resolution: the leadership team genuinely believed that it would be passed without fuss. Conference delegates understandably, however, regarded every hint of a shift as portentous: they quickly read the inclusion of the word 'multilateral' as a tactical manoeuvre. CND set to work on the union delegations. The unilateral motion was passed by 3,715,000 to 2,471,000, a majority of 1,244,000 in favour. The motion promoted by Kinnock's office, and recommended by the national executive, was defeated by 3,277,000 votes to 2,942,000 – a 335,000 gap.

The result was seen by outsiders as a severe blow; indeed Kinnock was disappointed. Closer calculation gave cause to be content. As a snapshot of the state of party opinion, the vote was not only useful, but encouraging. The narrowness of the second vote suggested that it might be possible to muster a majority for a changed policy – especially when it subsequently emerged that some of the union delegations who had voted against the leadership formula might actually have been happy to vote in its favour. Even the majority on the first, 'no change' unilateralist motion was surmountable: it would only take a switch by two medium sized unions, or one of the larger ones, for the results to be reversed. O'Neill was not alone when he left the conference sanguine that change could be achieved a year later. He was also becoming more sure that Kinnock was fully committed to change, despite his bruising summer.

Two incidents confirmed O'Neill in his view that Kinnock was committed to change. One was almost inconsequential. The evening after telling conference the policy had to change, O'Neill was at a reception when Glenys Kinnock pointedly crossed the room to tell him: 'Thanks so much for what you are doing.' More explicit was a later meeting with Clarke, who told O'Neill: 'There must be no last minute cock-ups at the end. Neil has reconsidered his position, and it is not a million miles from yours.'

It was self-evident that the policy would shift. No one, including Kinnock and Kaufman themselves, knew at that stage how far, or what form the final policy would take. The precise formula would await a visit to Moscow in the New Year. Between the conference and the visit, O'Neill saw it as his task to help prepare the party for change. He set about systematically highlighting the drawbacks of decommissioning Trident unilaterally and ejecting the US from their British bases, only for the Americans to set up new bases elsewhere in Europe. At the same time he was careful to ensure his argument for multilateralism remained implicit.

The explicit argument for multilateralism was reserved for an influential Fabian pamphlet, 'Working for Common Security', published in January. Ostensibly written by four people, the bulk of the work was done by David Ward, John Smith's clear-minded and persuasive researcher. The initiative was entirely that of the authors, but the party leadership was kept closely informed. Both Mike Gapes, and Kaufman's own researcher Mathew Hooberman, also attended some of the meetings. O'Neill suggested some drafting changes and Clarke was given a proof. The pamphlet presented the first sustained and convincing case for multilateralism to come from within the party for decades. Equally importantly, by focussing heavily on the informed debates in Europe on the future of short range weapons and Nato defence strategies, it exposed the shameful insularity of Labour's obsessive and superficial debate about the best means of dismantling the British bomb. The pamphlet was launched at a special Fabian two day conference in Oxford in January and soon became a best-seller, by Fabian standards, with prominent extracts, reviews and commentaries appearing in all the heavy newspapers.

'Working For Common Security' appeared as the final details of the visit to Moscow were being arranged with the Russian Embassy in London. The Russians made it plain that they would be laying on some senior people to talk to Labour's review team; the problem was that Kaufman did not know who he would be taking with him.

There were dangers in taking Todd. The London press were planning to fly with the delegation, and Todd had shown at the previous party conference that he could be an unguided missile. Against that was the possibility, admittedly small, that Todd might be converted by what he heard. If he were converted, it might be possible for the review group to deliver a unanimous report to the executive, and the party. Most importantly, however, Todd's presence was indispensable to the credibility of the trip. Without a unilateralist on the delegation, it could easily be dismissed by party activists as a cynical mission to harness Russian endorsement for a multilateralist policy.

Kaufman invited Todd, who quickly assented. The party's press office denied that Todd would be present, but the press was not so easily put off. The *Sun*, the *Daily Mail*, *The Times* and the *Daily Telegraph* said they would be accompanying the Labour delegation on the *Aeroflot* flight, regardless. The possibility of Red Ron breaking ranks and denouncing Kaufman's perfidy in the shadow of the Kremlin was too good to miss. Not surprisingly, Kaufman decided it was essential to have Mandelson accompany the party, in order to minimise the glasnost. Before departing from Heathrow, Kaufman laid down conditions, which Todd uncomplainingly accepted, that he would be the only official spokesman for the group during the trip. In his daily briefings at the British embassy opposite the Kremlin, the foreign affairs spokesman chose to give inconclusive accounts of their meetings with men such as Vladimir Petrovsky, the deputy foreign secretary, and Alexander Yakovlev, the head of the Communist Party's International Department. The reporters, increasingly frustrated by Todd's refusal to utter a word of any consequence to them on defence, took to doorstepping the delegation and pouncing on them as they left the various grey offices of the Russian military and political establishment. But Todd smiled benignly and remained silent on every occasion, before being whisked off in the official limousine. Even a late night encounter between the reporters and Todd at an alcohol-free Moscow jazz dive elicited nothing from the union leader except a panegyric on Charlie Parker.

BY THE end of the visit Kaufman was willing to unbutton his thoughts, most of which he had developed long before his arrival in Moscow. He chose the centre of Red Square in mid-afternoon to give his final briefing to the travelling British press. Surrounded by curious and bemused Russian passers-by, Kaufman buried Labour's unilateralism a few yards from Lenin's tomb. The Russians had impressed upon him that they saw the next stage of disarmament, after the conclusion of Start I, as a process which should involve all five nuclear weapons states. France and China, as well as the USSR, the US and Britain, should be negotiating to rid the world of nuclear weapons by the year 2000.

If there was a hidden agenda to the trip, it was to kill the third option of a bilateral deal, an approach which Kinnock still considered possible. O'Neill had long opposed bilateralism, because he believed that voters were hardly likely to be enamoured of a deal in which Britain abandoned all its nuclear weapons in return for the Russians giving up the most expendable four per cent of their nuclear arsenal. Fortunately for himself and Kaufman, the Soviets seemed equally uninterested in reviving bilateralism. Yakovlev told them that the Soviets had no interest in splitting Nato; they preferred one centre of decision-making.

The next step was due to be a two-day visit to Washington to check with the new administration of President Bush on how it expected strategic arms reductions talks to develop after the completion of Start I; what, in other words, the prospects might be for British nuclear weapons being included in a Start II. But, armed with the answers they wanted from the Russians, Kaufman did not feel the need to wait longer. On 14 March – Budget Day, when everyone's attention was on the contents of the Chancellor's leather case – Kaufman sat down at his battered electric typewriter in his tiny room along the Shadow Cabinet corridor and wrote the first draft of the report. O'Neill paced around behind him offering technical guidance, acting as a sounding board for the phrases Kaufman was tapping out. The Moscow trip had crystallized Kaufman's thinking and he felt he knew exactly what he wanted to say. Much of what he wrote had, in fact, been floating disconnectedly in his mind during and immediately after the Moscow trip. He wanted to cast the policy as part of a process, with an argument moving forward to its logical conclusion about the future of long range weapons, including Trident. He would judge it a failure if the thesis could be seen simply as a way of getting the party out of an electoral problem; it had to be intellectually persuasive too. The draft took about five hours to complete. It was deemed a joint effort: but the prose was all Kaufman's.

That first one-day draft was barely altered in substance between its completion in March, and its passage through the executive two months later. It began with a dissertation on the extent to which the old Cold War thinking was now out of date. There was both a political and economic need for Russia to seek disarmament. The historic coincidence of change within Russia, with a positive US response, transformed the context in which defence policy must be examined. Kaufman then went on to try to isolate Thatcher by showing the extent to which she alone in Europe, by continuing to argue that nuclear weapons should remain indefinitely in Europe, had failed to grasp the scale of change.

Drawing on his 1988 talks with the key ministers in Bonn, and Gorbachev's own statement to the UN, Kaufman argued that it was now the view in Europe that short range land-based nuclear weapons could be eliminated by linking their future to the talks in Vienna on major asymmetrical cuts in Russian conventional forces. That policy – known as the 'third zero' – in turn required the abandonment of Nato's strategy of flexible response, at the core of which stood Natos' willingness to use nuclear weapons first to repel superior Warsaw Pact conventional forces.

The report then scythed the nettle of Britain's own strategic deterrent: 'If Labour had won the 1987 election, we would have cancelled the Trident programme as wasteful, unnecessary and provocative. The new reality is that by the time of the General Election, three of the four Trident submarines will either be completed or under construction. There would be no financial savings available from halting their construction.' That was the pill for the party to swallow, followed immediately by the small peck of a unilateral sweetener: 'The fourth submarine is a different matter. We will cancel that as soon as we come to office. Further, we' shall cancel Tory plans to increase the number of warheads on Trident compared with the existing number of Polaris warheads. Therefore if a second stage of Start has not begun by the time a Labour government takes office, we shall as our highest foreign policy priority take all immediate action open to us to initiate such negotiations, involving the other nuclear powers. Labour will immediately seek to place all of Britain's nuclear capability into international disarmament negotiations. The important objective of first decommissioning Polaris and then Trident could be pursued by

Britain within the context of the Start II negotiations, depending on their pace and progress. Our aim is to bring about the elimination of that capability.'

Kaufman left a copy of the draft with Kinnock before leaving for Washington, agreeing that they would need to discuss it on his return. Up to that point Kinnock had not been directly consulted, nor had he sought to discover the direction of Kaufman's thinking. But, while reports indirectly flowed back to Kinnock through Charles Clarke, no formal discussion was held between the party leader and his foreign policy spokesman until after the Washington trip. Before returning from Washington, Kaufman went to New Zealand and it was from there that he first learnt that Kinnock was likely to accept the draft. The reassurance came via a telephone message from Hooberman who had been to see Clarke to find out the leader's response. Kaufman returned to London on 8 April and, despite Hooberman's reassurances, entered the Leader's office the following morning with some apprehension. He had little doubt that he would have to resign if Kinnock rejected the document outright.

He need not have worried. He found Kinnock entirely happy with the thrust of the draft. He suggested some stylistic changes and some amplificatory amendments to spell out the steps the party was taking independently, and those it was taking in concert with other countries. Other than that, Kinnock gave it his unqualified approval.

At that point the draft was ready to go to a full meeting of the nine-strong defence review team. Kaufman was confident that he had a majority, but was determined that there could be no complaint from any of them about not being able to argue their case. He opened the first meeting on 10 April by making two announcements. First, the group would meet as often as necessary, for as long as necessary, to discuss the issues in full. The discussion was one of the most fundamental to happen in British politics for 25 years: everyone should have their chance to speak, he said. Secondly, he insisted that 'National Security Council rules' (referring to the meetings of the most powerful and secret American defence and security body) would apply. To prevent leaks, Hooberman made nine copies of the report and wrote the name of a review group member on each of them. At the beginning of each meeting he distributed each review group member his personalised copy. At the end of each meeting Hooberman collected every copy back in again. Anyone who needed to see the draft between meetings had to read it in Kaufman's presence, in Kaufman's room. Stuart Holland protested that he needed to keep his own copy so that he could work on the drafting of his amendments. The rest of the committee rejected his request, but compromised by agreeing that Hooberman should be on call 24 hours a day to bring the review group member's copy to him. However, Hooberman would remain in the room whilst it was being read. In the event Holland made two visits to Kaufman's room. Only one man outside the review team or Kinnock's immediate office managed to sneak a preview of the report – and even he was not allowed to take it away overnight. Unable to control his curiosity, Roy Hattersley finally crossed the Shadow Cabinet corridor one day in April and asked to read the report. Kaufman acceded, but politely turned down Hattersley's request to let him read it quietly at home that evening. The deputy leader, like anyone else, had to study it in Kaufman's presence, in Kaufman's room. That was what the leader's office team meant when they responded, to anyone who asked how the defence review was going: 'Leave it to Gerald.'

The review team's deliberations required three sessions, each lasting about two hours, all held during the week of 17 April. The opposition came mostly from Stuart Holland, and partly from Joan Lestor. Ron Todd was unable to attend any of the meetings, because of illness, and the dock strike. He sent a proxy, Regan Scott, who took no active part in the debate. Although neither Holland nor Lestor pressed for Trident or Polaris to be immediately decommissioned on Labour taking office, they wanted a clear timetable for the dismantling of Britain's deterrent. They pressed for the retention of the commitment to rid Britain of nuclear weapons within the lifetime of a parliament. It was the only point at which the group 'voted', in the sense that differing voices were counted. Holland and Lestor were in a minority, and Kaufman and O'Neill were adamant that there would be no such binding timetable. But, in order that they could emerge from the sessions with the support of both Holland

and Lestor for the document as a whole, they agreed to an innocent amendment making it clear that Labour supported the objective of the elimination of all nuclear weapons by the year 2000. To Kaufman's astonishment, no one challenged the abandonment of the policy requiring the removal of all US nuclear weapons from British bases, which had once been one of the most important aspects of Labour defence policy. That meant that US nuclear armed aircraft (the F-111's and their modernized successors) would continue to fly from British airfields until they, too, were negotiated away.

The internal culture of the Labour Party – particularly the low premium placed on slavish loyalty – traditionally meant that deliberations on important policy could rarely be kept secret from either other Labour politicians or the press. Kaufman felt it was crucial, however, to prevent a leak this time, because early disclosure of the precise proposals in the paper would enable unilateralist opponents of the policy to build up momentum for their attack in advance of the executive meeting. Kaufman was relaxed about people outside the group having some broad idea of what was likely to emerge. But he felt it essential that any attacks should be launched blind. Delighted that only one, partially accurate leak had dribbled from the three review group meetings, Kaufman was even more determined that the press should not get hold of the document before members of the executive received their copies on the Saturday before the two day meeting – to approve all seven review group reports – set for Monday and Tuesday 8 and 9 May. Kaufman instructed Hooberman that no mistake should be made at this last stage. Hooberman drove his car from the Commons to Walworth Road with copies of the draft and personally oversaw the insertion of the copies of the report, first through a photocopier, and then into envelopes for Red Star dispatch to members of the executive.

RESPONSIBILITY for squaring the key national executive members lay with Kinnock and Clarke. On every other main element of the review, Kinnock could be confident of a commanding majority on the executive. But a mainly multilateral nuclear defence policy was different. Many of the trade union representatives, normally loyal to

a fault, were committed by their unions' conference policy resolutions to undiluted unilateralism. The reaction of the soft-left
members of the executive was also unpredictable. If Robin Cook,
Joan Lestor, David Blunkett, Clare Short, and Margaret Beckett, as
well as the representatives from Usdaw, the TGWU, Nupe and one
or two of the print unions, voted for an amendment setting a binding
timetable for the removal of Trident, Kinnock's normally secure
majority would be eroded dangerously thin. In the event the soft-left
MPs on the executive did not attempt to lobby many of the trade
unionists. They assumed that the document would go through, and
that the best they could hope for was to win improvements.

To co-ordinate tactics, Blunkett called a meeting of potential soft-
left dissidents on the night before the defence paper was set for
debate. Some declined the invitation. Diana Jeuda from Usdaw said
she could not come, because her union had just changed its conference policy. Lestor said her loyalty to Kinnock, and her already-
given assurance of backing for the report, overrode doubts. Tom
Sawyer was eager to see improvements made, but said he would have
to follow the unilateralist policy of his union until it was changed.
Robin Cook said he would come, but only so long as Joan Ruddock
was not there: she was not a member of the executive. So a group of
five – Blunkett, Cook, Beckett, Richardson and Short – headed off in
the late evening sun after Monday's day-long meeting, to see if they
could co-ordinate. The first pub they entered did not like Blunkett's
dog, and they ended up sitting outside at a pavement table at a pub
round the corner. Cook, a long standing unilateralist and one of the
sharpest minds in the Shadow Cabinet, told them he had seen
Kinnock earlier that morning and reached agreement over an
amendment of his own: 'If the beginning of Start II is subject to long
delay, and there is good reason to believe that these negotiations will
not make the progress we require, a Labour Government will
reserve the option of initiating direct negotiations with the Soviet
Union or with others.' Cook's proposal was designed to leave a fallback for the removal of Trident if the Start II talks failed to deliver
the removal of British nuclear weapons. Cook said he had agreed

with Kinnock that, in that event, the bilateral option would be revived.

Blunkett had been to see Kinnock in the leader's office at 9.15am that morning. Pressed to explain why the document did not set out a strategy to remove US bases, Kinnock simply replied: 'Trust me. It's manageable.' It was almost a courtesy call. 'I know you don't need my vote or you would have been on the 'phone by now', Blunkett joked. He stated his case and left, sensing defeat. Blunkett said Cook's amendment did not go far enough. There had to be a timetable, with a deadline for the removal of Trident set at the lifetime of a parliament. Cook, to Blunkett's surprise, said he could not support such an amendment; he had struck a deal with Kinnock and would not go back on it. Clare Short said Blunkett was right: the Kaufman draft had no failsafe strategy for the removal of Trident. Keenly aware of her own ignorance about defence, Short had spent much of the previous year in the sometimes lonely process of educating herself about defence, reading books, meeting women peace campaigners in Europe and becoming increasingly irritated by the semi-religious nature of the argument about Trident within her own party. She came to feel that much of the unilateralist argument had been made out of ignorance. She said she would be putting a series of hastily prepared amendments of her own on the dangers of proliferation, the uselessness of nuclear weapons as a deterrent, and finally a proposal not to commission Trident pending negotiations.

The gang of five left for home clearer about each other's intentions, but pessimistic about their chances. They were right to be. They had no collective agreement among themselves to support each others' proposals. Blunkett's timetable amendment was defeated by 16 to nine. Kaufman decided to accommodate most of the proposals from Clare Short, including a statement that there were no rational circumstances in which Britain would use its independent deterrent when Nato was unwilling to do so, and that the only relevant role for Britain's nuclear weapons now was to further the process of disarmament. To retain nuclear weapons was to invite proliferation, as other countries assumed they were only safe with a nuclear capability of their own. He refused, however, to include anything about the commissioning of Trident specifically.

The argument between Kaufman and Cook was less amicable. Kaufman did not trust Cook to stick by his agreement. Cook pressed his option that the party should reserve the right to initiate direct negotiations with the Soviet Union or others. Kaufman, determined to avoid anything that smacked of bilateralism, pressed for the wording to be altered so that it promised direct negotiations with the Soviet Union 'and others'. Cook countered that it was contradictory to propose bilateral talks with the Russians 'and others'; the whole objective of his amendment was to deal with a situation in which negotiations with the 'others' were failing to deliver the removal of the British weapon. Faced with an impasse John Evans, the socialist societies' executive representative, proposed that the text be altered to say that there would be negotiations with the Soviet Union 'and/ or' others. It was the closest thing to fudge that Kaufman was forced to swallow.

That tussle between Cook and Kaufman might well have turned out to be the main event of the two-day executive, were it not for Kinnock's decision to deliver a wholly unexpected and dramatic address of his own, in which he firmly and finally repudiated unilateralism. Now that Kinnock felt sure of where he stood he could, without notes, tell the executive that he would never argue for one-sided disarmament again. His words were bell-like in their clarity and firmness. No longer the prevarications and qualifications which people had come to expect of every Kinnock utterance on nuclear defence. No longer the hedging phrases, or the convoluted and cumbersome sentences which betrayed a mind ill-at-ease with the message its mouth was trying to convey. Kinnock told the meeting: 'We have the British people with us. We have their backing if we seize the opportunity of negotiation. Many in this room have protested and marched in support of nuclear disarmament. I have done something else: I have gone to the White House, the Kremlin, the Elysée, and argued the line for unilateral nuclear disarmament. I knew they would disagree with the policy. But above that, they were totally uncomprehending that we should want to get rid of nuclear missile systems without getting elimination of nuclear weapons on other sides too – without getting anything for it in return. I argued for the policy because of the integrity of the objective of eliminating nuclear weapons. But I am not going to make that tactical argument for the unilateral abandonment of nuclear weapons without getting anything in return. I will not do it. The majority of the party and the majority of the country don't expect me to do so.' With those words Kinnock crossed the review Rubicon.

He went on to confront directly the inevitable accusation that he was betraying his own long-held principles. The world had changed, and he was changing with it. 'If we had the opportunities for nuclear disarmament in the '80s that we have now, I would not have needed to advance the unilateral argument then. If we get the full support I firmly expect for this new policy, we will gain the credibility necessary to promote nuclear disarmament and stop the nuclear re-armament being undertaken by the present Conservative Government. The choice now is between a nuclear-disarming Labour government, renewed negotiation, or a re-arming Tory Government whose policies will set back all the progress, all the development we have seen since Gorbachev came to power. Gorbachev wants partners in negotiation to secure nuclear disarmament – not only the US, but also France and China too. Out of power we don't have the opportunities of unilateral or any other sort of nuclear disarmament. We only have the chance to talk about it. In power we can act, and make dramatic progress. My pledge is that the Labour Government will do that, and do so unstintingly, and I want your support for that.'

Kinnock was heard in silence, and most of those present applauded when he finished. For the first time, they genuinely felt that Kinnock was not making the shift out of a cynical need to grab votes, but out of a real belief that the world had changed and that his former view was no longer tenable. The paper was passed by 17 votes to 8. Only Benn, Blunkett, Skinner, Beckett, Richardson, Sawyer, Haigh and Hannah Sell, the Young Socialist representative, voted against. Clare Short abstained saying she would wait to see how her amendments were incorporated in the final draft. Ron Todd submitted an intricate critique of the Kaufman paper, written in flowery prose, describing the document as timid, and an insult to intelligence. It had no impact.

Journalists immediately hunted for the inconsistencies and omissions. Cracks there were none; gaps there were many. The first was shouted at Kinnock by television reporters the moment he emerged from Transport House: would he press the button? That question, while hardly central to the strategy behind Kaufman's draft, would inevitably be one of the tests by which voters judged the change. The second omission was more important to defence policy analysts: was Labour accepting the protection of the US nuclear umbrella, as the policy formulation implied? That issue was settled almost in an aside by Kaufman at a press conference on the Thursday after the two-day executive, when he said he accepted the full implications of membership of Nato. The question of whether a Labour Government would be willing to press the nuclear button so long as the weapons remained in place was more lethal. Kaufman had decided months before that, for his own part, he would pad the question away by saying it was too stupid to answer. It was clear, however, in the immediate aftermath of the executive that Kaufman's formula would not work. Commentators were withholding fulsome declarations of a policy change until they saw a plausible Kinnock answer to the question. The demand for a reply continued unabated: indeed for some television journalists it took on the status of a mantra to be chanted in the presence of any available member of the Shadow Cabinet. Kinnock's questioners were suggesting that, if he was not prepared to say he would use nuclear weapons, then the weapons had no deterrence value. They would therefore be worthless as bargaining chips in multilateral negotiations. Why should the Soviet Union take any notice of weapons which the British Government had vowed never to use?

The demand for an answer to the button-pressing question was always absurd; but so too was Kinnock's previous assertion that he would never use nuclear weapons. There was only one answer consistent with the new policy: the difficulty was to decide when it should be tried out on the public, and (perhaps more importantly) the party. Kaufman felt powerless to persuade Kinnock to say he was willing to press the button. Something so sensitive had to be Kinnock's personal decision. Kinnock was due to give his first big speech following the two-day executive at the annual conference of the Welsh Labour Party on Friday. His advisors said he should answer the question immediately, or else the whole policy might crumble. The party, they said, could not afford to lose the impetus generated by the passage of the policy review through the executive. Other colleagues warned, however, that Kinnock could play into the hands of the left by taking one step too far. At last Kinnock agreed to take the risk and carry the policy to its final logical conclusion. Until late on the Thursday night, Kinnock and his team argued over the formula, trying different wording, and trying to anticipate the likely follow-up questions. In the end, he adopted the formula, long current in the nuclear debate, that the very possession of nuclear weapons deterred, in the sense that the enemy could never rule out their use. 'We will negotiate with Trident and with the policy line that comes with all that operational weaponry, the policy line that never says "yes" or "no" to the question "will you press the nuclear button?"'. That is the combination of nuclear weaponry and the doctrine of uncertainty that is woven into it that we shall inherit. And it is that combination, the whole package, that we shall use in negotiations to secure nuclear disarmament by ourselves and by others. It is an inextricable combination, and the reason for that is that as long as the weapons exist, the assumption by others will be that there may be circumstances in which those weapons might be used.' The mere possession of nuclear weapons deterred a potential aggressor, simply because an aggressor nation needed only to know that enemy weapons were available for use, and therefore could be used. Specific protestations about their use were irrelevant.

Ken Livingstone seized on both additions to the policy line, and tabled amendments to the meeting of the executive the following week, on 17 May, insisting that Labour commit itself against the umbrella and deterrence concepts, and against ever using nuclear weapons. Kinnock hit back in the same terms: he tabled his own counter resolutions to the executive enshrining the two formulas as executive policy. Both views on deterrence and the nuclear umbrella were, therefore, formally endorsed by the executive – though they were not incorporated into Kaufman's document. The document as a whole was endorsed by 18 to 8, with Clare Short voting on the second occasion with the majority because she felt the main thrust of her amendments had been incorporated by Kaufman. Her decision delighted Kinnock. Sawyer was forced to vote against because of his union's unilateralist stance. But on 22 May, he gave probably his greatest service to Kinnock when he delivered the vote of the National Union of Public Employees, the fourth largest affiliate to party conference. To do so Sawyer, for the first time ever, had to challenge Rodney Bickerstaffe, his own general secretary and closest colleague, at a meeting of their union's executive. The executive backed Sawyer's argument in favour of the policy review and rejected Bickerstaffe's unilateralism. The delegates to the Nupe annual conference at Scarborough then backed the executive. They voted by a margin of three to one to welcome the defence review and to commit Britain to disarmament talks with foreign powers only when multilateral talks failed. It was that vote – swinging Nupe's block of 600,000 votes behind Kinnock – which effectively sealed the party conference result. Alongside the decision taken by Usdaw, the 365,000-vote shopworkers union, to broaden its unilateral stance to include multilateral options, the Nupe vote meant that the 1.24m majority for unilateralism at the 1988 party conference would be overturned.

It also meant that the decision of the TGWU, Kinnock's own union and the largest party affiliate, no longer mattered. A month later the TGWU ended a year of speculation and decided to stand by Todd's unilateralism. The vote disappointed Kinnock, but nothing more. One of Norman Tebbit's favourite jibes – that Kinnock could do nothing without the support of Todd's 1.25m block votes – would be proved untrue on the most controversial policy change the party could recall. Over a clamour of boos and applause, Kinnock told the TGWU conference in his fraternal address two days later: 'If our party was to go to the people of Britain after ten or 12 years of Thatcherism, and say we are going to disarm without negotiations, or that we were going to obey a deadline, regardless of all other

considerations, we would not be supported. And I put it to you –
every one of you a negotiator – that you know that if you set a
deadline and say that whatever happens, it will be met, there will be
no negotiations. There is no reason at all for anyone to negotiate.'

By the time conference came to vote on the defence paper in
October 1989, it felt anti-climactic. The policy did, however, suffer
genuine setback, when delegates passed a motion which called on
the party to reduce defence spending to the average European level –
the equivalent of a long-term £9bn cut, representing the annual cost
of running the entire Royal Navy. Such was Kinnock's authority, he
was able to ignore the resolution. But the vote gave the Conservatives
a stick with which to continuing beating Labour on defence. It also
demonstrated delegates' unease at being obliged to adopt a policy
which seemed to them excessively militaristic, particularly at a time
when the Iron Curtain was coming down.

Other lines of attack remained for the Tories. Labour still wanted
to abandon Britain's deterrent without any assurance that all Soviet
weapons would also go. That was true, but Kinnock was happy to go
into an election campaign arguing that he wanted to rid Britain of
nuclear weapons somehow, whereas Thatcher's emphasis was on
modernizing nuclear weapons. The Tory criticism also pre-sup-
posed that Britain had the same nuclear status as the superpowers.
Labour would anyway remain a full member of Nato's US-domi-
nated nuclear alliance. The remaining Tory charge was that the
transformation in Kinnock's personal belief was bogus – merely a
form of words, as Thatcher told the Conservative Party conference a
week later, to take Labour through the next election campaign. That
cut little ice: Kinnock's conversion was obviously authentic.

Apart from the defence spending vote at the 1989 conference,
however, there remained one critical inconsistency within the agreed
new policy. Robin Cook's amendment, incorporating an apparently
bilateral option in the event of Start II talks failing to take off, was
regarded by Kaufman as meaningless. But the issue may well return
to plague Kinnock, since the sequence of events suggests that he, in
all sincerity, approved of Cook's aim in submitting the amendment.
That meant that Kinnock remained sympathetic to the possibility of

a bilateral fallback halfway through a Labour Government's period in office, while Kaufman believed that a bilateral option would undermine the purity of the policy he so carefully compiled.

Party managers knew throughout the two years of the review that all their work, and the public reception of every other aspect of policy modernization, hung on defence. That was true, irrespective of the merits of the case on either side. Defence was the paramount symbol of the review. Without a significant shift away from unilateralism, Labour could have taken huge strides in other policy areas, and yet failed to convince the wider world of its commitment to change. The defence shift was achieved, and both Kaufman and Kinnock deserved the credit.

9

THE ECONOMY AND TAX
Fit to Govern

'IT'S NOT our policies they don't like, it's us', Bryan Gould, trade and industry spokesman, and convenor of the review group on the economy, argued soon after the 1987 election defeat. Trust between the party and the people was vital. In no field was that more true than the running of the economy. If defence policy was the pre-eminent symbol of Labour's willingness to change, confidence in the party's commitment to sensible economic management was the other pre-condition for electoral acceptability. Central to that confidence was the need to assuage the long-standing fear among aspiring earners that their income would not be drained away by a penal Labour tax system, only to be frittered away on wasteful public services. The 1987 campaign had anyway taught the party that perceptions of personal prosperity had the power to make or break the party's chances of electoral success. Doubts about Labour's competence were not only tied to its tax policy; they were further linked to impressions of the party as a whole. Voters could hardly be expected to depend upon Labour to manage the economy, if the party was patently incapable of managing itself.

Polls showed strong support for many of Labour's general economic aims – redistribution of wealth, reduced unemployment, stronger direct support for industry. Nevertheless, people remained firmly convinced that a Labour Government would let slip the public spending reins. No matter how much Labour's Shadow Chancellor pledged financial rectitude, the suspicion remained that once in office the party would revert to its true self. During the 1987 general election Labour polled four times on economic issues. Throughout the campaign 48 to 50 per cent believed Labour would manage the economy badly, while only 43 to 45 per cent thought Labour would handle it well. Among the target group – those who were intending to vote for the Alliance – only a third thought a Labour Government would handle the economy well. The north-south divide was sharply defined. Labour scored a net deficit of 6 points in the north of England, and 8 in the Midlands, compared with minus 16 points in the south. On the related issue of whether Labour would raise people's standards of living, the party performed particularly badly among middle aged voters (57 per cent thought they would not), those in work (54 per cent) and owner occupiers (53 per cent). In a paper to the Shadow Cabinet economic committee in the autumn after the election, Patricia Hewitt summed up the message of the research: 'There was a strong feeling that the benefits of voting Labour would be short term and that no real wealth would be created to pay for public spending. Our strong lead on unemployment is seen as an extension of our social commitment, rather than as part of our economic approach.'

Labour had struggled to overcome those deep seated fears prior to the election, when it published in quick succession a series of policy papers on the economy entitled 'New Jobs for Britain', 'New Skills for Britain', 'New Industrial Strength for Britain', and 'Work to Win' (jointly with the TUC). The papers were intended to convey prudence and a more market-oriented approach. Indeed Kinnock believed he had finally jettisoned the remnants of the Bennite economic strategy which had been party policy since the mid-1970s. Exchange controls, import controls, planning agreements, and massive reflation were all dropped. A diluted version of the tripartist approach to economic management – unions, government and employers acting in planned concert – remained. But the stream of policy papers made no difference. Voters were largely unaware that Labour had adopted any new economic policy. The documents failed to trumpet change; they were instead written with a bureaucratic cautiousness, as if the leadership was wary of raising alarm. More importantly, publication of the policy papers was swamped by the internal dissension on defence and the collapse after the Greenwich by-election defeat.

It was against that background that Gould recognized that the economic review could not afford ambiguity, on two or three key economic issues in particular. There had to be a clear approach to the utilities (water, electricity, gas, telecommunications) which had been or would be privatized in Thatcher's second and third governments. A fresh case for the state's role in boosting training, investment and research had to be made. Labour had shifted before 1987 away from a reliance on demand management towards what John Smith, then trade and industry spokesman, termed the three engines of growth. In autumn 1988 the party rechristened that approach 'supply side socialism', to pinpoint the contrast it was seeking to make with the increasingly apparent failure of the Tories' self-proclaimed 'supply side miracle'. Finally, there needed to be an overall message that the party's unalterable commitment to increased employment and improved social welfare would not jeopardise the balance of the economy as a whole.

Gould and his full time advisors – Henry Neuburger, a former Treasury official, and Nigel Stanley, the former secretary of the Labour Co-ordinating Committee – were unusual among the review groups, in that they commissioned no fewer than 75 papers on all aspects of the British economy, its decline, prospects, and its international position, from a mixture of academics, practitioners and politicians. Each section of the final report was supported by background papers, some of which were later published. Neuburger, an intensely studious researcher, had quit Kinnock's office after the general election to join Gould; he worked inseparably with Stanley, and the pair between them dominated discussion in the secretariat of review group research staff.

On the most politically sensitive issue – public ownership – some groundwork had already been done, with the statement on social ownership agreed at the 1986 party conference. That statement explicitly rejected the post-war Labour policy, modified during the seventies, that the state itself should own large swathes of British industry. There was little opposition from the left: most had become disillusioned with the unimpressive performance of nationalized industries. Smith and Hattersley found they were pushing at an open door. The door was nudged further ajar with the passage of 'Aims and Values' through the 1988 conference. Gould framed the new consensus in an internal paper drawn up for his review group. 'When we talk of social ownership', he wrote, 'we are not necessarily referring to who owns the equity, but the extent to which control over the enterprise is socially regulated . . . No one in the Labour Party supports old style Morrisonian nationalization any more. We have no interest in treating the Tory privatization programme as a video we wish to play in reverse.'

The more important task, Gould felt, was to adopt a clear approach to the regulation of utilities, whether or not they were left in the private sector. Without a great deal of discussion, members of the group assumed that their report would not advocate returning to traditional forms of public ownership, mainly because the cost of compensated renationalization would be prohibitive. In a paper that heavily influenced them, John Vickers, from Nuffield College, Oxford University, wrote: 'By the end of this Government's current term, there is little that a successor Government could do in the foreseeable future to reverse the privatisations of BT, British Gas, the electricity and water industries. If the shares were to be bought back, the cost would run into tens of billions of pounds, and it would be extremely odd for a government to have that as a top priority expenditure item.' Vickers went on to argue that the emphasis on ownership was anyway mistaken. Traditionally owned public monopolies had not always acted in the public interest. Attempts to clarify public interest objectives, such as the 1967 guidelines on pricing and investment, were sound and coherent; but they made little headway. A more creative approach to the utilities in the 1990s would be to build on the inadequacies of Conservative regulation of the privatized utilities and develop effective instruments of competition and regulation policy to promote the public interest. 'This will not necessarily require major regulatory institutional innovation, because recently created bodies such as Oftel and Ofgas now exist. The issue is how best to modify their powers and duties,' Vickers suggested. Gould proposed that all the utilities be defined as public interest companies and brought under a new regulatory framework.

Finding the right mix of regulation and competition for each utility proved difficult. In too many cases the regulatory bodies were insufficiently independent, and had to depend on the industry they were supposedly regulating for the necessary information. Limited competition could merely lead to price cuts in the competitive area of the industry being balanced by price rises in monopoly fields. Gould's solution of utility commissioners conducting open hearings was developed after Nigel Stanley heard a member of the Wisconsin Public Services Commission give a speech to a seminar organized by the National Consumer Council in December 1988.

As the review process approached its conclusion in March and April 1989, Gould came under pressure from David Blunkett, who argued that it would be possible for Labour to take the utilities back into public control without incurring the prohibitive cost burden of buying the equity. A Labour Government, Blunkett claimed, could simply create bonds. Both Gould and John Smith dismissed Blunkett's suggestion as utterly impractical; they thought he was being typically difficult, and – equally typically – that he was setting up for himself a position from which he could emerge seeming more left than the review. Smith stifled Blunkett by telling him in a series of one-to-one meetings that Government bonds would still count as public spending.

Blunkett's rather pointless tussle was used to hide a more serious challenge to Gould. At the very last stage two Shadow Cabinet members, Gordon Brown and Tony Blair along with John Eatwell, Kinnock's economic advisor, trooped into Gould's room over the road from the House of Commons to suggest that all decisions on the private sector utilities be deferred to a special working party. The Kinnock-inspired deputation appeared to Gould to be less concerned about the noise that Blunkett might make, than about their desire to exclude any commitment to repurchasing privatized shares from the review group's final report. Gould suspected that the trio had been sent to prevent any hint of a public utility shopping list emerging from the review. Gould himself was often regarded by colleagues as being too honest for his own good – naively so, on occasions. He sensed connivance in this case, however, and therefore resisted the pressure for deferral, saying that he would look ridiculous if, after two years of deliberation, the review group made no decisions on central issues. The suggestion was again pressed in a meeting between Gould and Kinnock, but Gould diverted the pressure.

Gould handled the treatment of shareholders in privatized companies less successfully. The party's commitment to prevent shareholders in privatized companies enjoying 'speculative gain'. Gould argued early on that the party could not sensibly seek to punish those who had bought shares in the privatized companies, particularly since so many of them were trade unionists. Labour could not afford to leave any trace of a policy which would enable the Tories to argue that shares would be 'confiscated' by Labour. The final review group paper baldly stated: 'There will be no question of paying other than a fair market price for any equity or other ownership rights we wish to acquire in the public interest.'

That formula left room for alternative interpretations, although it seemed fair to assume that Labour was proposing to allow normal payment of dividends to private shareholders. As the 1989 party conference approached, however, Gould declared in a BBC television interview that dividends would not be paid, because any surplus – profit – would be used up on investment, or carried over to hold prices down. Kinnock stamped on that. He included a passage in a speech the following day saying that, after necessary investment and pricing decisions, Labour would allow dividends to be paid in the normal way. The episode demonstrated that, even after two years of careful consideration, Labour's emergent review policy contained remnant ambiguities.

The review group also needed a convincing analysis of the decline of British manufacturing industry, and a means by which government could help arrest that decline without direct state control. Keith Cowling from the University of Warwick – the chief advisor on that front – argued that government needed an industrial strategy with which to intervene in the market for three reasons: transnational companies could otherwise act against the national interest; the outer regions of Britain could fall behind; and smaller companies without access to their own funds for investment might suffer due to the short term perspective of British finance capital. Cowling argued that it would be essential for Labour to establish a strong new Department of Trade and Industry; equivalent to the Japanese Ministry of International Trade and Industry. He described it as a powerhouse dedicated to raising the quantity and quality of investment. The state had to intervene on workforce training, investment, and research and development, because neither employers nor the City could be relied on to provide the necessary capital.

The only member of the hard left group on the executive who had agreed to serve on a review group was Ken Livingstone. Both Dennis Skinner and Tony Benn declined at the outset to take part. Gould had expected that having Livingstone on his group might prove sticky, but Livingstone in fact played a constructive role right up until the last minute. He and Gould were the only two members of the group who were seriously enthused by the idea of proposing a national information technology cable network; without Livingstone's eager promotion of the scheme, Gould might have found it hard to persuade the rest. Livingstone was advised throughout by John Ross, the editor of *Socialist Challenge*, a Trotskyist journal linked to the defunct International Marxist Group. With the help of a computer bought on the proceeds of his appearance in an advertisement for Red Leicester cheese, Livingstone tried to operate an alternative economic review.

Towards the end, however, it became clear to Gould that Livingstone needed to find a way of disassociating himself from the final report. At that point Livingstone ignored Gould's strictures against leaking details of the group's drafts and discussions, and disclosed to the press an internal dispute between Neuburger and Eatwell over nationalization, and the role of markets. He then wrote an article in *Tribune*, saying that he thought the review group's original draft – written by Nigel Stanley – was one of the best analyses of Britain's industrial decline he had ever read. He was rejecting the final report because pressure from Kinnock's office diluted that sharp analysis.

Gould was sceptical: he believed the real reason Livingstone liked Stanley's original was that it contained colourful phrases that appealed to the Brent East left-winger. There was, for example, one Stanley-written passage, which Gould subsequently deleted as being inappropriate to a staid policy paper, in which the right-wing monetarists were compared to 'Roman tribunes consulting the entrails of the dead'. In Gould's view, the central analysis, the cause of Britain's economic decline, remained unchanged.

EVEN IF voters accepted the extent of those changes in Labour's economic approach, there was a danger that they would still suspect that Labour's social spending programme would override the drive for competitiveness. In a paper written in February 1988 Neuburger argued: 'At the last two elections the centre piece of Labour's economic policy was reduction of unemployment. Our concern with unemployment looked too much as if it were no more than a desire to help a particular set of victims of Thatcherism. We made it look like there was a conflict of interest between the million people who were going to get jobs and the rest of the population who were going to pay for it.' Instead Labour should have a full employment target, but make clear that its delivery depended on the prevailing economic climate. Job creation figures, which had been the main plank of the 1987 campaign, were dropped in the first phase of Gould's review.

Neuburger suggested that the economic policy review group would want to reiterate the case for public spending, and prepare costings of its own to pre-empt the anticipated Tory accusation of Labour profligacy. That never happened. Kinnock – fearful that the review groups would emerge with a long list of costable policies, giving the Conservatives a field day pricing Labour's programme – appointed Gordon Brown to carry out a public spending check on all the review proposals. Brown, who shadowed the Chief Secretary to the Treasury, went around every convenor during March and April 1989, removing costable proposals, or draping them with the qualification that they would be carried out only when economic circumstances enabled a Labour Government to afford it. At the last two convenors' meetings, on 16 March and 18 April, Brown warned

convenors about the public spending implications of specific items in
the review reports. Finally, Dan Correy, a member of the economic
secretariat at Walworth Road, used his expertise as a former Treasury official to try and cost the programme. A proposal that the
British Enterprise Fund be funded with a gilts sale worth between
£5bn and £10bn, for example, was excised from the trade and
industry review group report itself. Similarly no cost was given for
the party's training programme. Robin Cook and Harriet Harman
were barred from including a target figure for health spending as a
proportion of the national product. Apart from that, two figures
escaped Brown's scalpel: the £2.80 an hour statutory minimum wage
in John Smith's report, and the commitment to immediate and
specified cash increases in pensions and child benefit in Cook's
report. For the rest, the sums to be spent on high-cost social services
– the NHS, education, and housing – were left vague. Kinnock's
introduction to the published review emphasized the principle on
which Brown had been instructed to work. It said that a Labour
Government's implementation of the review objectives would
necessarily depend on the rate of growth: 'We will not spend, nor will
we promise to spend, more than the country can afford.' The same
passage in the review introduction committed the party to costing its
own manifesto at the start of the next general election campaign –
but no figures would be published by the party until then. The whole
enterprise was shown to have succeeded when Gordon Brown was
leaked a copy of a memo written by Sir Terence Heiser, permanent
secretary at the Department of Environment, to Nicholas Ridley,
Secretary of State. Sir Terence's note was a response to a request
from Ridley for specific Labour policies to be costed. The civil
servant admitted that the policy review had been so carefully written
that it would prove difficult to produce figures on which the minister
could rely.

ASK ANYONE how much tax they pay, and they are likely to reply:
'Too much'. Ask them again to put a figure on it, and they will rarely
be able to give an accurate answer. Britain's tax system is appallingly
ill-understood by the people it most directly affects. Its very com-

plexity has allowed the Conservatives to escape with twisted presentations about the tax burden and thereby to present themselves as the tax-cutting party. Even though the polls consistently showed that most British people said they favoured increased public spending to cuts in personal taxation, reductions in the rate of income tax were an essential element in the popularity of Thatcher's Government. But the overall tax burden on individuals actually increased during the decade after 1979, because indirect and hidden taxes rose as the rate of income tax fell.

In an effort to understand more about how key voters viewed tax, Labour, soon after the election defeat, commissioned the shadow communications agency to study popular attitudes to taxation and benefits. The work, typical of the agency's research technique throughout the policy review, painted the backdrop for Labour's review of its tax policy. Undertaken between November 1987 and the following April, it involved telephone interviews and in-depth discussions, first with the ABC1 social grouping of professional and managerial classes, and then with the manual employee C2, D and E groups. In-depth interviews were held with C1 and C2 Conservative voters from different parts of Britain, followed up by group discussions with Labour voters.

The agency's report made depressing reading for redistributionist socialists. It seemed to confirm that Tory social ideology had succeeded in associating collective provision with inefficiency, passivity, indignity and lack of choice. It found an intense hostility towards the payment of tax, scepticism about the needs of the poor, and a qualified acceptance of the new individualism. Typical responses included: 'Britain's getting richer and so are we, but it's a new society with new rules and I've got to look after my own. Besides it's our money, and poverty's exaggerated.' Many felt proud about Britain's wealth. C1 and C2 Tories even imbued Tory economic buoyancy with a patriotic conviction that it was linked to Britain's new found diplomatic prominence on the world stage. Increasingly, people's role models were not carers, but those who had escaped from social responsibility. The 1980s were symbolised by self-starters who had cashed in on the boom.

The agency went on to describe the extent to which traditional class delineations had broken down. The key lower-middle class group, which had drifted away from Labour, now regarded itself as middle class. Most now owned their own homes, and nurtured ambitions for private health care and education. Better-off workers took a less sympathetic attitude towards poverty than the more comfortable middle classes. Poverty, so far as middle class interviewees were concerned, affected families with children in which both parents were forced to work. It also, they believed, affected old people on state pensions, school leavers facing unemployment, and single parent families. Those respondents were right. The C2 and D groups took a much narrower and more brutal view, defining the poor as tramps living in cardboard shelters, beggars, the handicapped, the unemployed and the low paid such as nurses. Indeed the C2 and Ds felt there were misconceptions about poverty. One of those interviewed said: 'Nowadays, they'll call anyone poor if they don't have a colour TV or video.' The research argued that the C2 and Ds 'were so hostile towards the undeserving poor, and focussed so heavily on the scroungers, that they forgot about the deserving poor'.

Labour voters saw tax as a means of redistributing wealth and managing the economy, but Conservative C1 and C2 groups took a much more restricted view of its purpose. The latter, for instance, regarded redistribution of wealth through social security as a form of hand-out. Where they were eligible, Tory voters' pride and status often made them reluctant to accept such hand-outs. Conservative C1 and C2s also had a poor conception of how tax works. There was little or no understanding of graduated tax bands or the differences between local and national tax, or direct and indirect tax.

Attitudes towards equality were ambiguous. Racial, sexual and educational equality of opportunity were accepted so long as the government was offering a leg-up and not a crutch. Attitudes to economic equality were more complex. Fairness, as opposed to equality, was accepted. Full financial parity was seen as extreme and since extremism was unfair, so was parity – that anyway, was how the agency expressed it. So much for Croslandism.

Britons believed that tax as a proportion of national product had fallen dramatically during the 1980s, when it had in fact risen slightly. There was little awareness of the degree to which the Conservatives switched from direct taxes such as income tax, to less visible indirect taxes, such as VAT – or of the fact that the cuts in income tax had been compensated for by cuts in benefits.

In summary, the agency argued that the government had 'broken down the traditional system of analysing social problems'. It had succeeded in instilling its message that government should be morally neutral. Poverty was not a problem; where it existed, government was neither culpable, nor strictly responsible. Taxation, anyway, was not the proper way to redistribute wealth.

Against that opinion background, Smith, the Shadow Chancellor, had to frame a tax policy for Labour which would achieve the party's redistributive aims, while assuaging voters' fears that Labour would place both the national economy and their own families in tax servitude. Smith was neither surprised nor particularly diverted by the agency's research: it confirmed, broadly, what he would anyway have guessed. Nevertheless, it underlined the degree to which Labour's loss of the lower-middle-class vote was directly related to the party's attitude to personal tax and individual prosperity. In his typically pragmatic and direct Scottish lawyer manner, Smith simplified his task into a set of straightforward political demands. The son of a headmaster, he prided himself on a frill-free, commonsense approach to politics. He never believed he could make tax a plus for Labour over the Conservatives. The best he could hope for was to neutralize the issue by refuting the charge that Labour would not reward enterprise.

Smith argued that the party had to build an entirely new house on tax and benefits, because the old one had been demolished by Labour's own incompetence during the election, and by the scale of the tax changes subsequently carried through in the 1988 Budget by Nigel Lawson. It meant that the party had to return to its tax policy foundations in the first phase of the review, and restate simply the case that tax could be fair and effective, without undermining economic competitiveness.

Fortunately, that radically tax-cutting Budget in March 1988 gave Smith the perfect platform for pressing home his case for the restoration of the principle of fairness. The Budget abolished the higher rate tax bands of 46 and 60 per cent, leaving only one higher rate of 40 per cent for those earning more than £19,300, and one lower rate of 25 per cent for the rest. In income tax cuts alone, the 250,000 richest taxpayers received the equivalent of the entire increase in the social security budget. The announcement caused chaos in the Commons, and brought gasps of astonishment even from the Tory benches. According to Labour's private polls, a sharp increase in the public's already stated preference for more public expenditure on better services, rather than more tax cuts, registered soon after the Budget. The gradual removal of the progressive principle in the tax system by the Conservatives, Smith argued, gave Labour far greater freedom to propose returning to a more progressive system, without needing to advocate punitive tax rates of 80 per cent or more.

The tax and benefits review group was able to put a simple but compelling argument in its first phase report: 'The progressive principle that contribution should vary according to the ability to pay, and rise as income rises, is fundamental to tax systems throughout the world. Britain's tax system is unique in levying the same income tax rate from the poor as it does from those earning well above the average: an income of £5,000, £10,000 or £19,000 a year attracts the same rate of income tax. Fewer than one in twenty taxpayers pay at the higher rate . . . the rate at which in Britain people start to pay tax is among the highest in the world, yet our top rate is now lower than any other European country.' To advocate a vastly more progressive income tax, Smith only had to argue that Britain's tax rates should match comparable European systems.

He rested throughout on the advice of John Hills and Tony Atkinson, the two leading tax specialists at the London School of Economics. Hills' work – 'Changing Tax', published in 1988 – formed the basis for many of the final tax and benefits review policies. Without fixing it as definite, Smith made his most politically important move during the first phase – fortunately, since he collapsed after a heart attack only two days past the closing of the 1988 party conference, and had to spend six months losing weight, walking the Scottish heather to recuperate. At the 1988 conference Smith floated the idea that Labour's tax bands should fall somewhere between a lower rate of 20 per cent and a higher rate of 50 per cent (plus 9 per cent national insurance contributions). There was no protest from within the party, and a calm reception outside.

That enabled Smith to press ahead in the second phase. Instead of the existing two bands, there could be five. The purpose was to combine the impression that the party was abandoning its allegiance to the old punitive tax levels, while seeking to inject greater fairness. By forgoing restoration of the formerly high marginal tax rates levied on British earners, Labour hoped to refute the charge that it was churlish in its reward of enterprise. Hills estimated that the financial loss to an incoming Labour Government would be minimal. Increasing the top rate from 60 per cent to 70 per cent, for instance, (on taxable income above £43,500) would have raised only £500m in 1989. Smith declined to disclose the more important information – the starting points for the various higher rates. They were more important because for example, simply restoring the 45p and 60p in the £ higher rate bands, without any further change in tax rates, could raise an extra £700m simply by reducing the starting rate from £19,300 of taxable income to £16,400.

Pressed to give more detailed figures, the Shadow Chancellor said it would be imprudent to decide until the time of a Labour government's first Budget. But it was clear from some of the computer models prepared by Hills that Labour hoped to be able to go into the next election promising to retain revenue roughly at present levels, while reversing the distributional shift in the tax and benefit system effected by the Conservatives over the previous 12 years. According to 'Changing Tax', Hills' study, the top-earning 10 per cent might lose an average of nearly £46.50 per week, a total of nearly £7.2bn per year, of which nearly £6bn would come from the top 5 per cent.

The level of taxation remained one of the most potentially controversial elements in Labour's programme; until the party provided precise figures, the Tories would be free to place their own interpretations on its impact. But Smith's contribution to the review passed through the 1989 conference with barely a whisper of protest. David Blunkett objected at a fringe meeting to the 50 per cent upper limit, saying it was too low. His was a lone voice. Not a single amendment was tabled to the tax policy review at the 1989 conference.

10

INDUSTRIAL RELATIONS
The Policy of Discontent

ONLY ONE of the seven review groups – 'People at Work', run by Michael Meacher, the employment spokesman – did not deliver the report the party leadership wanted. That failure caused climactic tensions between Meacher, Kinnock's office and the leadership of the trades unions. At one point the unresolved conflict threatened to overwhelm the 1989 party conference in Brighton.

Meacher always displayed an independent streak, notably when he distanced himself from Bennism in the mid-eighties. Up until then he had been nicknamed 'Benn's representative on earth', a reference to his decision to stand for the deputy leadership in 1983 when Benn's loss of a Commons seat made him ineligible to stand. But Meacher never entirely broke his sympathies with the left, and often, therefore, found himself trying to reconcile the irreconcilable: in this case, he struggled to wed the trade union's industrial interests with the party's electoral needs.

A well-meaning but impressionable politician, Meacher at least equalled his Shadow Cabinet colleagues in cleverness. He enjoyed a scholar's capacity to consume information. Once his interest in an issue was aroused, he showed a tenacity with detail. Having gripped a problem, he worried at it and could no more be shaken off than a dog from its bone. His intellectual enthusiasms sometimes lent him the unworldly air of an abstracted cleric and at other times, he demonstrated an unnerving political innocence. For instance, his decision to sue the *Observer* for libel in a dispute over his class background was ill-judged. His critics dismissed him as being too easily swayed. They blamed Mary Walker, his young, bright, and tough left-wing researcher, for the struggles that befell the industrial relations policy review.

Kinnock and Clarke's plan to deal with industrial relations had been to let the Trades Union Congress make modest proposals in the politically sensitive field of law on trade unions and industrial disputes, and place those mild changes alongside sweeping reforms to the law on individual employees. The idea was that reforms to collective labour law need cover only four or five issues to redress the most blatant imbalances in favour of employers, while making it clear that not all the legal immunities enjoyed by the unions prior to 1979 would be restored. The leadership of both the party, and the TUC, were in other words intending to bend over backwards to avoid the impression that the party was in thrall to the unions. In particular they wanted to stifle the Tory accusations that newly powerful trade unions would be able to dictate political terms to a Labour Government.

The strategy was agreed at meetings between members of Kinnock's office and the most senior TUC officials. Charles Clarke reasoned that the policy could be presented as comparable with the step by step approach adopted by the Conservatives in the early eighties, when the Government had extended the range of their trade union and employment law with a series of Bills over a long period, rather than a single 'big bang' item of legislation. Labour would set out a broad framework on collective labour law, but avoid being committed on each aspect of the subject. That would not only help the party avoid internal rifts; it would also shift the debate onto individual rights at work, Britain's laggard training record, and the need to help more women into work and at work. All that would make industrial relations a better political terrain for Labour.

As far as Clarke understood, Meacher had agreed that approach. All seemed set fair. The TUC's employment law committee duly delivered a submission for the Labour Party policy review, drafted by John Monks, the TUC deputy general secretary. The submission focussed on the need to set a minimum standard of individual rights at work covering issues such as sick pay, the rights of part-timers, protection against unfair dismissal, employee status and rights of consultation. In a short section at the end, it stated that some issues of collective union rights needed to be given priority. A Labour Government should repeal five of the most unfair aspects of the Tory employment laws: the ban on unions disciplining members that continued to work in defiance of a lawful strike ballot; the practice of a company artificially dividing itself in order to render strike action unlawful secondary action; the right of companies to seek injunctions banning strikes without the union being given the opportunity to put its case before a judge; and the entitlement of companies to dismiss its workforce solely for going on strike. All other issues of collective labour law should be the subject of a review in Government, with a commitment to consulting both unions and employers.

The TUC formula never explicitly stated, but was plainly intended to imply, that other employment laws passed by the Conservatives would not be the subject of immediate repeal. Large tracts of the government's one-sided laws would remain on the statute book, for the time being at least – including the tight restrictions on secondary action and picketing, the ban on the closed shop and the narrow definition of the issues over which a strike could be called. A battery of financial penalties against unions would also remain: the possibility that unions could still be subject to damages claims if they called unlawful strike action, that they could be fined for contempt if they pursued a strike in breach of a court order, and that their entire funds might be sequestrated on behalf of the courts if either the contempt fine had not be paid or the unlawful strike action was continuing in defiance of the courts.

The TUC's submission was not published until months after it had been sent to the Labour Party. Even before then, as the hidden agenda became more widely known, left wing unions began to challenge the document's status, saying that it had never been sent to the general council for endorsement. Opponents of the TUC formula spread the rumour that Ron Todd, the general secretary of the Transport and General Workers Union, had never agreed to the document. Meacher began to worry that the TUC strategy was unworkable. He told the review group that the idea that Labour could go into the general election without clear views on the key issues of collective labour law was laughable. It would not survive ten minutes in a television studio. He proposed instead to spell out the party's position on some of the contentious issues.

Meacher prepared a paper outlining his view, and presented it to a meeting held on 17 March at the TUC headquarters in London. It was a meeting of one of the Labour movement's most exclusive and secretive institutions, which has no formal status in the party. Its very existence is known to only a limited number of people inside the movement; its membership (or rather those who attend, since it has no formally fixed membership) is known to even fewer. Many Labour MPs, for example, knew nothing of the Contact Group. It was set up before the 1987 election with the intention of acting as a small, more private body than the large and formal TUC-Labour Party Liaison Committee. The Contact Group's role was to thrash out issues in private before they reached the Liaison Committee. Kinnock had become increasingly uneasy with the Liaison Commit- tee – once the movement's leading decision-making body – because its very existence seemed to authenticate the claim that union barons dictate policy to the party. The Liaison Committee's importance had anyway for some time become more apparent than real. Cynical participants felt that meetings had degenerated into a pattern of Neil Kinnock telling jokes for half an hour, followed by Norman Willis telling slightly funnier jokes for another half hour, after which the audience would gather its papers and leave.

By contrast, the Contact Group enabled important discussions between the main powers in the two wings of the movement to take place in comparative privacy. That was the case on 17 March. In attendance for the unions were Rodney Bickerstaffe, John Edmonds, Brenda Dean, Bill Jordan and John Monks; the party was repre- sented by Kinnock himself, Roy Hattersley, John Smith, Bryan Gould and Meacher. Meacher presented his paper as a new start, saying he wanted to 'commit Labour to replace whatever Tory legislation is necessary to achieve the new modernized industrial relations system we envisage'. To the horror of most of those present Meacher's proposals included a statutorily enforceable right to union recognition, a broader definition of trade dispute so as to allow solidarity (secondary) action, and the return of immunities to remove a union's liability in tort. Meacher was firmly told he was making a mistake: he should not go beyond the outline agreed in the Monks paper. John Smith, in particular, attacked him, saying there was absolutely no point in the party offering more than what the unions themselves wanted. 'You are in a minority of one', Brenda Dean told him bluntly. Meacher's Shadow Cabinet colleagues were impressed by the trade union general secretaries' unanimity, and left feeling confident that the TUC position would now prevail.

However, Clarke immediately discovered that Meacher was not only unconvinced, but also unclear about what the meeting meant. Later that day Meacher reported the views of the Contact Group to the sub-group of specialists he had set up on industrial relations law. That sub-group was formed, not from members of the whole review group but from the most formidable left-wing labour lawyers. It included the two peers Lord McCarthy and Lord Wedderburn, as well as one of the leading young barristers, Jeremy McMullen. The other members were Jim Mortimer, the former general secretary of the party, Ian Mikardo, the former Labour MP, and Joe Irvine, one of the most important backroom officials at the TGWU. Every one of those specialists believed that the Conservative employment laws should be extensively revoked, and so it was unsurprising that they advised Meacher to press on as he intended. That decision placed the trade unionists on the executive in a dilemma. Most of them would have been happy to follow the strategy agreed between Clarke and the TUC. But, confronted with Meacher's insistence that the party should repeal more of the government's laws, many of them felt bound to follow him. Their own unions' policies, after all, said much the same thing. One example was the right-winger Cordon Colling, the National Graphical Association full time official on the full review group. He personally disagreed with Meacher's approach; but once confronted with the choice, had to follow the NGA's policy and call for wholesale repeal. Colling's view mattered because he carried weight as the unofficial whip for the national executive right wing. Without the support of someone such as Colling, Kinnock's office knew that it would be impossible to overturn Meacher on the executive.

The battle lines between Meacher and Kinnock's office hardened when Meacher agreed to be interviewed about the policy review by BBC television's *On the Record*, before the report was finally drafted and issued to the executive. Kinnock had specifically urged that none of the convenors agree to be interviewed about the review while it was being prepared. Meacher, however, saw it as an opportunity to press his point, and decided to go ahead, despite a request from Mandelson not to do so. Meacher expected to be able to use the interview to discuss all aspects of the review, including the training proposals, and future relations between Labour and the unions. Instead of which Jonathan Dimbleby made the proposals on secondary picketing and secondary actions the fulcrum of the discussion. Hours after the interview was screened, Colin Byrne, Mandelson's deputy, spoke to political journalists on the broadsheet papers and effectively disowned Meacher's remarks. Acting on the instructions of Mandelson, who was in turn acting with the agreement of Clarke, Byrne told them that the interview was unauthorized and did not represent party policy.

The resulting stories in the Monday newspapers made Meacher bitter, a feeling which was intensified when a draft of the section on industrial relations appeared in the *Sunday Telegraph*. Meacher was convinced that the story had been planted by Mandelson, a neutral party official, to try and bounce the committee into an interpretation of the review draft that Meacher hated. The story suggested Labour was going to be tough with the unions, that the freedom to carry out secondary picketing would be limited, and that sequestration of union funds would continue as necessary. Any proposals on industrial relations reform, beyond the TUC paper's list of five injustices, would be subject to consultation. That implied some kind of veto by the Confederation of British Industry – an approach which Meacher's staff strongly detested.

Meacher fought back by claiming that, once that interpretation of the review was abroad, it became imperative for any ambiguous wording to be removed from the report, to prevent such misinterpretations being repeated. Meacher and his staff – Mary Walker, his researcher, and Andrew Slaughter, his press officer – started to counter-brief, while battling against Geoff Bish, the head of policy research, to secure the kind of wording they wanted. The precise circumstances in which unions should be allowed to take sympathy secondary action was redrafted repeatedly. The key issue, though, was whether or not unions and their funds should be liable if they breached the law. Meacher would not allow full sequestration of union funds; he contended that it would be possible for a union in contempt of court to have only some of its assets sequestrated. Bish argued that that was impossible because judges could not be issued directions on how to deal with anyone in contempt.

Meacher sought a succession of meetings with Kinnock and Clarke, at which he complained that the report was being undermined. Redrafts were sent to Kinnock for his personal approval. Some of the fundamental issues in the whole policy review were still being fought over during the final, farcical, 48 hours before the draft had to be sent out to executive members. Meacher spent much of a day at Walworth Road arguing with Bish. Mary Walker – treated by Mandelson as the *eminence grise* behind Meacher's obstinacy – spent two days in front of the Walworth Road word processor reinserting Meacher's views into the document, while Bish struggled to reinstate his. In the end, both sides ran out of time, and the key issue of union liability remained unresolved by the time the paper went to the May executive. The uncertainty and muddle was such that, after the first day of the two day special executive meeting, the trade union group stayed behind with Meacher to try to find a solution.

The review document, when published, left Meacher more or less the first bout victor, in the sense that the review gave trade unions more rights than those originally proposed in the TUC document. Notably, the boundaries of lawful action would be widened to include secondary action. At present, the review said, the laws were drawn with such excessive narrowness that the right to withdraw labour was effectively prohibited. 'We do not think it is fair that all forms of sympathetic action by other employees following a majority vote should be unlawful. Balance requires that if workers have a

genuine interest in the outcome of a dispute and democratically seek
to take appropriate sympathetic action in response to those in dispute
they should be able to do so within the law'. No elaboration of the key
phrase 'genuine interest' was given in the review. Meacher later told
journalists that the phrase, which was drawn from social security law,
would be interpretable in the courts.

The review failed to say how Labour's legal framework would be
enforced, because the issue could not be resolved. It was clear that
judges finding a union in contempt of court would no longer be
entitled to sequestrate the entire assets of a trade union. The
wording, however, left unanswered the question of whether a
union's funds would be liable to civil action taken by employers. In
short, it was impossible to discern how Labour's proposed laws were
to be enforced.

The vague wording the party was forced to use, due to the
formidable internal political pressure, soon began to present more
puzzles than it solved. The lacuna at the heart of the report – unions'
liability – became apparent at the TUC Congress in Blackpool. The
Transport and General Workers Union tabled a motion both to the
TUC and the Labour Party demanding that union funds be protected entirely from civil action. Norman Willis, seeing his elaborate
strategy tumbling down around him, begged the TUC not to press
the issue. However, the TGWU executive refused to budge. Its
members were furious at the way in which the courts had intervened
over the summer to neuter the union's strike in defence of the
National Dock Labour Scheme, and believed that the judges had
shown themselves to be irredeemably biased. The only solution, the
TGWU insisted, was to render union funds not liable.

Willis knew that he did not have the votes to defeat the TGWU
motion, so when the TUC Congress met in Blackpool it went
through without any opposition. Kinnock's team met and agreed it
was best for the party leader to say as little as possible. He merely
asserted, while visiting union leaders in Blackpool after the vote, that
the TUC position was 'broadly compatible' with the policy review.
Mandelson, down in London, briefed that a decision of the TUC did
not bind the Labour Party. Meanwhile, Norman Fowler, Secretary

of State for Employment, was making late summer hay with the disarray, accusing Labour of wanting to set the unions above the law. He could not believe his luck, and wondered for how long Meacher could be left in place.

The more immediate worry for the Labour leadership was the need to settle the issue before party conference a month later. The TUC vote had exposed the fact that the central pillar of the party's industrial relations policy – enforcement of the law – was missing. Emergency work was needed. Only three weeks remained to erect a policy which should have been developed over two years. Over those weeks Clarke effectively assumed the role of shadow employment spokesman. He brought the unions together in the search for a formula on enforcement. In a series of private meetings he told Meacher that Kinnock insisted that the party could not go into an election campaign without a clear commitment to bring the unions within the jurisdiction of the law. Todd, faced with severe political infighting within his own union, began to succumb to the pressure.

Significantly, Clarke by-passed the specialist advisors used by Meacher. Instead, he asked Lord Irvine, the distinguished Labour peer and barrister, to map a way through an increasingly dangerous political crisis. Irvine offered, and Todd bought, the idea that industrial relations issues should be taken out of the hands of the civil courts and handed instead to specialist labour courts. Those courts, analogous to those in the Family Division, would not be plagued by the ignorance and prejudice displayed by High Court judges. They would not have the power to sequestrate a union's entire assets in the event of a repeated breach of the law. In return, Todd had to accept that union funds would be liable. A clarifying statement was prepared, and issued in the week before conference: 'Industrial action outside the ambit of a lawful trade dispute will not enjoy immunity in tort or protection from damages . . . trades unions, like any other body which does not comply with court orders, will be subject to normal enforcement procedures to obtain damages awarded and to secure compliance with the law.'

Eight days before the conference, a facsimile transmission reached the party leader's office from Malta. It was Todd finally agreeing to accept the new formula. After the previous year's conference, in which he had inadvertently ruined Kinnock's big speech, Todd was anxious not to do the same again. The industrial relations policy parcel was, at the time of the May executive, a handful of torn wrapping which barely covered its contents. Within ten days, Clarke managed to rebundle the package for conference delivery. A month after the conference, Kinnock moved Meacher out of the Employment Portfolio in his Shadow Cabinet reshuffle.

The battle over union liability obscured much that was innovative and potentially popular in the report. For the first time Labour industrial relations policy shifted away from the national corporate level and institutions, and instead focussed on people at work and how their work environment affected them. Under a Labour Government the law would provide all workers, trade unionist or non-unionists, part-time or full time, a basic set of legal rights. Instead of the government setting formal rights which were to be enforced by third-party agencies (mainly trade unions) the law would concentrate on providing individual rights. The policy also offered flexible approaches towards the increasingly diverse needs of the modern workforce, such as the need for women to have a balance between work and home, and the need for those over 60 to choose when to retire. It was closely in tune with the tenor of European law, and the European Commission's Social Charter. Some of the most radical proposals in the review were swamped by an unnecessary and time-consuming dispute over the important but wholly foreseeable problem of trade union law.

II
PEOPLE POLITICS
Citizens and Consumers

THE OPINION research was unequivocal. Voters' two strongest impressions about the Labour Party were that it was dominated by 'extremist' activists, and that its philosophy leaned towards directing people into a drab, uniform culture determined by trade unions and bureaucrats. Behind the television studio facade of nice, clean-cut frontbenchers, Labour was seen as 'loony left' and anti-libertarian. It was associated, not with the quality and diversity that people increasingly sought to enjoy, but with levelling down to a commonly determined condition. The party was seen in that respect as being out-of-date. The Thatcher Government had swung with the 1980s political pendulum away from state planning and provision, towards individually-led consumption and privately-generated growth. By persuading people that their improved personal prosperity arose out of increased social and economic liberty, the Conservatives had succeeded in entrenching a view of Labour as politically anachronistic. There was, therefore, nothing abstract for Labour about the 1980s agenda of consumer-oriented services; no agenda was more important for Labour to reclaim.

Similarly, citizens' rights issues had shifted away from the protection of collective rights – Labour's traditional ground – towards the safeguarding of individual legal and constitutional rights. Labour again found itself cornered. However much the party leadership protested its faith in personal freedom and consumer choice, voters would adhere to their inherited perceptions of the party for as long as there remained evidence to the contrary. As the policy review went on, the test of commitment to democracy became increasingly defined by attitudes to electoral reform, and proportional representation.

As Labour had been out of government for so long – longer than nearly half the voting population could properly remember – the only source of images for what a Labour Government might look like were Labour-led councils. For every 'loony left' story that the party could prove to be false, there was another story with a vein of truth. It made no difference to protest that the 'loony left' was represented on only a tiny minority of councils: a tiny minority was too many – particularly if they were in close proximity to Fleet Street. The picture book about a little girl who lived with two homosexuals – *Jenny Lives with Eric and Martin* – was never issued to schools, let alone pupils, in inner London. It was held in the resource centre stores for teachers to use if they chose. For which voters read: 'no smoke without fire'. The banning of black bin bags by Islington council for being allegedly racist never happened. Neither were Islington schoolchildren instructed against singing 'Baa baa black sheep'. The stories fed off a strong feeling among perfectly sane and perceptive consumers of council services that left-led local authorities were not interested in what they as parents or householders thought. Labour voters themselves frequently felt that their councillors cared only for redesigning local society according to preconceived notions. The successful 'loony left' story therefore typically linked commonly held illiberal prejudices (against gay or black people), to the idea that Labour-run councils forced people to conform to their 'extremist' social theories. It was a powerful concoction with which to poison the party, because it contaminated every limb of Labour's social programme: not only local government and education, but housing, the local environment, transport, policing and the law.

The perception of Labour as authoritarian in its social philosophy, with a potent extremist ingredient in its membership, spread wider: it cast a shadow over people's faith in Labour's commitment to political liberties. The publication of Charter '88 – a non-party rollcall for enhanced constitutional and political liberties – was presented as being as much a challenge to Labour's traditionalism, and its conservative attitude towards constitutional and electoral reform, as a bid to counter the threat to political freedoms perceived in Thatcher's dictatorial approach to government. To succeed electorally, Labour had to regain its appeal to the centre ground without abandoning its commitment to community values, or its belief in the potentially liberating benefits of public provision.

The task fell to David Blunkett and Jack Straw, convenors of the 'Consumer and the Community' review group, and Roy Hattersley, the leading convenor on the 'Democracy and the Individual' review group. Straw, although Blunkett's Shadow Cabinet co-convenor, necessarily devoted the bulk of his attention to rewriting the party's education policy within the 'Consumer and the Community' group.

Blunkett's task was made easier than it originally seemed by the 1987 general election defeat. The 1985 campaign against rate-capping had collapsed in a Tory rout of Labour's local government left. To some extent the left, particularly in London, reacted by splitting into mutually recriminating groups; though there was already a strong 'new realist' strand among those on local councils, who saw that their rate-capping campaign defeat was partly caused by their lack of local support. Councils who were running 'Save our Services' campaigns suddenly discovered that a large body of voters did not believe the services were worth saving. Left councillors had too readily assumed that because they had been elected locally, they would be supported locally: in fact local voters quickly withdrew their backing from representatives whom they felt were sometimes flaunting financial martyrdom as a badge of left-wing purity. Many, such as Blunkett himself, and prominent left-wing leaders such as Margaret Hodge in Islington, began to feel that left-led councils had to rebuild support among their local communities. That feeling had in fact begun to develop during the 1987 general election, partly as a result of anger throughout the party about the Greenwich by-election defeat, which left-wingers outside London attributed to what became known as 'the London factor'. Leaders of Labour councils mainly prayed for Labour victory in 1987 because they hoped it would save them from otherwise inevitable financial crisis; their creative accounting and lease-back borrowing deals, designed to escape the worst consequences of rate-capping, took their finances to the edge of a terrifyingly vertiginous precipice. The re-election of the Conservatives, therefore, in one way played into the hands of a leadership which was eager to drag its recalcitrant left-wing local councils into pragmatist line. Labour performed particularly badly in London. Though the left retained power on inner London councils, they quickly appreciated that there was nothing they could do to frustrate the Government's enforced spending restrictions. In several London boroughs left-wingers had to fight their way through a thorny hedge of service and cash cuts. They knew that local authority resistance to Thatcherism had to be scaled down and alternative tactics adopted. That led, in turn, to a realization that Labour might not have been so heavily defeated at the general election if Labour councils had been more widely popular. The most evocative expression of the changed mood came with the publication in spring 1988 of a Labour Co-ordinating Committee pamphlet, called 'Labour Councils in the Cold', which argued that Labour councillors had abnegated their managerial responsibility. They had come to see themselves as servants of local authority trade unions and professional groups, rather than the servants of their electors.

The 'Consumers and Community' report was far and away the most prolix to emerge from the seven review groups – partly reflecting the wide range of material it had to cover, and partly because Blunkett believed that the idea of socialist consumerism needed to be explained at length. Blunkett believed passionately that socialism should be about the empowerment of individuals through indentifiable and democratically accountable community organizations. He started with the conviction that Labour could seize the consumerist political advantage from the Conservatives by emphasizing that the quality of a service came before any question of whether it should be publicly or privately owned.

The report achieved those aims. In the local government section the emphasis was placed heavily on quality and efficiency, with proposals to enable the consumers of public services to penalize their local authority if it fell short of set standards, and included performance related pay and fixed term contracts for chief officers. The Audit Commission would be converted into the Quality Commission. On one significant point the policy review group shied away from a complete break with inherited policy: it maintained Labour's commitment to end expensive compulsory competitive tendering of council services to outside contractors, but it muffled that policy under a blanket of vagueness. The report said that a council which received repeated poor quality audits 'would be required to test the effectiveness of its services by inviting alternative provision'. Alternative provision is not quite the same as market competition; and it would anyway only be enforced as a last resort. It would have been more convincing to spell that position out in sharp terms.

In one major area Blunkett's original aims were baulked. Immediately after the 1987 general election there was wide-spread discussion as to whether the Government's privatization programme had, by creating a new class of small shareholders, effectively captured a sector of voters that were formerly Labour. Those voters – the group identified in Ron Todd's memorable formula of the £400 a week docker who owns British Telecom shares and takes his family on holiday to Marbella – were precisely the southern voters which Labour needed to win back. During the summer of 1987 one of the most frequent topics of conversation, among soft-left national executive members and frontbenchers, centred on whether Labour, instead of appearing to threaten confiscation of such shares, should instead offer share holdings to everyone who used the utility's services. 'Citizen's shares', it was thought, might pay dividends to consumers, and give them a right to vote at annual general meetings. Blunkett strongly favoured the proposal, and backed a paper given by Peter Hain, the left-wing union researcher, to his review group, which advocated ways of donating share-holdings to all consumers of public services and privatized utilities. On this single issue Blunkett's review group plainly overlapped with Gould's. The two convenors started the review with a mutual agreement that Gould would stick to the regulatory aspects of industrial control and ownership, while Blunkett dealt with the consumer end. But when it came to the penultimate convenors' meeting – at which the convenors tried to scissor such overlaps – Hain's 'citizen's shares' were snipped out. Gould objected that shares which are, in effect, owned by every citizen in equal measure, would be merely gimmicky.

Proposals to empower consumers by the means of multi-tiered consumer councils, alongside legally-enshrined rights of consumers to be represented on company boards, were the other main elements in Blunkett's package. He suggested the creation of a myriad of utility councils, part-funded by a new Department of Consumers' Affairs. At the two-day national executive meeting in May, Blunkett's advocacy of a Cabinet minister to head the new department was challenged by Roy Hattersley. Blunkett was delayed in returning from a Commons vote, and arrived to be told by Straw what was happening. He delivered a ten-minute speech arguing that consumer organizations would become the unions of the twenty-first century, unifying ordinary consumers into collective action much as trade unions had done for workers in the nineteenth and twentieth centuries. Kinnock stepped in to suggest that they alter the wording to 'a minister of Cabinet rank', and Dennis Skinner – chairing the session – quickly shut down the debate by interrupting: 'I think we've settled that'. At no point did anyone ask Kinnock to clarify what a 'minister of Cabinet rank' might be, if not a member of Cabinet.

Straw produced a politically brave education policy, which accepted parts of the Tory agenda in a way that enabled him to concentrate on what parents and pupils wanted from the system, rather than what traditionalist teachers thought they should want. By concentrating on a parent-friendly programme to raise standards in the state sector, and accepting the need for a national curriculum, Straw enabled himself to attack the Government's specific and restrictive proposals more persuasively. The executive frustrated him on only one small item. The original paper which went to the two-day executive meeting included a proposal that Labour should inaugurate a Queen's Award for Schools, to be awarded by independent arbiters to schools which demonstrated high standards in any given sphere. The idea came from Stephen Benn, a London borough councillor. In a light irony, the proposal was converted into a mere 'national award' (to remove the monarchical connection), at the behest of Stephen's father, Tony. Patricia Hewitt was amused, but disappointed: she had even gone to the trouble of consulting Buckingham Palace to make sure that a Queen's Award would be acceptable.

Robin Cook and Harriet Harman worked on health policy in parallel with the Government's secret review of the NHS. They adopted some innovative methods of sampling opinion about the health service: in one session, for example, they talked directly with a group of about 50 chronically mentally ill and mentally handicapped patients, asking them what they wanted out of the system. However, apart from the incorporation of more consumer-oriented institutions, the content of the policy was uninventive. The health team worked on the assumption that Labour's health policy was already broadly trusted by voters. On health probably on more than any other issue, Labour's stance was felt to reflect a public consensus, if not a consensus within the health service itself.

By the time the review went to conference it was regarded as the most uncontroversial in the review. It ought to have been fiercely debated, because the paper was in many ways a monument to quango socialism – for which it failed to make a convincing case. But the only conference argument was over a sterile and ritualistic call from the hard left to defy the law in protest against the introduction of the poll tax. Ironically, the sole aspect of local government which the review had deferred for later decision was Labour's alternative to 'the Tory tax'.

The degree of Labour's commitment to devolution of government had been referred to a working party, chaired by Jack Cunningham, environment spokesman, before the 1987 election. That group was still at work when Roy Hattersley's review group was created, with constitutional reform a central part of its remit. Hattersley was already bound by the party's unalterable commitment to a Scottish assembly – a commitment which needed to be reinforced after the Govan by-election defeat at the hands of a temporarily buoyant Scottish Nationalist Party. Cunningham's group had, in a pre-election interim report, proposed a new regional tier of government for England and Wales, too. The only dissent of substance came from Kinnock himself, who feared that his famed opposition to Welsh devolution might be compromised by a generally devolutionist policy. Kinnock raised objections at the final convenors' meeting, but he was on his own. Hattersley told the party leader at that meeting that if he took Wales out, while leaving the option of devolution for the English regions, it would amount to saying that Wales was, like Northern Ireland, under direct rule.

ABOLITION of the House of Lords remained one of the vestigial tests of left-wing conviction. Hattersley's personal predilection at the start of the review was to stick with straightforward abolition – leaving Britain with a unicameral system. But as the second phase of the review developed, and Hattersley faced the Charter '88 challenge, he realized that he could sideline the most explosive issue in his remit – proportional representation – by tying it to regional representation and reform of the Lords. On 20 September 1988 Hattersley opened the second phase of his group's policy review by delivering a speech at Dartford community centre outlining for the first time his idea that a reformed second chamber might be elected by 'some other form of suffrage'. Although he was still unsure about whether to have a second chamber at all, he argued at Dartford that the peers' power to require the Government to think again might be worthwhile in the arena of constitutional and civil liberties. The debate – which was largely confined to those intellectuals, academics, journalists and writers who make up the metropolitan élite – centred on Charter '88's call for a Bill of Rights, a written constitution, a fair electoral system of proportional representation, a democratic, non-hereditary second chamber, and an equitable distribution of power between local, regional and national government. The first issue – the Bill of Rights – came down to the question of whether or not to incorporate the European Convention on Human Rights into British law. Hattersley thought that had been dealt with in the first phase. The only member of the review group who advocated incorporation was Paul Boateng, a successful defence barrister, as well as the MP for Brent South. He argued that a generalized civil liberties safeguard would be most effective in ensuring that the law ceased to discriminate against minority groups, particularly blacks. Hattersley opposed incorporation on the grounds that human rights needed to be entrenched in specific statute law if they were to be effective: equal rights legislation, in particular, he felt would need to be specifically targetted. He also queried the wisdom of a Labour Government opting to let appeal court judges and law Lords decide fundamental civil rights: that, he said, should be the business of a Labour Home Secretary and Cabinet. In addition, he argued that the European Convention was flawed; it protected, for example, the individual right to buy private education, without insisting on anyone's right to minimum standards of education. The primacy of one right over another, in other words, was a minutely debatable issue, and should be decided according to each case.

No one on the 'Democracy and the Individual' review group favoured proportional representation. But, as the party flapped its way through the doldrums of late 1988, Kinnock himself flirted with the possibility of proposing electoral reform. If he could only become Prime Minister as the head of a coalition, he would have to accommodate the centre parties in advance. In December 1988 John Evans, a staunch leadership supporter on the national executive, wrote an article advocating electoral pacts with the minority parties. His words were correctly interpreted as a sign that Labour MPs doubted the party could win the next election on its own – particularly since John Reid, MP for Motherwell North and a former advisor to Kinnock, publicly agreed. Advocacy of electoral reform had been running throughout the autumn. Jeff Rooker, having voluntarily quit his front bench post as local government spokesman partly so that he would be free to speak his mind on the issue, compiled a compelling analysis of the problem that would face Labour after the 1993 review of constituency boundaries. He demonstrated that, on existing population trends, the boundary review would lead to Labour losing around 20 seats without losing a single vote. It was the same point that Paul Ormerod had made in 'Labour and Britain in the 1990s' – the shadow communications agency report after the 1987 general election. Rooker spelt it out in brutally hard terms. He argued that even if Labour won the next election under the first-past-the-post system, failure to introduce PR immediately would almost certainly ensure that it lost the next election after that. Labour should therefore proclaim as soon as possible its intention to introduce PR during the next parliament. Jack Cunningham, a member of the Shadow Cabinet, 'came out' in favour of electoral reform in an autumn 1988 speech. He joined Robin Cook, the one member of the Shadow Cabinet whose conversion to PR was repeatedly and forcefully expressed.

Fear of defeat was, Hattersley countered, the worst reason for supporting PR. He also objected that it would unpredictably transform the political system. Whichever PR option Britain adopted, he said, it would probably lead to unrepresentative coalition governments dominated by minority partners. It would therefore fragment the British party structure and pull politics towards a consensual centre, which might exclude the kind of socialism to which he personally aspired. Hattersley further argued that the doctrine of the mandate would be undermined by PR: a Labour Government elected as a majority government could properly claim – as Thatcher had claimed – that it had a mandate to deliver the full contents of the manifesto which it presented to voters at the election. A coalition government would decide its policies by negotiation after the election, in ways which might substantially differ from voters' expectations.

The deputy leader confidently expected the party's interest in PR to ebb, as Labour's fortunes rose. He therefore sought a means of ensnaring the argument, by trapping electoral reform in the lobster pot of constitutional reform. By arguing that PR would undermine the doctrine of the mandate, he enabled the option of PR to be entertained for any government body elected according to some doctrine other than the mandate. He therefore dovetailed pressure for Lords reform with PR. In an article in the *Independent* in January 1989 Hattersley floated the notion that the Lords be abolished, but that it should then be replaced with a new elected second chamber. The new chamber would be unable to initiate legislation, but it would have a specific brief to scrutinize Commons-initiated legislation to ensure that it did not undermine fundamental human and civil rights. It would therefore be elected to represent 'the regions and nations of Britain'. Since no ministers would be drawn from the second chamber either, it could be elected by (in the words of the final review paper) 'a scheme different from that by which Members of Parliament are elected'. That small outlet for PR pressure was designed to allow the group to devote the final six paragraphs of its report to a condemnation of proportional representation. The report concluded by saying that the review group had 'found no merit in replacing the present system of voting with an alternative which inevitably entails the confusion of coalition government and grants to the smaller, and increasingly irrelevant, parties a degree of influence over policy which is utterly disproportionate to the size of their vote'. Labour's task was to convince people that it was fit and prepared for power: 'Talk of proportional representation or any alternative voting system would cause the electorate to question our resolve, our commitment and our self-confidence. Most important, we are opposed to change in our present system of election to the House of Commons because we believe that, far from increasing democracy in Britain, it would decrease it.'

Electoral reform cut across traditional left-right demarcations. Arthur Scargill, for example, supported PR, as did Ken Livingstone. Yet at the two-day executive meeting Tony Benn applauded the anti-PR passage as the best in the whole of the seven review documents. But it failed to remove PR as a continuing source of controversy within the party. The unexpected success of the Green Party at the European parliament elections a month later jolted the PR debate back into life. This time the debate centred, not on Labour's anxiety about the fading prospects of a future majority, but on the Greens' claim that a truly pluralist approach to tackling planetary problems required a fully pluralist method of electing democratic representatives. The Greens, looking fresh for all their political naivety, were winning support because voters felt disillusioned with a political system that felt stale and out-of-touch with a new internationalist mood. Public support for PR grew: an eve-of-Labour-conference poll showed three out of five voters favouring electoral reform. That

strengthened the movement within Labour's ranks. Of 40 constitutional reform motions submitted for inclusion in the party's 1989
conference agenda, 22 backed PR. The evidence among MPs was
that support for PR was similarly rising. The same opinion poll,
carried out for the Campaign for Electoral Reform, suggested that a
pro-PR Labour Party might stand a better chance of winning those
seats in the south of England which would make the difference
between victory and defeat at the next election.

Neil Kinnock had never personally favoured the introduction of
proportional representation, but he had long suspected that it might
at some point become politically unstoppable. He wanted to seem
open to debate within the party, so long as that debate was not
allowed to breach the firm anti-PR line during the run-up to the
election. He was therefore happy to leave Hattersley's policy mould
uncracked; it contained, after all, room for discussion about whether
to adopt some alternative form of election at the regional, European
and second chamber levels of government. That could not be
expected to satisfy the electoral reform campaigners, who pressed a
conference composite seeking the establishment of a working party
to look at the options. Adoption of PR, they argued, was the final step
towards modernizing Labour. Without it, the party's attempt to
capture the agenda of democratic reform would seem fraudulent,
because Labour would be seeking to retain a system which had been
finally discredited by its abuse over more than a decade of Tory rule.

The conference rejected the pro-PR argument by an overwhelming three to one vote. The party leadership, and Roy Hattersley in
particular, relaxed in the faith that the size of that majority had killed
the PR issue for the foreseeable future. The majority was largely
made up of union block votes: it was clear that opinion was more
evenly divided among constituency parties, with southern constituencies in particular favouring PR. If Labour were to be defeated at
the next general election, pressure within the party might become
irresistible. That alone meant that PR could not be sidestepped as a
running issue before and during the next election campaign. The
question will be asked. Even though the campaign will be fought as a
two-horse race, the demand for electoral reform will be top priority

for all the minor parties. That will maintain a pressure on Labour from below. Hattersley dismissed PR at the 1989 conference by arguing that it would only serve to breathe life back into the Owenite SDP. The point was naturally popular. Destruction of the SDP would give malevolent gratification to the architects of Labour's revival; to someone like Roy Hattersley, who had spent the 1980s striving to prove David Owen wrong, the possibility of resuscitating the SDP seemed a final insanity. But the Green Party's accusation that Labour remained out-dated in its attitude to political reforms carried the potential critically to undermine Labour's modernist image. PR will not go away.

12
PRIVATE AGENDA,
PEOPLE'S AGENDA

GIVEN THE political demands placed on the review, it was
surprising that the party leadership did not conspire more
completely to predetermine its outcome. In one sense there was such
a plot. Patricia Hewitt, Peter Mandelson, Larry Whitty, the shadow
agency, Charles Clarke, and others in Kinnock's office did contrive
to direct the review. They partly succeeded; only Michael Meacher's
industrial relations locomotive managed to shunt up a siding of its
own. But management of the review was characterized as much by
paralysis as cabal. Among the back room aides, Charles Clarke
played the central role in engineering the review politically – as the
foregoing chapters on defence and industrial relations show. There
was an equally important job, however: to package and present the
review in a way which ensured that the party derived maximum
electoral advantage from it. Mandelson and Hewitt – protected by
Whitty – were the key figures assigned to that mission. Two attempts
were made to impose a thematic cohesion, or at least to funnel the
groups' activities into one vessel. The first – a search for symbolic
policies along the lines of the Conservatives' 1978 paper, 'The Right
Approach' – ended as a series of speeches and presentations to the
secretariat and the convenors. The second led to two secret seminars
being held at the Institute for Public Policy Research, the new
independent left-wing think-tank.

Not long after her return from maternity leave in late spring,
Hewitt was moved from her post as Kinnock's press secretary.
Doubts about her position, and conflict with Charles Clarke in

particular, peaked during the summer. Prior to her appointment to Kinnock's office, she had been a successful general secretary of the National Council for Civil Liberties. She was quick-thinking and inventive, well-versed in Labour policy, an articulate writer and speaker, and an imaginative proselyte. Blame for Kinnock's bad press was unfairly laid with her; much of the fault lay with Kinnock himself. Nevertheless, Hewitt's sometimes school-teacherly manner, combined with the forceful personality of a public relations consultant, irritated many journalists, some Labour MPs, and a number of her colleagues in Kinnock's office. Hewitt and Clarke raised each other's hackles. Kinnock – recognizing her attributes – decided to create a new post for her as 'policy co-ordinator'. His idea was that, from that position, she could continue helping to manage the review and liaise with the shadow agency.

By the time the second phase was fully under way, Hewitt and her colleagues on the campaign management team realized that the review had become hydra-headed. The groups themselves had burgeoned their own bureaucracies of expert advisors, researchers, and sub-groups. No unifying theme emerged, nor any conceptual framework. It seemed improbable during the autumn of 1988 that the review groups would be able to complete on time.

The campaign management team first attempted to pull the review together in November 1988, when Hewitt submitted a note to her colleagues, headed with a quotation from Bruce Babbitt, on the American Democrats: 'The Party has succeeded in scrubbing the graffiti of its past off the wall, but we still have not painted the mural of the future.' She began by arguing that 'the policy review should be a central component in the task of positioning Labour for the next general election'. Labour's vision needed to be symbolized by 'two or three memorable policies which will make life better for you and your family'; and it needed to be 'a party in tune with what people want – a party they trust'. In a follow-up note she said that the party's success depended on winning voters' trust: without trust the 'issues agenda' would not work in Labour's favour. That trust, Hewitt continued, would be founded on an impression of economic competence, of a leadership victory over extremism, and a sense of 'We know where we're going'. Hewitt argued that, apart from the fundamental need to produce a convincingly competent economic strategy, the priority was therefore to find vote-winning policies, with the second priority being to eliminate or neuter vote-losing policies. Everything else should receive either 'broad brush' treatment only, or be left until after the 1989 conference. Some policy areas, Hewitt said, could easily be left until after the next general election.

Hewitt knew that 'vote-winning policies' would not simply drop like windfalls as the review groups' deliberations ripened: the campaign management team would have to go out and pluck them from the groups' first drafts. In some cases they might have to conjure them out of thin air themselves, she implied. 'We are looking for symbolic policies. The classic Tory symbolic policy was selling council houses. A good Labour symbolic policy was the Open University.' Vote-winners were defined by Hewitt as policies linked to values; which affect people's lives directly and immediately; which concern individuals not interest groups; which are properly thought out and costed, and capable of creative development. 'We only need a few symbolic policies. The Tories in 1979 stood for lower taxes, the right to buy your council house and stronger defences. The more policies we try to publicize, the less chance people have of remembering any of them.'

Hewitt had garnered for potential 'vote-winners' from the review groups, and proceeded to propose a menu. She added that the shadow agency were ready to 'develop and test creative ideas' on selling its items. She first suggested the 'right to train or retrain for everyone aged 16 to 60' – but then suspected that the Government's expensive training advertising campaign might persuade voters that training was a Tory issue: 'We will need a strategy to capture this area if it is to work for us,' she commented. She then offered child care, and shorter or more flexible working hours. The drawbacks there, Hewitt said, were two-fold: tax relief for child care was controversial inside the Labour Party, and there was a danger of being outflanked by the Government's recently-signalled intention of encouraging employers to provide child care to recruit women in the 1990s. The consumer's charter which Blunkett's review group was working on was, Hewitt thought, in danger of 'becoming bogged down in detail'. On education she said: 'We need clear targets (e.g. 3 languages taught in every school by 1995) for secondary schools.' On transport there had been 'little progress so far'. On the environment she picked out as possibilities: a Green Ombudsman, preventive health, cleaning up Britain. On science and technology she chose 'cabling every home', but doubted whether Bryan Gould's review group had the time, resources or the interest to produce an exciting scientific symbolic policy. On tax reform she advocated a lower standard rate without allowances (which had been advocated by Frank Field, MP for Birkenhead, and Paul Ormerod, one of the shadow agency's advisors). She noted, however, that John Eatwell – Kinnock's economic advisor – thought that Field's ideas would lead to too many losers. On the constitution Hewitt suggested that a 'House of Lords/PR/Bill of Rights' package might have symbolic impact – but then noted that a Bill of Rights had been ruled out by Hattersley's group in the first phase.

Geoff Bish wrote a sceptical commentary on Hewitt's note, which perfectly defined the tension between him and the newer, younger team around Kinnock. Bish was happy to press the secretariat about the importance of sticking to the tight timetable, but he did not believe it would be proper or sensible to intervene on the groups' deliberations in the way Hewitt proposed. He argued: 'Symbolic policies can seldom be developed successfully in isolation from the broad policy areas they concern. Nor can they be properly developed without working through their implications for other policy areas.' That, to Hewitt, was antique thinking. But, while Hewitt felt Bish's approach to the policy review was deadening, he thought hers would run into a dead end. He objected that the review groups would not be able to come up with 'specific "popular" policies' until they had looked at 'all the key issues within their policy area'.

Bish was not the only doubter. For quite different reasons Philip Gould, co-ordinator of the shadow agency, opposed testing policies in that way. He believed that successful presentation of Labour lay in anticipating and steering the public mood, rather than appearing to acquiesce abjectly in public opinion. From his perspective, the prevailing state of public opinion was important in the sense that it was essential to have a map of the terrain over which you were preparing to march – to know, in other words, where the bogs lay, where there were steep hills, where there might be short cuts. But it was absurd, in his view, to believe that the destination could be decided by opinion polls: the central purpose of a political strategy was to shift and lead opinion. Gould's simultaneous preparation of a set of strategic themes was used primarily to orient the party for its whole 1989 campaigning drive. But the key ingredients were linked by Hewitt into her symbolic policies programme, and thence into the review presentation.

Bish rewrote Hewitt's note before submitting it to the secretariat. All the researchers saw of Hewitt's aggressive and punchy original was a paper headed 'A preliminary note on priorities', which opened: 'The range of policy issues now under review is extremely wide. It might be useful, therefore, if we were to begin thinking about which are the issues which will feature most strongly in our election campaign: and especially which ones are likely to be potential vote-winners.' Bish then set out Hewitt's menu, minus her more hard-nosed remarks. The secretariat was, understandably, neither antagonized nor excited; they paid meagre regard to the demand for symbolic policies.

Hewitt's menu of 'symbolic' or 'vote-winning' policies – plundered from the researchers' early drafts – was handed over to Deborah Mattinson, who carried out qualitative research on 10 or 12 items. When Hewitt came to sub-edit the review group reports and discuss their presentation with the secretariat, she suggested, for example, that the Environmental Protection Executive being proposed by Jack Cunningham's group should be called the 'Green Watchdog', and the Food Standards Agency, the 'Good Food Council'. Both brand-names had proved more popular in qualitative research groups, but were rejected by Cunningham. A suggestion that Harriet Harman's health sub-group could use the name 'One-Stop Health Shops' to describe their 'going local' health centres was similarly bounced back.

Hewitt's November note to the campaign management team,

calling for symbolic policies, did form the basis of a pep talk which Kinnock delivered to the convenors on 7 December 1988. He told them that he was alarmed at the way in which the review was creating, even among the members of the groups themselves, an unrealistic expectation that the second phase would answer every question about what Labour would do in power. While the review had the objective of giving Labour a comprehensive programme for Government, more attention needed to be paid to policies which would symbolize Labour's vision of Britain. Kinnock wrote no prescriptions: he merely outlined areas he regarded as important, such as the European single market, industrial competitiveness, and proposals to widen individual choice. Each group should decide how to describe the respective roles of the state and the market, and how to break down sexual inequalities. Kinnock concluded by repeating that the top priority was to bring forward two or three 'leading edge' policies. They were not trying to publish an 'encyclopaedia of socialism', but to decide which issues to fight the next election on. That election would not be fought on 'loads of detail', but on 'a few big ideas which we take from the people's agenda, and which people can understand'.

Originally, Mandelson and Hewitt had wanted the party leader to announce that, instead of seven separate long reports, Labour would publish a single short sharp paper at the end of the second phase. The 'symbolic policies' and 'flagship themes' in that condensed version of the review could be tested on sample sets of voters by the shadow agency, and presentationally adapted to gain maximum impact for a minimum number of words and policies. A single short report would be more digestible, and could distill the best elements of the review: it would be presented almost as an interim manifesto. The review group reports themselves could be published as background papers. The idea of one paper for the 1989 conference was mooted at the November meeting of the secretariat by Hewitt. She suggested a paper along the lines of the Tories' pre-1979 pamphlet, 'The Right Approach', which had highlighted a small batch of 'symbolic' policies, such as extension of home ownership and freedom from trade union domination. In December Bish wrote a note to the campaign management team, which argued that it would be difficult to deal with defence or other sensitive issues like industrial relations law in that format. Important policy fields, such as housing, would be covered in only a couple of paragraphs. And if the review group reports were submitted as background documents, they would not then be submitted to conference. 'The public could be confused about the status of the different documents', Bish protested. Sawyer also opposed the idea of a single short publication; he thought it would anger both the review groups, and the party at large.

Sawyer's scepticism was decisive: the convenors caught only the backwash of the discussion within the campaign management team, when Kinnock told their 7 December meeting that not all the detailed work needed to be published. The plan for a single short document to the 1989 conference was doomed, because the convenors would never have allowed their reports to be subsumed. Instead, Mandelson proposed that a 'campaign document' be produced during 1990 – a distillation of the policy review which would serve as a mid-term manifesto pamphlet.

ANXIETY about the progress of the review, at the heart of Labour's operation, coincided with a sharp slide into despair as the party's fortunes plunged to their nadir in late 1988. Kinnock's aides were anxious that the review was out of control, that convenors were leaving the work to their researchers rather than taking a political grip themselves, and that they were conducting their work in an abstract state of mind, rather than keeping their eyes on the electoral imperative. On 28 November – shortly after Hewitt began her search for symbolic policies – Mandelson also wrote a paper for the campaign management team offering an alternative way of invigorating the review. He proposed an all-day seminar, to which they would invite a small group of inventive thinkers. 'I believe we need to take a view now of what we want to fight the next election on, and then work backwards in our policy development from that. This will also include what we don't want to fight the next election on, but which we have to get right to avoid disqualification at the outset.' The *'sine qua non* policy areas', according to Mandelson, were defence, public ownership and industrial relations. 'We have other problems, but these three are in an electoral category of their own, and require separate and special treatment. So far all these have received spasmodic or half-baked attention, and if agreed solutions are not found by next conference, our other policy achievements will be put in the shade. How is this being carried out?'

The rest of the paper urged 'the need for brainstorming'. Mandelson wrote: 'If we think back to the lessons of 1979, the Tories successfully identified the obstacles to economic growth as excessive public spending, trade union power and low productivity in industry. These formed the political agenda, we were on the defensive, and they won. We have to attempt the same on the economy. But we also need to liven and freshen up our social agenda and make it both more topical and more tailored to individual choice and freedom. We should also take an imaginative leap and give more breadth and vision to our programme – we should offer a view of society that takes us into the next century and the public policy needed to underpin this direction.' That, then, was the communications imperative of the review. The problem, as Mandelson saw it, was that there was no guarantee that the review groups, left to themselves, would meet those demands. Hence, in his view, the need for a brainstorming session which would 'only be useful if its thinking and conclusions are used to form our immediate private agenda for the policy review'. That private agenda would, in essence, seek to create the 'people's agenda' which Kinnock subsequently urged on the convenors.

Mandelson's idea for a one-day secret session outside London ended up as two half-day sessions held under the aegis of the IPPR, the independent think-tank. No one other than Kinnock, and those who attended, knew that the sessions were taking place, because the participants did not want to risk offending the many politically important figures who were not invited. Sawyer, Mandelson, Clarke (at the first meeting only), Hewitt, Bish and Whitty from the campaign management team were joined by Tony Blair, Gordon Brown, and Jack Straw from the Shadow Cabinet, Philip Gould, and some others. Baroness Blackstone, who chaired the Institute, chaired both seminars. They discussed, not specific policies, but

overarching themes on which the next election could be fought.
Several alternatives were tried. The freedom of the individual was
dropped because it seemed unlikely that Labour could wrest that
theme from the Conservatives. They kicked around choice in the
public sector, and community versus centralization. High hopes
were raised for using the concept of citizenship as a unifying theme,
which Hewitt had been discussing with Raymond Plant. That was
eventually rejected, too, on the grounds that it would not grab the
imagination of ordinary voters. A Bill of Rights had anyway already
been rejected by Hattersley's group. Eventually, the overarching
presentational theme for the review emerged: modernization and
change. It determined the slogan-title of the published review –
'Meet the Challenge, Make the Change' – and was intended to show
that the party had changed and was now ready to change the country.
The theme, devised by Barry Delaney on behalf of the agency, was
eventually incorporated into a pop song which would have ranked
second rate even as the Norwegian entry in the Eurovision song
contest. Arguably, it was one of the less inspiring themes devised by
Mandelson and the agency, but it endured long enough to carry the
review through the party conference.

WHEN ALL the first drafts of the review group reports were submitted
at the end of April, every one of them over-reached the target length
of 10,000 words. Bryan Gould's group came in closest, at 11,000:
the 'Consumers and the Community' group, co-convened by David
Blunkett and Jack Straw, came in the longest, at 27,000 words.
Hewitt rewrote and sub-edited all the papers (except for the sacro-
sanct defence document) before and after the two-day executive,
negotiating with the convenors and secretaries as she went along.
She cut the 'Consumers and the Community' paper by 10,000 words
and completely restructured it. Hewitt and the agency wrote brief
summaries of the contents and presented them in highlighted
squares within the published text. The agency also wrote new titles
for each report, based on briefs from Hewitt. Much of Hewitt's work
was a stylistic spring cleaning. In some places she introduced new
policy – such as an annual health check in the health section.

The introduction to the published review was drafted by Hewitt, from Kinnock's speeches. An ironic eye could find there an answer to those who had been wondering whether there was any distinction between political principle and the communications imperative. 'All measurements of public opinion', the introduction said, 'show that the Labour Party and the substantial majority of the British people continue to hold common values. It is those values which will guide Labour in government.' Hewitt drew that favourite Kinnock theme from the leader's speeches. There was, in his argument, no distinction between public opinion and Labour's long-held principles, for the simple reason that there was no actual conflict between the two. Labour's values and the people's values were – abracadabra – identical.

13

THE TURNAROUND

T HE ABYSS of Kinnock's disillusion and dejection at the end of 1988 only partially registered with outsiders at the time. As far as most observers were concerned, the worst period for the party leader had passed; the miserable summer period of June and July. He personally, and the party generally, in reality travelled through its most profound low point at the end of the year – a fact that was well-concealed at the time.

Mandelson cast around for a communications initiative that could be used to reactivate interest in Labour's reconstruction, but he quickly realized that no such initiative would fire until the review was in place. From the centre of Labour's operation the party seemed to be drifting in space, with no obvious means of propelling it back into a politically breathable atmosphere. The appearance of policy vacuum was beginning to debilitate those who were charged with selling the party. Philip Gould warned Mandelson that Labour was in a serious polls slump. Although the absolute level of support for Labour was not falling, the gap with the Tories remained wide. One factor rang deafening and dissonant alarm bells to the shadow agency co-ordinator: the Government was staying ahead in the face of widespread and deepening economic pessimism among voters. If Labour failed to make opinion poll gains when people were beginning to doubt the Tory economic 'miracle', then it seemed hard to imagine how Labour could ever pick up.

The slide shelved even more sharply away with the humiliation of the Govan by-election in November. It hit Kinnock personally very hard that Labour should be deprived, by a protesting Scottish electorate, of one of its largest majorities in the country. He told a snap television interviewer in the early hours of that Friday morning: 'We got a lesson in Govan. It's one we will never forget, and will never need teaching again.' Rarely did Neil Kinnock speak in public in such an evidently disheartened tone. The Shadow Cabinet met the following week at Rottingdean, the Sogat trade union centre near Brighton, to discuss its 'quality of life' push over the coming months. Politically, the party was concentrating on the right issues: the environment, transport, private affluence versus public squalor. But its increasingly demoralized leader showed little interest in new schemes; and without his decisive lead, his aides were more or less helpless.

Looking back over the year, Kinnock felt he had expended every last ounce of will to heave the party to its feet. He had failed. MPs gossiped; their tea-room talk laid the blame for Labour's inertia on poor perceptions of Kinnock's leadership. Kinnock moved against the gathering grumbles by appointing Adam Ingram – a popular Scottish MP of the 1987 intake – as his new parliamentary private secretary in early November. Ingram told the party leader to go out and talk to his backbenchers; he organized groups of Labour backbenchers to dine with Kinnock, and mustered others to join the leader for drinks in his room when there were late night votes. Nevertheless, MPs and commentators continued to talk and write about Kinnock's poor performances at Prime Minister's question time in the Commons. Instead of blowing poisoned barbs at Margaret Thatcher, he was floating long-winded questions that drifted blithely by their target. There is no hiding place in the House of Commons chamber; any politician standing at the despatch box feels, like a chill draught, every breath of unspoken judgment from the MPs sitting behind on his own benches. A party leader rising to the despatch box should be greeted with cheers, and waving of order papers; Kinnock would stand each Tuesday and Thursday, and be greeted by utter silence from his backbenchers. No judgment is more public, in Westminster terms, nor more damning.

In the second week of December Clare Short and Andrew Bennett resigned from the front bench so that they could vote, along with 41 Labour backbenchers, against the Government's entrenchment of the Prevention of Terrorism Act. They were in flagrant breach of the party whip, having been told to abstain. For Kinnock it was the last straw; he took the vote as an indication of the party's obstinate refusal to buckle down. As Kinnock left Westminster for the Christmas break, some of his closest staff feared he might quit, or that he would be so undermined by his own sense of impotence that his colleagues would conclude that they should replace him. When he re-appeared after the New Year to conduct a radio interview on 2 January, Mori was showing Labour 10 points behind. He blamed divisions in the party – the Prevention of Terrorism Act vote – for the poll slump; but the same Mori poll set his personal rating at its lowest ever : 27 per cent.

Charles Clarke absorbed the periodic depressions to which Kinnock was subject. He felt throughout that Kinnock's blackness was no worse than others in the past: it was merely the flipside of a periodically volatile temperament, which rose to great highs and sank to severe lows. Kinnock's character was always self-fuelling. He could be dragged back by his own turbulence, or ride on his own adrenalin. Others entered the 1987 election campaign in a mood of trembling dread; Kinnock literally bounced from the starting block. The converse was also true: his own doubts simmered in themselves, and then spilt like an oil-slick around him. Clarke had seen it all before. On previous similar occasions his boss had emerged with renewed vigour, and Clarke fully expected him to do so again. He told Kinnock that Labour was still scoring between 36 and 38 points in the polls, and that once they reached 40 per cent they would start benefitting from Government unpopularity. In his view it was not the gap between the two parties that mattered, so much as Labour's absolute share. They need only wait for mortgage rate rises to bite, for all the other disaffections to take their toll on Tory support: water privatization, the health service, splits within the Government over Europe and the economy.

Despite all that, Mandelson and Clarke met and reached a deal at the turn of the year that they should make a renewed effort to boost Kinnock personally – while urging the party leader into a high risk, high stakes political strategy to carry them through until the 1989 conference. Clarke and Kinnock between them devised a new speech-writing system, which helped the leader prepare a series of six policy lectures. Their content was based on the main themes emerging from the as yet unpublished policy reviews, and they were used by Mandelson to try and project Kinnock as having 'bottom' – the weighty quality which commentators almost unanimously believed Kinnock lacked.

Kinnock himself later told friends that his spirits rose over the Christmas break when he painted a bedroom for Rachel, his daughter, and laughed unstoppably at a National Theatre comedy. He just needed personal release. His staff, however, believed that the main factor in his personal recovery was his sharpened perform- ance at question time. Kinnock was bad at taking advice on his political style: his instinct was to try and prove people wrong. He very often responded to well-intended counsel with a dismissive 'yep', yep'. All his staff and colleagues had been telling him how he could improve his question time performance, with shorter, jokier ques- tions. The two MPs who acted as his pre-question time sparring partners – Derek Fatchett and Bruce Grocott – had told him often enough as they kicked around ideas. The nudge finally came from outside; it was a 3 November column in *The Listener* by Stephen Fry, headed 'Don't Kneel, Neil', which reminded Kinnock of the value of deflating his adversary with mockery. Fry argued that Thatcher in particular, who depends on an inflated reputation to overblow her stature, could be most wounded by a puncturing humour. The serious political point could sneak in behind the smile. 'However monstrous Mr Kinnock may find the Prime Minister, it is no good taking that as his starting point. It merely builds her up', Fry wrote. Kinnock only needed to find Thatcher funny, and show that he assumed everyone else found her funny too – to 'demonstrate that he, and all of Britain behind him, know this to be so: that she is weird, and a laughing stock for apparently never having noticed it'. From the first week the Commons returned in the New Year, Kinnock began to score. Conservative backbenchers, who had been gleefully baying at Kinnock's unease in the autumn, found themselves chuckling at his gibes; there were evidently plenty of Tory backbenchers willing to enjoy a wisecrack at their leader's expense. Thatcher herself sometimes walked into it, providing such ample opportunity for mockery as announcing that 'we are a grandmother', for example. Tories took the change as a signal that the Opposition was in business. It was also proof (evidence which some of Labour's newer backbenchers needed to witness) that the Commons is no side-show. Such apparently small things as a brief exchange of maybe 100 or 200 words twice a week could alter the perception of a whole party, and even the national political mood.

IT WAS already clear that Labour would have to conduct a period of intensive election campaigning running through the local elections in early May, straight on into the European parliament election in mid-June. Labour's local election campaigning had improved under the party's new communications direction. Under normal circumstances, it would have devoted scant resources to the European parliamentary polls but Mandelson and Gould, backed by Clarke, prepared during January a campaign plan which was designed to haul Labour out of its rut.

Gould composed on two sides of A4 a set of simple, but not easily attainable targets. First, the party should enter a period of continuous election campaigning. Instead of slowing down after the local elections, and then ticking over into the European polls, Labour should steadily crescendo right through the two to three month period, until the party hit treble fortissimo on 15 June, European parliament polling day. Second – the most hazardous element – he suggested that Labour should publish its policy review in the middle of May, like a cymbal crash at the centre of its continuous election bolero. It would have been possible to delay publication of the review until after that two-month march. Kinnock agreed, instead, to the review being presented to the national executive after the May local elections, and before the European elections. If the executive's approval of the review went awry, the European elections might prove disastrous for Labour. The timetable placed an astonishingly tight schedule on the review groups. But if the review proved a success, however, it could provide the extra impetus needed to lift Labour's ratings off the ground.

Alongside those discussions lay a shadow agency brief, prepared at the turn of the year, titled 'Policy Review Research and Communications Strategy', which provided a framework for the presentational delivery of the review. The focus should, Philip Gould said, be on 'trusting Labour to form a Government' as the key attribute. That would mean 'demonstrating that the leadership is delivering a new Labour Party, ready for the 1990s'. The communications aim should therefore be to 'use new policies as the central lever to shift attitudes towards Labour', by focussing on 'efficiency, quality of life and fairness'. It would be important to 'present Labour's team for Government', and to 'stress substance, not at the expense of style, but at the heart of it'.

The shadow agency co-ordinator said that three main areas were 'up for grabs' politically: industry/skills, the environment, and education. He later added women's policy, and Europe. Labour negatives were listed:

* Raising taxes – spend, spend, spend – to hit 'the ordinary man'
* (Re)nationalization – old Labour – means 'we' bail out loss-making industry
* Union rights – 'they' will hold the country to ransom
* Disarmament – soft foreign policy.

Tory negatives were:

* Health – destroying British institution, may 'affect me'
* Privatization – was a positive, now a problem – water
* Poll tax – may 'affect me'
* Education – breakdown of state system, discipline, lack of investment.

On attitudes towards the parties the agency found a continuing belief among voters that Labour lacked unity, and fears of left-wing extremism remained strong. But people also saw the party as being 'on the up'. Encouragingly, too, for Labour, there was a generalized perception of confusion in the centre ground of politics, with the former Alliance partners in utter disarray. Attitudes to the Conservatives revolved around perceptions of Thatcher herself; voters derived all the Tories' strengths and weaknesses from her. Philip Gould's thematic outlay was fed into the review launch, which was designed to convey the message that the party had changed, and that it was ready to change the country. Labour, Gould concluded, should set itself a campaign target of net gains in the European election, and a sustainable poll lead by June. Every target was hit, right through to the delivery of the review through party conference in the autumn.

SEVERAL pivotal points about Labour's modernized campaigning style have long been misunderstood. That the view was eagerly but misguidedly fostered that the party became, after 1985, utterly subservient to communications strategies dreamt up and perpetrated by Peter Mandelson, almost as if he were a kind of media-manipulating Merlin riding at King Kinnock's right hand. One of the easiest ways a left-wing Labour Party speaker could win easy applause was to mention Mandelson's name: he became, among suspicious leftwingers, an emblem of distrust. Even the Tories fell for the Merlin myth. They appeared to imagine that, if they attributed Labour's success solely to Mandelsonian image-making, they could create the impression that the review's outcome was mere tinsel.

Mandelson became enormously influential in the party, on matters of politics as well as presentation, as other aspects of our account have shown. But he always acted as a servant to his master. If he ever stepped out of line, Kinnock let him know. Or, more frequently, Charles Clarke did. Clarke's political command at the centre of the party was at every stage greater than Mandelson's. Although the pair were friends of many years' standing, Clarke's loyalty was all to Kinnock. As the leader's Chief of Staff Clarke was his closest advisor and ally. Mandelson never implemented any strictly political task without Clarke's prior approval.

A further misconception was that Mandelson and his shadow agency achieved all their aims by massaging the media. His manipu-

lative skills were frequently and vividly displayed. Mandelson
understood the needs and pressures of both written and broadcast
journalism perfectly. He knew how to use heavy newspapers to
describe a news agenda, which would then be picked up by broadcasters. He wheedled, cajoled, flattered, bullied and pestered political journalists into writing the stories that he wanted. He set up
young, clever, telegenic politicians – such as Bryan Gould, Gordon
Brown, and Tony Blair – in preference to less appealing ones. But
his real talent lay in sheer force of personality, not in sorcery.

Many of the strategems carried through by Mandelson were not
strictly of his devising: they were Philip Gould's. Gould, throughout,
regarded political strategy and communications as utterly inseparable. They never allowed themselves to drift on the day-to-day flow
of events. Having agreed a strategy, they uncompromisingly followed
it through. Without the substance of the policy review, all the glitter
of glitznost would be worthless. Mandelson and Philip Gould
succeeded, not because they exploited slick advertising and media
management more effectively than the Conservatives, but because
they forged between themselves an approach to political strategy
which has never before been seen – certainly in the Labour Party,
and arguably, ever in British politics. They welded policy, politics
and image–creation into one weapon.

THE temper of the time turned sharply in Labour's favour, sucking
the Tories into a whirlpool of hesitance and dissent. By spring 1989
the two former Alliance partners were fighting each other into
mutual oblivion at the Richmond and Pontypridd by-elections.
Their agonizing demise left a clearing in the political centre, and the
policy review was successfully completed in time to enable Labour to
occupy the space the centre parties vacated. To try and strap down
the inflation that threatened to resurge in late 1988, Nigel Lawson
had been forced to raise base rates. As Clarke and others had
predicted, the consequent rises in mortgage rates began to bite: they
were delayed because a number of people did not see the effect
of the increase until the beginning of the new year. Polls

started to move towards Labour even before the review was delivered.

Then, just as the review was cruising past the national executive with only a ripple of backwash, Margaret Thatcher's tenth anniversary of accession to prime ministerial power arrived to bore and irritate an unwilling populace. At the moment when people were finally beginning to feel fed up with her reign, they were reminded that it had lasted a long decade. The timing could not have been more unfortunate for Conservative Central Office.

Even worse, though, from the Tory point of view, was the Government's damaging split over Europe. Private polling by both parties showed what everyone knew: that British people were deeply sceptical about Europe, and especially about meddling Brussels bureaucrats. Pro-Thatcher Conservatives felt confident that her Bruges speech a year earlier, violently opposing the move towards greater economic and political union, struck a popular chord. But Labour's polling showed something else. People increasingly accepted that, for good or ill, Britain's future lay in Europe. Their concern was, what kind of Europe?

For the first time since Britain entered the Common Market, Labour found itself in a position to take advantage of public opinion on Europe. One of the key shifts made by Kinnock had been to ditch the reluctant or even plainly chauvinistic attitude to Europe which the party had previously adopted. As early as 1984 the party leader had declared a more pro-European line – accepting that Britain, once in, could no longer agonize about quitting the Community. During the review, leading Labour politicians made frequent visits to their socialist partners on the continent, and developed a more European perspective. The West German socialists, for example, brought home to the Labour Party the absurdity of trying to control multinationals with merely national measures. And the European agenda was moving in Labour's direction, with the presentation of the 'Social Charter' by Jacques Delors, president of the European Commission. Labour opponents of Community membership agreed to keep their heads down and their mouths shut. One of the most prominent doubting voices on Europe – Bryan Gould – was cleverly appointed to front the Euro-campaign.

By contrast, the Conservatives had to endure either Edward Heath, or Michael Heseltine, or some other Tory politician, almost daily attacking Thatcher for her insular and distorted vision of Europe. There were almost daily reports of divisions among Cabinet ministers over whether to join the exchange rate mechanism of the European monetary system, that powerfully linked the Europe splits to Tory economic management. On top of that, Conservative politicians and their advisors spent enormous energy producing a well-written manifesto that no one read, while Central Office ordered disastrous Euro-election advertising that everyone read. One notorious Tory election advertisement said: 'If you don't vote on June 15, you'll live on a diet of Brussels.' Voters either gave up trying to understand the message, or understood it to mean that they should not bother to vote at all.

As the shine rubbed off the Tory economic miracle, an additional factor broke its electoral spell: the environment – or, more widely, the quality of life. Labour had for some time been arguing that Thatcherism had brought sharp division between personal wealth and poor quality public services. That theme was unexpectedly nurtured by a series of disasters on public transport, and in public places – from the Clapham train disaster through to the soccer fans crushed in the Hillsborough stadium. The Government perfectly legitimately protested that it could not be held responsible for most of the incidents, but they nonetheless served to concentrate public attention on the disjuncture between increasing abundance of goods and leisure, and the shabbiness of public services. Besides, people felt, the Government could not go on disclaiming blame for everything that went wrong in the public sphere. The issues which the Shadow Cabinet had discussed at Rottingdean in November 1988 finally stepped centre stage in the late spring of 1989. Complaints about traffic congestion and housing development pressure, in turn entwined with the more strictly 'green' theme which the Prime Minister had sent to the top of the political agenda in her Royal Society speech in September 1988. Her proclamation of the need to

tackle ozone depletion and greenhouse gases led to wildlife protection finding its way onto the front pages of tabloid newspapers, and
nightly presentation on news bulletins.

The environmental agenda, which Thatcher had hoped to capture
and command, instead tied itself into a net which tangled and
trapped her. The Green Party's surge in the European elections –
which took all its opponents completely by surprise – dragged back
the Tory share of the vote. That helped Labour pull clearly ahead,
and attribute its advance directly to the delivery of the policy review.
That in turn enabled the party to claim with conviction that it was
now placed to win the next election. For the first time since Neil
Kinnock had taken over the party leadership, that claim was beginning to feel plausible.

The policy review did include a group which worked on the
physical environment, but it produced little that the party had not
already offered prior to 1987. Both the front bench and the executive
were relaxed – indeed, rather complacent – about their policies on
'green' issues, and related subjects such as housing. By contrast,
John Prescott, by then transport spokesman, took to the 1989
conference a whole new transport policy – and managed to be
elected on to the executive in the constituency section. Kinnock –
who only a year before had wanted Prescott stifled – suddenly started
referring to him in public as 'Johnny'. Peace broke out.

As the policy review sailed through the 1989 conference, the key
figures in the leadership team could not help kicking themselves that
they did not ask for more. The success of the review strategy, which
brought with it the realistic prospect of general election victory,
tamed the party into acquiescence. Suspicions remained. The rank
and file still felt as if it had been passed by. There were protests, and
one or two minor defeats. The gradual shift in the party's culture
towards independent unity and critical loyalty, was highlighted when
Ken Livingstone, the most outspoken executive critic of the review,
was voted off the national executive. No one doubted, least of all
Livingstone himself, that he lost his seat in the constituency section
because the party had decided no longer to condone anyone who
rocked the boat. The mood of the conference was best captured by

Dennis Skinner, who chaired it with dry humour and aplomb. He made no bones of his political disapproval for much that was in the review. Nevertheless he guaranteed his loyalty to the party – and unashamedly boasted in his final speech that an *Evening Standard* poll on the final day of conference gave Labour a firm 10-point lead. By that time the party had enjoyed its most prolonged and substantial lead over the Conservatives since Neil Kinnock had become leader. Skinner even deigned to quote to the conference the poll figures which showed that Kinnock's own satisfaction rating with the public was at last ahead of Margaret Thatcher's, and rising along with his party. Kinnock snatched the opportunity, and told a television interviewer on the last day of the 1989 conference that he was fit to be Prime Minister, not only because he loved his country, but 'because I truly represent the people of this country – their hopes for economic success and social justice, and their aspirations, because I'm from them . . . I'm not detached, remote, in the way this Government certainly has become.' He added: 'I know that I'm tough. I know that I can see objectives and drive after them. I think that tenacity is required too. I've got it.' When Kinnock could say such things, and be heard in earnest, it was clear the turnaround had been achieved.

Within a month the Cabinet rift over European monetary co-operation, on top of the intensifying pressure on sterling, ripped the Government apart. Lawson demanded that Thatcher sack her personal economic advisor, Sir Alan Walters, because Sir Alan's public comments against the EMS were swaying the markets. Thatcher refused, Lawson resigned in protest, and Labour's lead jumped to 15 points. Nearly half the population were willing to support Labour. Those fast-moving events swiftly proved that the review had enabled Labour to capitalize instantly on Government misfortune. In late 1988, Kinnock's team despaired because the Tories seemed immune from mounting economic difficulties. Only a year later the Government, and Thatcher herself, were placed in real electoral peril. The review, and the 1989 strategy, had been played for high stakes. Labour reaped every available reward.

14

PERESTROIKA

THE PARTY'S presentational strategy was frequently symbolized
with a triangle, in which the party, the leader and the policies
each represented one of the three sides. Each was regarded as
equally important. By the end of the 1989 conference the review was
in place and the leader's status was rising. Work on improving the
party's attractiveness, however, had only just begun. Top-to-bottom
overhaul of the party's structure was not merely communications-
led: it was central to Kinnock's ambitions. He was, in many ways,
always more clear about how he wanted to reconstruct the party
organization, than about the details of policy change. Indeed Kinnock's leadership has been distinguished from those of almost all his
predecessors by the importance he attached to what he called his
own version of perestroika. Though the analogy with Gorbachev's
reforms seemed overweaning, it was in in many ways legitimate. Just
as modernization of the Soviet economy depended on restructuring
and democratizing Russian society, so the durability of Kinnock's
policy reforms depended on spreading internal democracy and
broadening party membership. Only in that way – by becoming a
truly 'new model party' – can Labour ensure that it stays in step with
the times.

That drive had always been a strong ingredient in Kinnock's
thinking. Even before he became party leader, in one of his speeches
during his 1983 campaign, Kinnock set out his programme for
reform. On 12 September, at Stoke-on-Trent, he said that individual membership 'must be increased and made more representative'. He added, over-hopefully: 'A quarter of a million new

members in the next 18 months is not a pious hope, given the problems that the British people will face.'

The Kinnock group never set out with a precise outline of what the new model Labour Party would look like. They embarked on one-step-at-a-time reform, towards an only foggily-perceived horizon. If there was an ultimate destination, it was to convert Labour into a European socialist party. Europeanized Labour would have a continuously updated party programme, a mature means of discussing policy, an internal democracy based on individual ballots, and a representative mass membership. But any reform was also inextricably bound up with probably the most touchy issue within the party – its unique relationship with its founding affiliates, the trade unions.

Kinnock tried to take that bull by the horns in 1984, at only his second conference as party leader, when he promoted a proposal to give only party members the right to vote in the selection of their parliamentary candidates. Parliamentary selection was up until then determined solely by members of each constituency party's general committee, the membership of which was elected by the smaller party branches, plus delegates from local trade union branches and other affiliates. In some constituencies union delegates frequently outnumbered ward delegates to the general committee, in effect ensuring that the seat went to the candidate sponsored by the dominant union. Equally, delegates from the ward parties tended to be not only the most internally active members, but often the more left-oriented members. A ballot confined to party members would have deprived the unions of their patronage, while simultaneously undermining the strength of the activist left. The proposal was rejected by more than 900,000 conference votes. That defeat on its own set Kinnock's reform programme back by about three years. Having been beaten once, he had to wait before reintroducing new proposals for change. In effect – because of the dangers inherent in advocating controversial internal reforms too close to a general election – that meant waiting until after 1987.

The episode underlined the risk of instability which any Labour leader runs if he seeks to alter a party constitution which was carefully constructed in 1918 to balance the conflicting interest

groups which make up the party. But the question could not be
ignored. Every test of opinion showed that the link between Labour
and the unions was unpopular. The sight of union delegates at
conference holding aloft cards bearing fantastical block vote
numbers seemed politically prehistoric. The anachronism was made
no more acceptable by the fact that only the tiniest fraction of the
people which the cards supposedly represented had been consulted
by their union leadership. The very existence of the block vote
seemed to hinder the development of a politically active trade union
membership. The party's own internal surveys showed that very few
active trade unionists devoted much time to the party. Out of 6m
union members and 10,000 union branches affiliated to the party,
possible no more than 4,000 trade union activists were similarly
active in the party. The trade unions with the busiest Labour Party
members were white-collar professional unions which were not
affiliated. Ten per cent of the membership came from the white-
collar local government union, Nalgo, and 13 per cent from one or
other of the teaching unions. The manual unions, the financial life-
blood of the party, had relatively few members in the party. Activism,
evidently, had become a predominantly white-collar – even middle-
class – pastime.

The undemocratic character of the block vote became more
glaring as unions themselves merged and grew larger, thereby
concentrating the votes into a smaller number of hands. At its birth
in 1900 the Labour Representation Committee, the forerunner to
the Labour Party, allowed 176 unions to join, with 1.1 million
members being affiliated in total. That diffusion of power made it
impossible for one or two unions to override the others. But by 1956
only 87 unions remained, affiliating 5.6m votes: the big six unions
accounted for 3.7m votes. By 1988 the total number of affiliated
unions had dropped still further to 38, representing 5.8 million
votes. Within those 38 unions, four giants wielded 3.3m votes, more
than half the total number of votes to be cast at the conference. The
proportion of the constituency parties' vote shrank, in parallel. At the
1945 conference the unions held 81 per cent of the votes; by 1988,
their share had risen to 90 per cent. Any one of the three biggest

unions could on its own cancel the entire vote cast by constituency party delegates.

The unpopularity of the trade union/Labour bond was not, however, the only reason for Kinnock to consider recasting the party's relations with its founding affiliates. Many of the unions, themselves hit by membership losses, had begun trimming their affiliation figures, or were finding it a strain to pay their affiliation fees on time. Plans to raise £5m from the unions for the 1987 election fell short; £3.76m was gathered. Only a small group of unions – the GMB, the TGWU, the printing unions, and the railwaymen – had maintained their political funds at an adequate level.

The long-delayed financial crisis struck soon after the 1987 general election. By the end of 1987 the party's overdraft with the Co-operative Bank had risen to £1.8m. A few months later it rose to £2.2m. Interest charges were rising uncontrollably and the Co-op called a halt. Urgent remedial action was demanded. Over 40 of the party's 160 staff were made redundant and *Labour Weekly*, the party's loss-making newspaper, was shut down. The measures were intended to reduce spending by £1m in 1988, nearly a sixth of total spending. The process bruised Larry Whitty, who as general secretary was responsible for carrying it through. It enabled him to clear out some of those staff he regarded as a drag on the headquarters operation, but it damaged staff morale. Even then the cuts proved inadequate: in spring 1988 the party's auditors, Peat Marwick, were called in.

Tighter control on spending hardly dealt with the underlying problem of declining income. The unions could do their best by trying to restore the balances in their political funds, but the real difficulty was a low and falling individual membership. Extraordinarily, the party only first compiled a true picture of its individual membership in 1981. Up until then each constituency party was automatically affiliated to the national party on an assumed membership of 1,000, even though only a handful of the 633 constituencies had anything approaching that number. As a result, the party sustained throughout the seventies the fiction that around 670,000 members belonged. In 1980, the first year that real figures were presented, it emerged that the party's true membership stood at 348,000. The numbers then fell rapidly by 68,000 to 280,000 in 1982, possibly reflecting the impact of the Benn campaign and the party's loss of office in 1979. Officials had no real means of analysing the cause, because no records of individual membership were kept centrally – only totals compiled from constituency returns. By the end of 1988 the figures had declined to a record low of 267,000. Regardless of fluctuations, both the absolute figure, and the declining trend, presented a desperate problem.

There is a perverse sense in which Norman Tebbit can be held responsible for the development of the Labour's mass membership drive. As Secretary of State for Employment he legislated to force unions to ballot their membership on whether they wanted to continue contributing to political funds. Tebbit – along with many union leaders – anticipated that thousands of trade union members would rise up and order their leaders to step aside from politics. They were proved wrong. During 1985 and 1986 the unions balloted and won: 37 ballots ended with 87 per cent out of 3.5m members voting to retain their unions' political fund. Gordon Brown argued that if union members has shown themselves so willing to vote to retain political funds, the time was surely ripe to persuade them to take the next logical step, and join the Labour Party.

Brown worked together with a group of similarly young Labour MPs, mainly from Scotland and the north of England, to present a solution. Determined to force the issue of building a mass party up to the top of the party's internal agenda, the group wrote an influential, near evangelical, pamphlet. Published by the Tribune Group just before the 1987 conference, it was signed by nearly half of the parliamentary party. The pamphlet began by pointing to the party's low membership relative to European socialist parties. In Sweden, for instance, the Social Democratic Party had more than 300,000 individual members and 700,000 local union members, together representing a sixth of the total population and nearly half of all Social Democratic voters. In Britain, by contrast, less than 3 per cent of Labour voters were members. 'British socialists have an army waiting in the wings, ready to be mobilized for socialist change, and yet little has been done,' the pamphlet argued. 'If a sustained recruitment campaign were mounted under which union levy payers could enjoy full membership rights at little expense, then thousands, perhaps millions, could be attracted into party membership.' Instead of being forced to pay out £10, new union applicants should be offered a membership card at an additional minimum fee of £1 or £2. A mass membership, recruited primarily from the trade union levy payers, would allow the party to evolve a new relationship with the unions. It would also mean that union involvement in the party would cease to be confined to general secretaries casting phantom votes at party conference; instead, real breathing trade union members would cast their individual votes in their constituency parties. For nearly a year Brown toured Labour clubs campaigning.

Party officials were cautious. Though not opposed in principle, they saw huge financial risks. If too many union members took up the cheap rates, one internal memo pointed out, the members paying the full £10 a year would fall, and the party would end up losing income. Similarly, a drop in the subscription from £10 to £5 for all members could lead to a net loss of £600,000 (at 1986 prices) even if the total membership rose by 15 per cent. Research showed a strong vein of hostility to joining the Labour Party. Qualitative research by the shadow communications agency revealed that people were alienated. Labour Party members were seen as strange and fanatical people who were 'extremely knowledgeable about current affairs', 'only interested in minority issues', 'brilliant at debate', 'unfriendly', 'middle aged men wearing cloth caps', 'scruffy teenagers who sell *Socialist Worker* and shout', and 'so committed that they give up all their free time'. People were no more enamoured by the prospect of attending a Labour meeting, something they regarded as compulsory for a Labour member. Such meetings only happen in the evenings and are very boring and bureaucratic, the agency was repeatedly told. Similarly interviewees often said: 'You have to know how to behave at meetings, you have to know the right words and language, you have to speak.' Labour Party meetings were associated with smoking, drinking and bickering. Many interviewees spoke of the administrative barriers to joining Labour, even if they wanted to join. Typical statements included: 'It's impossible to join the Labour Party', 'you have to write to your MP', 'you have to know who your MP is', 'you have to write to Neil Kinnock', 'you have to write to Walworth Road', 'you have to know where Walworth Road is', 'you have to know what Walworth Road is', 'you have to be an active trade unionist' -and so on. Party officials knew that a very large number of people in Britain had at some stage belonged to the Labour Party, but that only a small proportion belonged at any one time. In other words, Labour found it difficult to retain members, once they had been recruited.

WITHOUT THE intervention of John Edmonds, general secretary of the GMB, the Tribune plan might have died. During the election Edmonds had willingly signed his unions' cheques for the occasional £50,000 here and there. But a begging bowl seemed to him an impractical way of running the party. He called a meeting with the general secretaries of those unions which enjoyed healthy balances in their political funds – Tony Dubbins from the National Graphical Association, Jimmy Knapp from the National Union of Railwaymen, Alan Tuffin from the Union of Communication Workers, Ron Todd from the Transport and General Workers Union, and Brenda Dean of Sogat, the print workers union. Out of that meeting was born an Edmonds's plan to stabilize financial relations between the party and the unions. On 8 May 1988 the GMB general secretary wrote to Whitty with a scheme which incorporated the Tribune proposals. Given Edmonds's authority, it was an offer the party could not refuse. 'I understand the difficulties facing the party', his letter began, 'but we must find a way to deal with the immediate crisis in a manner which is consistent with the longer term need to develop a robust and permanent funding base for the party.' He accepted a phased increase in union affiliation fees, but attached stiff conditions. A corporate plan had to be agreed by the executive, identifying the party's spending programme right up to the next election. A specific committee should be established charged with monitoring spending. A joint group of trustees made up of MPs and union officials would ensure that money flowing in from the affiliation fees, and earmarked for the general election fund, would not again be plundered to pay off debts.

In return for those controls, Edmonds said his union would underwrite the cost of the hardware necessary to process and service a national membership. The procedure for processing and approving applications to join the party would be simplified. 'When we develop a central computer system, it should be possible to receive applications at Walworth Road, or at the regional office and then process that membership within a matter of weeks. Trade unions should be given the opportunity of proposing their members for party membership in this way. At the same time, a new membership rate should be introduced for trade union members who already pay the political levy. The discounted membership for trade unions should be no more than £5 for members in work.' Finally, the GMB offered to cover the costs which poorer unions would incur in the transition from annual payment of party subscriptions to quarterly payments. Edmonds concluded his letter by saying he believed 'the package would transform the financial position of the party and give us the financial stability we have been seeking for so long'.

Edmonds's purpose in writing had not been to advance original ideas, but to coerce the party into action. The letter had the desired effect. After months of prevarication, the executive acted. Every one of Edmonds' proposals was carried out. At the 1988 conference delegates accepted a reduced membership rate of £5 for three years for trade union political levy payers. Recruitment of members by the party's national and regional headquarters would be allowed from 1989, ending the recruitment prerogative which local constituencies had enjoyed since the party's formation. A national computerized membership list would be ready by 1990, with party headquarters processing all membership cards from January 1991.

No one, least of all Kinnock's office, saw the measures purely in terms of efficiency or modernity, They were regarded as intensely political. The leadership believed – indeed the 1988 leadership election proved – that the character of the party's membership had already changed. The new generation of younger members was much more self-disciplined, business-like and single-minded in its ambition for power. Successive election defeats, and the enlistment of a post-sixties generation, sobered the party. But Kinnock knew that more was needed. A mass party, drawing its membership from a wider social range, would not only reflect the views of Labour voters better: it would also help guarantee realism. The party's institutions would be less vulnerable to take-over or neglect.

At the launch of the mass membership drive in January 1989 Kinnock unwisely asserted that the party's low membership was an administrative, not a political problem. He predicted that membership would double within 18 months (the same reckless prediction as he had made in 1983) and reach a million by the time of the general election. It was foolish and ineffectual hype. No preparatory work had been done on organizing trade union officials into recruitment campaigning. Silly mistakes were made. The party launched its drive in the West Midlands the month that the regional organizer took long leave in America. It soon became clear that there was no substitute for one-to-one recruitment in workplace canteens and on windy doorsteps.

However, Kinnock, having delayed so long in delivering reforms which he had promised in 1983, did not allow the early disappointments of the mass membership drive to hold up the next round. The reliance on union finances to keep the party afloat made it impossible to abolish overnight the right of unions to vote at conference. It was unrealistic to expect unions to give up such power while they were still being asked to bankroll the party. But it was realistic to ask the unions to agree to reduce their share of the vote. A Larry Whitty paper, submitted to the 1989 conference and subsequently sent out for party-wide consultation, proposed options for diminishing the union block vote. If votes were weighted in favour of constituencies – reflecting the larger sum which each constituency affiliate paid to the national party in comparison with the unions – it would be possible to create a built-in democratic incentive for individual constituencies to recruit more members in order to enhance their voting power at conference. Only one formula appeared to achieve both goals. Each constituency could have a minimum single vote for its first 500 members, and one additional vote for every additional 250 members.

Unions would have one vote for every 3,000 members. In 1988 the unions wielded 90 per cent of the conference vote, while the constituencies had the rest. Under the favoured option, a doubling in the party membership would swing the proportions to 45 per cent for constituencies, 55 per cent for unions. A trebled party membership – nearly one million members – would give the constituencies a majority of the vote.

As yet the unions are not prepared to countenance a further reform, whereby they would split up their block vote to reflect minority opinion within the union. The homogenized expression of mass opinion is supposed to reflect solidarity within the union behind the agreed stance. But nothing in the party's constitution requires unions to cast their vote at party conference as a single block. They have always been free, if they chose, to hold internal ballots and cast their block vote in proportion to the result, so as to reflect substantial minority views within the union. Some leading left-wing MPs, such as Prescott and Meacher, argued that it was hard to understand, in the late 1980s and early 1990s, why a unions' opinion should be treated as monolithic. But there is nothing the party can do to instruct unions how to use their votes: reforms in that direction have to be left to the unions themselves.

There was a prior question: why should the party leadership want to break up the block vote, when its relative predictability provided one of the few sources of dependable loyalty on which any Labour leadership could rely? Without the block vote, conference – and the party – would become less easy to manage. Sidney Webb, devisor of the party constitution, once remarked: 'If the block vote of the trade union were eliminated it would be impracticable to vest the control of policy in the Labour conference.' Some contemporary trade union leaders, such as Bill Jordan, president of the Amalgamated Engineering Union, took a similar view. They told the party they were prepared to see the block vote reduced or changed, but only if it were linked to a review of the role of conference, policy-making and the executive.

A second consultation paper, largely written by Whitty himself, was therefore despatched alongside the block vote options, setting out two different approaches to transforming the party's policy-making process. It may yet prove the most significant reform undertaken by Kinnock's leadership – not least because it will go further towards 'Europeanizing' the Labour Party than any policy shift. Comparisons have been made between Labour's policy review and the dramatic, revisionist renunciation of Marxism which the West German *Sozialdemokratische Partei* undertook at Bad Godesburg. A more profitable comparison, however, might be made between the smoothly efficient method with which the West German socialists went about writing their party programme at the end of the 1980s, and the bumpy, haphazard progress which the backfiring Labour Party machine managed.

The experience of conducting the policy review taught the party that it was only halfway towards a streamlined policy-making process. Under Labour's inherited structure, conference policy derived from resolutions submitted by affiliated organizations, and from national executive statements. The former were composited behind closed doors, usually by union leaders trading support for each others' proposals against mutual concessions. Most constituencies received the final conference agenda – containing the motions and amendments – in time to be able to mandate their delegate how to vote. But the compositing mincer meant that the policy meat was rarely served to the conference floor in an edible form. During one conference week up to 30 issues could be perfunctorily debated, while the national executive peppered complex new policy statements across the rows of delegate seats at the start of each session. The rules did not allow constituencies and unions to amend those statements: they had to be accepted or rejected as a whole. The entire structure of the conference militated against either consensus, or the exploration of alternative ideas. Confrontation and denunciation was easier, and more likely to attract attention in the limited time available. Randomly-selected speakers were unrepresentative, or ignorant of policy substance. The people most influential in writing policy, or in selling it to the public, were often not allowed to speak.

That began to change with the 1988 and 1989 conference, when the presentation of policy review papers enabled Shadow Cabinet spokesmen to explain their own policy from the platform. Delegates received the review output long before conference. There was a justified protest, however, on the first day of the conference, against the executive's ruling that the policy review documents could not be amended.

Experience of the review has ensured that Labour will now move towards a completely new way of making policy. Like the socialist parties of Denmark, Sweden, West Germany and Italy, it will probably adopt a system of policy-making known as the 'rolling programme', in which policy papers are presented in a cycle, with only a limited number being put to each conference. The reports would be prepared by policy commissions drawn from an expanded and more representative executive, so that all policy initiates from a single source. Every other year the conference would be free to approve, amend or reject a policy commission's work. Local parties and unions would be entitled to table line-by-line amendments.

Many on the left opposed those proposals at the 1989 conference, arguing that they would sterilize the conference and turn it into an American-style party convention. One delegate warned that in subsequent years delegates would be expected to sing 'Happy days are here again' and wave balloons, rather than sing the Red Flag and move reference back. There was legitimate cause for concern about excessive centralization and creeping authoritarian control over the party. Kinnock after all had responded to the 1988 leadership challenge by introducing a new rule raising the threshold of support at which a challenger would become able to force a contest. Similarly, the executive agreed during 1989 that the shortlist for future selection of by-election candidates should be approved by the executive before the local party made its choice.

But the rolling programme, far from centralizing power with the leadership, would actually grant to party activists – and ultimately, individual members – a democratic policy oversight which they have hitherto enjoyed only in their imagination. Amendments could be considered by the policy commission and the national executive before the conference. If the two bodies accepted them, they would not need to be put to the conference. Or the policy commission could suggest an alternative wording which would not need to be debated if it was accepted by the movers of the amendment. The Danish socialist party, for instance, received 103 amendments for its 1988 conference. Most were either accepted by the executive or withdrawn by the movers in favour of the executive's new wording. Only eight needed to be debated at the party conference.

Labour reformers, however, also insisted that the party would not be fully reconstructed until it had been imbued with feminism. Research prepared by the agency for 'Labour and Britain in the Nineties' showed that for some time women had been less likely to vote Labour than men. That so-called gender gap existed, even though the same research showed that more women held socialist values than Conservative ones. Part of the explanation lay in the perception of Labour, and its bedfellow trades unions, as overwhelmingly male institutions, with virtually no female leaders. Women simply did not identify with a party run by, and for, men. Indeed, the most famous Labour woman politician continued to be Barbara Castle, who had departed the Commons a decade before. The MPs were finally shaken out of their complacency when the evidence, including a specially commissioned video, was presented to the Shadow Cabinet meeting at Rottingdean in autumn 1988, and to a special meeting of the parliamentary Labour Party. Despite resentment from the male MPs, the electoral urgency finally convinced them to introduce an element of positive discrimination for elections to the Shadow Cabinet. As a result, in the 1989 Shadow Cabinet elections, four women were elected and one of them, Margaret Beckett, was given the key post of Shadow Treasury Secretary.

The likelihood is that, by the time of the next general election, the Labour Party will have agreed in principle to these and other structural changes, including some form of separate representation for black party members. Their combined effect is inestimable. They will ultimately be more important in transforming the character of the Labour Party, and in preparing it for survival into the twenty-first century, than any other individual policy changes in the review. Labour will eventually be imbued throughout its organization with an extended one member, one vote franchise. All party members have already been given a guaranteed right to vote in the selection of their parliamentary candidate, and in any election for the leader or deputy leader. They will probably, also, eventually determine how their local constituency votes in the elections for constituency representatives on the executive. It is possible that the executive itself will be reconstructed to abandon national election for the constituency section of the executive, replacing the seats with representatives from the regions. If MPs have their own section on an expanded executive, they may be prevented from standing as constituency representatives. For the first time, the constituency representatives might actually be drawn from the ranks of constituency activists. Women may also finally be given the exclusive right to vote for their representatives on the executive. Quotas for women – incorporated in the constitutions of all the European parties – are probable.

Kinnock's version of perestroika is the true final phase of the policy review process. The details of its implementation will decide whether Labour turns into a massive but passive party, in which communications between the members and the party is increasingly conducted through head office rather than the local constituency, or a mass, active, new model party. Some activists genuinely fear that party membership might come to involve nothing much more than an armchair expression of support for Labour's values. The alternative is that local party meetings – which have put off so many new and potential members by devoting precious evening hours to petty squabbles, posturing speeches, and rule-quibbling – could be converted into attractive occasions which combine mutual political education with social fraternity. Labour's survival as a political force in Britain depends on it taking the second course.

CONCLUSION

C AN LABOUR win? Psephologically, the task is huge. The seat gap has been described as an electoral Everest. The Conservatives probably have to lose the next election as much as Labour has to win. Everest was climbed however. The question is not so much whether Labour can win, as whether it is properly placed to do so. Does the party deserve victory? And will the review changes endure?

The Conservative Party conference in Blackpool in 1989 sought to portray the review as a con-trick performed on the British people by a collection of politicians so consumed by their yearning for power that they were willing to follow any opinion poll, jettison any policy, and debase any principle, if it would take them a yard nearer Downing Street. The accusation was a caricature, but like all caricatures had an element of truth. Kinnock never disguised the single-mindedness with which he craved election conquest, and dreaded defeat. In an ironhanded but emotive passage of his speech to the 1988 conference (one of the best he has ever delivered) Kinnock strayed from his prepared text to say:

'Let me tell this party what so many in the party tell me: the greatest concession to Thatcherism is to let it win again. Those who are afraid of developing the alternatives that will gain the support of the British people, those who say they do not want victory at such a price, had better ask themselves: if they will not pay that price for winning, what price are they prepared to pay for losing, and who are they prepared to see pay that price? Because I tell you this – the price of defeat is not paid by the people on this platform or even in this hall. The price is paid by the poor. We feel disappointment, frustration, anger when we are beaten. We feel all that. But we will not have to live on poverty pensions. We will not have to go creeping and crawling to the Social Fund. We will not have to wait in dead-end training. We will not have to live on low pay. I am heartily sick of meeting people in anguish, and having nothing to offer them but sympathy and solidarity, when I know we should have the power to give them real hope, real support, real backing.'

The speech exemplified the extent to which the long years of opposition and repeated disappointments had hardened Kinnock's inner core and his obsessive determination to win power. By intermingling the demand for unity with an impassioned appeal to relieve poverty and deprivation, Kinnock exerted a pressure approaching emotional and political blackmail on the party. At times the intensity of his purpose and contempt for those party members who did not share his priorities was forbidding.

Notoriously, Neil Kinnock's quest for power forced him to shut down part of his character, and some of his beliefs, probably for good. Much of the innate ebullience and impulsive gaiety which made him a popular figure was stifled in the search for gravitas. Some of his natural traits were shed voluntarily; others were crushed by the burdens of office. Leading the Labour Party in opposition requires a rhinoceros's protective hide. Kinnock had to graft on that skin if he was to survive jibes from both friends and enemies dismissing him as incoherent, verbose, boorish, thick, or all four. Unbroadcast parts of an interview on BBC radio's *World at One* programme in the late spring of 1989 provided showpiece evidence against Kinnock's fitness to govern. Irritated by being repeatedly asked his alternative to the Government's economic policy, Kinnock swore and blustered, before angrily snapping that Labour had no alternative because it was not its job to specify alternatives from outside Government. Then he aborted the interview. Tory MPs rejoiced at proof of their belief that Kinnock was the weakest link in Labour's recovery. Nigel Lawson scorned the Opposition leader's pretensions to prime ministerial stature, saying that, so far from controlling the economy, Kinnock could not even control himself.

Kinnock was erroneously portrayed as a dullard. He did, too

often, make up for the poor quality of his words by increasing the quantity. Sometimes he filled reporters' notebooks with quotes, but nothing quotable. But no other leading Labour figure could have been so systematically successful in persuading the party to change, or so emphatically correct in believing that re-building and re-educating the party were preconditions for lasting reform.

For all his faults and shortcomings, Neil Kinnock created the new model party. The policy review was his construct. He believed profoundly that Labour had strayed too far from the people. For him, the review was a way of leading his party back to its proper place in British life. Cynics used fondly to repeat the nostrum – attributed to Herbert Morrison – that socialism is what a Labour Government happens to be doing at any one time. Kinnock despised that view of power: he took the party's policy programme seriously, as the indicator that Labour's truest values were Britain's best values. The review, for him, showed that the party was prepared to admit that British socialism had lost its way in the 1970s and 1980s, and that Labour, like its sister parties in France, West Germany and Spain, could respond to social change.

BUT FOR all its bulk, the completed review document was short on radical ambition. The review could most easily be criticized for providing a policy for every problem, and a quango for most policies. Far from being the gold-mine of extreme and expensive proposals proclaimed by Kenneth Baker, the Conservative party chairman, it was often too cautious. The party leadership misjudged how open to new thinking some of the party had become. An intellectual perma-frost had begun to melt. After years of hostility toward anyone who did not chant well-worn rubrics of the left, the party began in the mid-1980s to start free-thinking again. The review inadequately reflected that change.

Some members of the Shadow Cabinet, inured by years of being detested by the party membership, were slow to open up to the new spirit of enquiry. For too many of them, the review was simply an elaborate public relations exercise, in which the party could be seen to be dropping the main policies which had proven to be electoral negatives: punitive levels of personal tax, extended nationalization, the restoration of union rights, and above all unilateralism. Certainly there were those who saw the review primarily as a means of politically educating the party – including also some members of the Shadow Cabinet, and most of the national executive.

If the goal was covertly limited to expunging unpopular policies, then the review succeeded. But Labour did not thereby become Thatcherite, or an SDP Mark II. On defence the party remained firmly anti-nuclear. On tax, the policy retained the principles of wealth redistribution. In economic affairs, intervention remained – though its extent and purpose were constrained and clarified. In industrial relations the party sought to reinstate the legitimacy of trade unionism.

At its inception, the review was intended to be more ambitious than that. It was supposed to equip the party for a long-distance future, extending well beyond the next general election. In some little-noticed fields it achieved that radical aim. The emphasis on the individual in employment law is one example; the commitment to providing educational options from cradle to grave is another. But the overall impression was of Labour leaning sideways into the centre, rather than pushing forwards. That was reinforced by the review's lack of a self-contained set of values. It was not only metropolitan commentators who felt the absence of a theme. The most effective way of attacking Labour continued to be the insult that socialism was an out-dated creed. The review modernized the Labour Party – or started to – but failed to make socialism modern. True, few traces of welfarism, or corporatism, or any of the other cloying '-isms', clung to Labour's new programme. Public owner-ship and the pursuit of equality for itself – the traditional definitions of Labour Party socialism – were put to one side. But no dominant alternative, which could describe the relevance of socialism to the modern world, was offered as a replacement. 'Aims and Values' was never accepted by either the convenors or the party as a whole as the ideological foundation for the review.

Kinnock dismissed the accusation that the review lacked a 'big idea': he thought that was a mirage on which newspaper columnists had become fixated. It was not so much a 'big idea', however, as a harmonizing theme which people sought. The soft left Labour Co-ordinating Committee, which was sympathetic to the review, was forced to admit: 'What the review lacks is a core of analysis, and a coherent strategy for social change, which could explain and inform the policies of a Labour Government . . . the final review document provides no central logic – no framework of key ideas around which specific policies are built.'

Neglect of cross-cutting themes was partly the consequence of the way the review was put together. Sawyer's initial idea had been for a multi-disciplinary approach, with groups working outside the orthodox policy boundaries. He wanted to break away, both from 'shopping list socialism', and from the practice of party spokesmen and specialists beavering away in isolation. By the time the review was published, a new political agenda had taken shape, which demanded just the kind of intersecting and overlapping approach which Sawyer initially envisaged.

That failure was exemplified by the issue of the environment. A separate review group looked at 'the physical and social environment', including housing and transport. It followed on (and barely expanded) the party's 1986 environmental policy statement. That statement asserted that environmental concerns should be built in to the production process – a policy shift which had in its time been thought adventurous. But environmental policy barely touched economic policy. The main section on energy, including nuclear power, was presented and written within the trade and industry review group. More pointedly, the group working on economic policy never considered the questions of red-green economics (alternative ways of measuring growth, for example). The issue was mentioned in the review's introduction, but more as an addendum to the review proper than a vigorous element in its overall analysis. Bryan Gould did not start work on 'green' economics until after the Greens' success at the European elections in June 1989. Neither did John Smith's tax and benefits review group research ecologically-oriented levies and duties – proposals which were already at the heart of the other European socialist party programmes.

The groups did cross-cut, but they did so according to policy subjects, not wider themes. A sustained attempt was made, for example, to imbue all the review reports with an awareness of women's needs. They were bolted on, rather than integrated. The final document, as a result, contains a plethora of policies on child care, flexible working, equal opportunities legislation, independent taxation, and so on. Patricia Hewitt's introduction recognized that younger men and women in particular were questioning traditional divisions of labour in the home and outside. But the thematic bond between individual items was lost.

Thatcher was courageous enough to use the word 'revolution' to describe her own ambitions for British society. What, in the review, could honestly be proclaimed inspiring? The Green Party's vote was no mere protest. It revealed that there was a latent longing among British voters for the established political parties to break out of the ingrained habits of speech and attitude. People felt estranged from the conventional style of political discourse – particularly young people who could not remember either the winter of discontent or the International Monetary Fund, and women who were more concerned about the next generation than the next Budget.

People were also alienated, at the end of Thatcher's decade, by the feeling that one party (the Conservatives) would remain forever dominant, while another party (probably Labour, for the foreseeable future) recorded its prolonged protest. Thatcher came along promising to roll back the frontiers of the state, but her party and the state became overbearingly identical. The review rejected proportional representation on the grounds that a Labour Government would need every ounce of majority power to turn back Thatcherism. But some members of the Shadow Cabinet came to feel that they did not want power on those domineering terms. They did not want to impose socialism on a reluctant nation, any more than they accepted the validity of Thatcherite policies which had been thrust on a majority of opposed British voters with the spurious mandate of a minority. From that perspective, a friendly attitude towards electoral reform could have helped signal Labour's conversion to genuinely pluralist policies.

BUT PROPORTIONAL representation is not a solution in itself. Labour must primarily re-bed itself in the society which it exists to try and serve. That is why Kinnock's perestroika plans for the party are so profoundly important. The new model Labour Party already looks more competent and confident at the top, and more unified and less torn by extremism than ever. But the full development of its character will be determined by its membership, and its active members in particular. Even if Labour wins, the task of rehabilitating the party, at every level at which it touches the outside world, will remain.

Paradoxically, the most brutal test of the review will come if Labour loses, and is forced back from the upper slopes of Everest. If the party implodes in the misery of a fourth successive electoral defeat, the review will have failed. If it withstands the shock of defeat, and the culture and institutions established by the review survive, then Labour could still continue (with or without Neil Kinnock himself) as the most plausible political opposition which British politics has to offer. Labour is in a race against time to complete its conversion to membership democracy, and modernize its policy-making, before the next election. So long as those final tasks are carried through, Labour will not merely survive, like some nearly extinct species hanging on with the sympathetic benefaction of its dwindling, loyal supporters. It will become in truth a new model party, once again equipped to contest the political high ground as Britain moves towards a new century.

INDEX

advertising 49–59
  see also shadow communications
    agency
'Aims and Values' 64–75, 103, 205
Alliance (Liberal/Social Democratic
    Party) 21, 27–8, 30, 31, 33, 183
  defence policy 14
Andrews, Kaye 102
Atkinson, Tony 140

Baker, Kenneth 204
Banks, Tony 81
Barnes, Rosie 19
Barnett, Guy 19
Barrett, Eddie 96
Basnett, David 91
Beckett, Margaret 81, 200
Benn, Stephen 158–9
Benn, Tony 2, 9, 10, 36, 43, 60–1,
    134, 159, 163
  and Meacher 143
  attacks Kinnock 79–80
  leadership challenge 6, 8, 80–1,
    92–3, 94
Bennett, Andrew 177–8
Bevan, Aneurin 9, 25, 70, 107
Bevins, Anthony 84–5, 90–1
Bickerstaffe, Rodney 77, 125, 146
Biden, Joe 26
Bish, Geoff 37, 43, 65, 102, 149, 169,
    170, 171–2

'Policy Development for the 1990s'
    37–8, 41, 42
Blackstone, Baroness 173–4
Blair, Tony 132
Blunkett, David 9, 25–6, 27, 41, 57,
    64–5, 71, 77, 88, 119–20, 132,
    142
  1985 conference 10–11
  'Consumer and the Community'
    review group 102, 155–9
Boase Massimi Pollitt (advertising
    agency) 54–5
Boateng, Paul 160–1
Booth, Albert 49
Brecon by-election 12–13
British Enterprise Fund 136
British Social Attitudes Survey 61–2
broadcasts
  party political 52
  see also television *and names of
    programmes*
Brown, George 132, 135–6, 192, 193
Budget, *1988* 139–40
Burgess, Mark 30–1, 32
Butterfield, Leslie 55
Byrne, Colin 148

Callaghan, James 8, 9, 20
Cambridge 33
Campaign for Nuclear Disarmament
    105, 111

Campaign Group 9, 79–82, 95
campaign management team 22, 25, 29,
        102, 167–72
campaigns, conduct 52
    see also elections
Castle, Barbara 200
Chariots of Fire broadcast 26
Charter 88, 154, 160
citizens' rights 43, 153–65, 174
Clarke, Charles 3, 13–14, 20–1, 25,
        29, 30, 88, 102, 110, 116, 180
    career and character 13
    and Kinnock 7–8, 178–9, 182
    'People at Work' review group 102,
            144, 147–9, 151, 152
    policy review 166–7
Clarke, Richard 'Otto' 13
Clarke, Tony 12, 108, 110, 111
class structure 61, 137–8
Clause Four of *1918* constitution
        70–1, 73
Clements, Dick 7
Co-operative Bank 191
Coffman, Hilary 78
Colling, Gordon 12, 147
Commons, House of 177
communications and campaigns
        directorate 12, 14, 49
    see also Mandelson, Peter
communications audit 50–5
communications strategy 3–5
    see also shadow communications
        agency
community 71
conferences, Labour Party
    1945 190
    1984 7, 189
    1985 10–11, 26
    1986 14–15, 16, 26, 58
    1987 43–7
    1988 75, 95–7, 98, 141, 195, 197,
            198–9, 202
        defence policy 110–11
    1989 126, 142, 143, 164–5, 186–7,
            198, 199

    policy 198–200
    voting system 189–9, 196–7
Conservative Central Office 29, 31
Conservative Party
    attitude to Europe 185
    election victory, *1987* 2
    image of 61, 153
    Kinnock attacks 96
    1986 conference 15
    1986–7 campaign 19–20
    1989 conference 202
    1989 rupture 187
    see also Thatcher, Margaret
constitution, Labour Party 189–90,
        197
    Clause Four 70–1, 73
consumers 153–65, 168–9
    'Consumers and the Community'
        review group 102, 155–9, 174
Contact Group 146–7
Cook, Robin 22, 70, 71, 77, 82, 88,
        162
    defence policy 119–21, 126–7
    health policy 59, 136, 159
    and Prescott 83
Correy, Dan 136
Cowling, Keith 133–4
Craven, Mike 18, 78, 83
Crick, Bernard 65, 67
Crosland, Tony 67
Cunningham, Dr Jack 17, 56, 69, 159,
        162, 170
Curtice, John 60

Daily Express 32
Daily Mail 32, 91, 113
Daily Telegraph 113
Dartford 160
Davies, Denzil 89–90, 106, 108
Dean, Brenda 146–7
defence policy 3
    'Labour's Defence Policy' poster 29
    1986 14–17
        campaign document 104–5

1987 62, 104—10
  US visits 15—16, 20—1
  conference 45
  Frost interview 28—9
in 'Aims and Values' 72
1988 86—91, 110—25
  Independent 84—5, 90
  review group 43, 102, 108—12,
    116—18
  Kaufman 106—7, 108—27
'Democracy and the Individual' review
    group 102, 155, 159—65
Denmark 200
deputy leadership 76—8
  1988 election 91—2, 93
Derer, Vladimir 79
disasters, public 185
Dunwoody, Gwyneth 9, 108
Durham 89

Eatwell, John 18, 21, 95, 102, 132, 134
economic policy 17—19, 31—2, 71—4,
    128—42, 206
  review groups 43, 102, 128—36,
    157—8
  see also taxation policy
Edinburgh conference 79
Edmonds, John 11, 91, 194—5
education policy 100, 154, 158,
    169
elections, general
  1964 13
  1983 6—7
  1987 1—2, 34—5, 36, 155—6
  campaigns, Labour
    responsibility 12
    1983 6, 17
    1987 1—3, 14, 21, 22—35, 53, 62,
      191
    Bevin Room meeting 30
    committee 25
    media strategy 22—5
    1990 5
electoral reform 161—5

employment policy 15, 17—19, 20, 135,
    168
  'People at Work' review group 102,
    143—65
environment 169, 185—6, 206
equality 138
Europe
  attitudes to 184—5
  socialist parties 64, 73, 184, 192,
    198, 204
European Convention of Human
    Rights 160—1
European monetary system 187
European parliament
  elections 180
Evans, John 121, 161

Fabian Society 47, 89, 103, 112
Fatchett, Derek 179
Faulkner, Richard 55
feminism 200
Field, Frank 169
financial crisis 191
Financial Times 57
Fisher, Colin 55
Follett, Barbara 58—9
Foot, Michael 6, 8, 9, 17
Foreign Affairs 105
foreign and defence policy review
    group 102, 108—12, 116—18
Fowler, Norman 150—1
Fox, Andrew 22, 26
freedom 70—2
'Freedom and Fairness' campaign
    55—7, 68
Frost, David 28—9
Fry, Stephen 179
Fulham by-election 14

Gaitskell, Hugh 70
Gapes, Mike 105—6, 110, 112
Gau, John 52
'gender gap' 61, 200

General Municipal Boilermakers
    (GMB) 194—5
Glen, Roddy 58
Gorbachev, Mikhail 104, 106, 109,
    110, 122, 188
Gould, Bryan 43, 47, 70, 82, 206
    campaign co-ordinator 22, 24, 25,
        29, 31—2, 33—4, 41
    1987 conference speech 44—5
    after 1987 election 37—8, 128
    economic review group 128—35,
        157—8
    employment policy 18
Gould, Jeannette 92, 94
Gould, Philip
    career and character 49—50
    communications audit 50—5, 57
    shadow agency co-ordinator 54, 58,
        60, 169—70, 180—3
Gould Mattison Associates (advertising
    agency) 55, 58
Govan by-election 159, 176—7
government
    devolution 159—61
Grant, Nick 51
Greater London Council 55
Green Party 163, 165, 186, 207
Greenwich by-election 19, 20, 21, 155
Grocott, Bruce 179
Grosschalk, Brian 55
Guardian 32, 56—7

Haigh, Eddie 11—12, 41
Hain, Peter 157
Hanna, Vincent 2
Harman, Harriet 56, 58—9, 136, 159,
    170
Hattersley, Roy 9, 17, 100
    Shadow Chancellor 18, 31—2, 33—4
    deputy leadership 24, 37—40, 77—8,
        82—3, 88, 92, 93—5
    and Kinnock 65—8
    'Aims and Values' 67—70
    Choose Freedom 67—8

defence policy 107, 117
'Democracy and the Individual'
    review group 43, 102, 155,
        159—65
    economic policy 131
    on 'A Week in Politics' 39
Hatton, Derek 10—11
Healey, Denis 14—15, 17, 28, 45, 49
    defence policy 105
health policy 30—1, 59, 136, 159, 170,
    175
Heffer, Eric 9, 56, 64, 81, 82, 92, 94
Heiser, Sir Terence 136
Herd, Peter 55
Hewitt, Patricia
    career and character 166—7
    Kinnock's press secretary 19, 21,
        22—6, 29, 30, 34, 55, 60, 86,
        87—8, 95, 102, 129, 159
    presentation of policy review
        166—75, 207
Hill, David 78, 83
Hills, John 140—1
    Changing Tax 140, 141
Hodgson, Geoffrey 65
Holland, Stuart 108, 117—18
Hooberman, Matthew 112, 116,
    117—18
House of Commons 177
House of Lords 160, 162
Huckfield, Les 79
Hudson, Hugh 26—7

IFF Research Ltd 60, 62
image
    Labour 52—3, 153—4, 193—4
    personal presentation 58—9
Independent 84—5, 87, 90,
    162
industrial relations
    policy review 143—65
industry 133—4
    public ownership 44—5, 130—2
Ingram, Adam 177

Institute for Public Policy Research
    166, 173
Institute of Contemporary History 34, 53
'Investing in People' campaign 58
Irvine, Lord 151
Irvine, Joe 147
Islington 1, 154, 155

Jenkins, Peter 90–1
Jeuda, Diana 119
Jones, Doug 32
Jordan, Bill 197
Jowell, Roger 60–1

Kaufman, Gerald 27, 102
    career 109
    defence policy 106–7, 108–27
        visits Moscow 112–114
        draft report 114–118, 120, 122–5
    How to be a Minister 109
Kinnock, Glenys 1, 26, 28, 107, 111
Kinnock, Neil
    1986 14
    1987 position 1–3
    in *1987* election campaign 21,
        22–35
    after election 36–40
    summer *1988* 83–4
    1988 conference 95–7, 202–3
    end *1988* 176–9
    1989 conference 187
    character 6, 25–6, 178, 203–4
    promotion of 23–6
    broadcasts
        Chariots of Fire 26
        'Kinnock' 26–7
    leadership 5, 6–12, 21, 35, 48, 62,
        86, 188–9
        challenged 76–9, 88–91, 199
    defence policy 14–16, 28–9, 45,
        84–8, 89–91, 104–5,
        107–8, 110–11, 114, 116,
        118–27

devolution 160
economic policy 17–19, 32–5, 129,
        132–3, 135–6
electoral reform 161, 164
industrial relations 144, 146, 149,
        151
    and Militant 9–11
    party reform 188–9, 196, 201,
        208
    and policy review 41–7, 48,
        98–103, 171, 175, 205–6
    'Freedom and Fairness' 55–8
    'Aims and Values' 64–75
    in United States 15–16, 20–1
    and *Independent* 84–5, 87, 90, 162
    Benn attacks 79–80
    and C. Clarke 7–8, 178–9, 182
    and Hattersley 65–8
    and P. Hewitt 167
    and Prescott 186
    and Thatcher 179–80

'Labour: Putting People First' 56
'Labour and Britain in the 1990s' 49,
        60–3, 161
Labour Co-ordinating Committee 8, 9,
        82, 156, 206
'Labour Councils in the Cold' 156
'Labour listens' 46–7, 100–1
Labour Representation Committee 190
Labour Weekly 191
Lansman, Jon 80–1
Lawson, Nigel 31, 32, 33, 139, 183,
        187, 203
leadership dispute, *1988* 76–83
    election 88–9, 92–5
    see also deputy leadership
Leeves, Paul 55
Lestor, Joan 108, 117–118, 119
Lewis, Martyn 33–4
Liberal Party
    Assembly, *1986* 14
    see also Alliance
Liverpool city council 9–11

Livingstone, Ken 55, 80, 86, 124,
        134–5, 163, 186
Llandudno 26, 27
Lloyd, John 95
local authorities 154, 155–9
    conference 79
    elections 180
London
    'Aggy Hall' 1
    Greater London Council 55
    local authorities 154, 155–6
'loony left' 19–20, 153, 154
Lords, House of 160, 162

MacGregor, John 31
Madrid 85
Mandelson, Peter
    career and character 13, 49–50
    communications director 1, 2,
        12–13, 14, 16, 19, 20–1, 22,
        24, 25, 26, 27, 28, 29–30,
        34, 41, 43, 49–50, 52–8, 60,
        78, 85, 88, 89, 113, 176,
        178–9
    industrial relations 148, 150, 173
    influence 182–3
    'Moving Ahead' memo 3–5
    on policy review 172–4
market, role 71–4
market research see opinion polling and
        research
Mattinson, Deborah 55, 58, 60, 102,
        170
McCluskie, Sam 77–8
McDonnell, John 79
McIntosh, Andrew 60
McSmith, Andy 77
Meacher, Michael 9, 36, 41, 94
    career and character 143
    'People at Work' review group 102,
        143–52
'Meet the Challenge, Make the
        Change' song 174
    see also policy review
membership, Labour party 188–97

Militant 3, 9–11, 26
Moncrieff, Chris 89, 90
Monks, John 144
Moore, Wendy 79
Mortimer, Jim 12, 80
Moscow, Kaufman visits 112–14
    Thatcher visits 21
'Moving Ahead' 43
Mullin, Chris 81
music 53, 174

national executive 3, 158
    defence policy 118–23
    election to 201
    sub-committees 12, 98–9
    1985 11
    1987 election-inquest 36–9
    1988 elections 94–5
    1989 186
National Union of Miners 8, 9
National Union of Public Employees
        11, 125
nationalization 62, 130–1
Nato 105, 109
Neuburger, Henry 32, 130, 134, 135
New Statesman 71
Newbigin, John 95, 102
nuclear weapons see defence policy

Observer 56, 143
On the Record (television programme)
        148
O'Neill, Martin
    defence policy 106, 108, 109, 111,
        112, 114, 117
opinion polling and research 51, 60–3,
        100–2, 153–4, 170, 193–4
    1987 36
    conference events 58
    economic policy 128–9
    election exit 2
    tax attitudes 137–9, 140
Orme, Stan 92

Ormerod, Paul 60, 62, 161
Osborn, Rex 60
Owen, David 39, 69, 165

Panorama 14–15
parliament *see* House of Commons;
    House of Lords
parliamentary candidate selection 7,
    189, 201
  by-elections 199
Paxton, Robin 49
Peat Marwick 191
'People at Work' review group 102,
    143–52
perestroika 188–201, 203–4
personal presentation 58–9
photographs, publicity 23, 58, 83
Plymouth 100
policy review, *1987*
  proposed 2, 3–5, 35, 36–47
  shadow communications agency
      48–63
  structure 46
  groups 41–3, 98–103, 166, 167
  reports 174–5
  presentation 166–75, 180–1,
      198–9
  'rolling programme' 199–200
  achievement 203–7
polls *see* opinion polling and research
Pontypridd by-election 183
'popular socialism' 44–5
posters 56
  'The Country's Crying Out for
      Labour' 31
  'Labour's Defence Policy' 29
poverty 138, 139, 203
Powell, Charles 54
Powell, Chris 54
Prescott, John 20, 186
  employment policy 17
  challenges deputy leadership 76–9,
      81–3, 93–4
press conferences, policy 24

Price, Charles 14
Primarolo, Dawn 81
privatization 157
proportional representation 160, 161–5
public ownership 44–5, 130–2

racism 138–9, 154
Radice, Giles 64
Ragman, L.Cpl. Colin 29
Rawls, John 68
Reagan, Ronald 15–16, 20–1
reform 188–201, 203–4
regional election results 36
Reid, John 161
research *see* opinion polling and
    research
Richardson, Jo 81, 94
Richmond by-election 183
Ridley, Nicholas 136
Rights, Bill of 160–1, 169, 174
Roberts, Allan 81
Robertson, George 108
Rooker, Jeff 161
rose, red 52–3
Ross, John 134
Ruddock, Joan 45, 81, 88, 119

Saatchi and Saatchi 15, 53
Sawyer, Tom 4, 9, 12, 27, 101, 103,
    172
  character 40
  defence policy 119, 125
  and Militant 11
  proposes policy review 40–4, 46, 98,
      99, 206
Scargill, Arthur 8, 163
Scott, Regan 117
Scottish Nationalist Party 159
services, public 155–7, 185
Shadow Cabinet 12, 83
  1987 meetings 17–18, 48
  Rottingdean meeting, *1988* 177, 185,
      200

and 'Aims and Values' 69–70
attitude to policy review 204–5
women elected 200
shadow communications agency 24, 31,
    46, 48–63, 174
  'Labour and Britain in the 1990s'
    60–3
  presentation of policy review 181–2
  see also opinion polling and research
share ownership 44–5, 157–8
Sharples, Adam 40–3
Shaw, Andrew 60
Sheffield 10, 65
Shore, Peter 91
Short, Clare 80, 81, 177–8
  defence policy 119–20, 122, 125
Skinner, Dennis 9, 43, 60, 70, 80, 82,
    134, 158
  chairs *1989* conference 187
Slaughter, Andrew 149
Smith, John 29, 31, 69–70, 72, 82, 91
  economic policy 17, 130, 131, 132,
    136
  industrial relations policy 146–7
  tax policy 139–41
Social Democratic Party (SDP) 6, 19,
    33, 64, 165
  see also Alliance
socialism 64–5, 67–9
socialist parties, European 64, 73, 184,
    192, 198, 204
Southwark Council 17
Soviet Union 21, 188
  arms policy 85, 87, 89, 104, 106,
    112–15
  Kaufman's visit to 112-14
'Stak' (photographer) 58
Stanley, Nigel 130, 132, 134–5
Strang, Gavin 81
Strategic Arms Reduction Talks (Start)
    106, 114
Straw, Jack 155, 158
Sun 19, 119
Sunday Telegraph 148
Sutherland, Jim 101

Sweden 192

taxation policy 31–5, 38, 128, 136–42,
    169, 206
Taylor, Robert 77
Tebbit, Norman 19, 20, 28, 29, 31,
    125, 192
television 22–3, 49–50
  election exit polls 2
  electronic news gathering technology
    22, 34
  Frost interview 28–9
  see also names of programmes
Terrorism, Prevention Act 177–8
Thatcher, Margaret 6, 20, 21, 30, 31,
    93–4
  defence policy 115
  environment 185–6
  image 25, 61, 179–80, 182
  Kinnock's attitude to 179–80
  tenth anniversary of power 184, 207
  1989 187
This Week, Next Week (television
    programme) 86–7
Tilly, Alan 55
Times, The 113
Todd, Ron
  defence policy 108, 112–13, 117,
    122–3
  'People at Work' review group 145,
    151–2
  Tribune rally, *1988* 96–7
trade unions 7, 8–9,
    11–12
  'People at Work' review group
    143–52
  block vote 189–91, 196–7
relations with Labour party 189–92,
    193, 194–8
  representation on national executive
    12
Trades Union Congress
  1988 meeting 96
  Blackpool meeting 150

'People at Work' review group
    submission 144–50
TUC-Labour Party Liaison
    Committee 146
transport 185, 186
Transport and General Workers Union
    (TGWU) 96–7, 125, 145
Tribune 57, 134
Tribune Group 8, 9, 79, 94, 192–4
    1988 rally 96
Trident 108, 111, 115–16, 117,
    119–20

unemployment *see* employment policy
United States of America
    defence policy 14–15
    Kinnock visits 15–16, 20–1
    Republicans 53
utilities, regulation 130–2

Vickers, John 131–2
voting rights
    party members 200–1
    trade unions 189–91, 196–7

Wales 160
Walker, Mary 143–4, 149
Walters, Sir Alan 187
Ward, David 112
Webb, Sidney 197
'Week in Politics, A' 39
Weekend World (television programme)
    49
Welland, Colin 26
Welsh Labour Party 124
Welwyn, Herts 33
West German SPD 73, 184, 198
Whitty, Larry 12, 29, 46, 52, 63, 191,
    194, 196, 197
Willis, Norman 146
Willmore, Ian 97
Wise, Audrey 80, 81
Wolf, Michael 53
women 61, 200, 201, 207
Wood, Deirdre 19
Worcester, Bob 55
'Working for Common Security' 112
World at One (radio programme) 203
'World This Weekend, The' 38